Marshfield Columbus
Football Compendium

Columbus Catholic Schools

710 S Columbus Avenue
Marshfield, Wisconsin 54449

To all Columbus football players
who ever donned a uniform,
especially the linemen

...and the Columbus Catholic High School Class of 2024

Marshfield Columbus Football Compendium 1950–2000

MIKE VARNEY

The reach of Columbus Dons football

MINNESOTA

WISCONSIN

MICHIGAN

IOWA

ILLINOIS

Superior

Ashland

Rhinelander

Saint Paul

Chippewa Falls

Stanley Thorp

Medford

Antigo

Menominee

River Falls

Wausau

Apple Valley

Eau Claire

Mosinee

Brussels

MARSHFIELD

Stevens Point

Green Bay

De Pere

Pepin

Wisconsin Rapids

Wabasha

Nekoosa

Little Chute

Menasha

Two Rivers

Rochester

Necedah

Winneconne

Oshkosh

Manitowoc

Onalaska

La Crosse

Mauston

Fond du Lac

Plymouth

Austin

Reedsburg

Portage

Baraboo

Oconomowoc

Prairie du Chien

Madison

Delafield

Milwaukee

Oregon

Cudahy

Janesville

Racine

Waterloo

Monroe

Burlington

Kenosha

Dubuque

Abbotsford   Edgar

Colby   Stratford

Spencer

Loyal

MARSHFIELD

Pittsville

CONTENTS

Foreword

Columbus Dons football went beyond the school and reached the entire Marshfield community and points more distant. That is well documented within these pages.

I graduated from Columbus High School in 1996. I was on the football team for two seasons at Columbus near the end of Coach Kroll's time here. I was not a good football player. I played football because football was the face of Columbus High School. It was what every young student wanted to do. While I was not a standout, I can assure you I am a better person for playing. Coach Kroll taught life way before football. Unfortunately, he died the spring of my junior year.

After graduation, I attended UW-Milwaukee. During my final year there, I was surprised, like most people, when the fateful June 2001 decision was made by Columbus to drop the sport of football. I could not imagine the school without the program that meant so much to so many people. Over the years, I have come to accept the decision.

In 2004, I was hired at Columbus as the athletic director and in 2005 I became the boys basketball coach. On the surface, the school was different. We now had a successful cooperative football program in addition to many more athletic offerings. Like the rest of the world, Columbus had changed. However, I realized quickly the qualities Coach Kroll instilled in the school were still here. Many of the staff had been influenced by Coach and they continued to provide a high-level education. The students still followed a dress code, went to weekly mass, and had a level of respect toward each other that Coach Kroll had always demanded. The perception of Columbus had changed with the loss of football, but the values he held dear remained the same.

I have now been the basketball coach here for 19 years. We've had success, and much of it flows from Coach Kroll. I still retain methods from observing his operation up close my freshmen and sophomore years. I was impacted greatly by coaches and teachers he hired and influenced. I remember how he always put Columbus High School first and how he influenced his student-athletes to do the same. I know he loved Columbus and he'd want it to remain great. It's a responsibility everyone here takes very seriously.

Columbus played its last football season as a stand-alone program in 2000. It's been 25 years. I hope the alumni listed in these pages know how much they still mean to our school. The values they hold dear are still here, and I am hopeful our current students will impact future generations the way they have impacted mine. Your school still needs you.

I am grateful to Mike Varney and his efforts in creating this book. Recording events from the past allows us to move forward. This book does both.

Joe Konieczny
Class of 1996

Preface

The impetus for this book came in March 1992. That's when I interviewed coach Walt Kroll on six separate occasions from our respective homes, mine in Marquette, Michigan, and his in Marshfield, Wisconsin. At the time I was back from two European tours with the Air Force and stationed at K. I. Sawyer Air Force Base.

Having completed all the course work and written exams toward a doctoral degree in educational leadership from Western Michigan University, I now found myself all but dissertation. The idea was to write a small treatise for new high school football coaches on how to succeed based on the methods of a successful model (Kroll).

As so often happens, life intervened and larger priorities prevailed—namely family and career. When Kroll died in March 1995 the urgency of the project took a back seat. I never did complete the degree.

Years passed. In 2017 at my 45th high school class reunion, the current Columbus Catholic High School athletic director, Joe Konieczny, gave a light-hearted yet inspirational school tour to classmates. He had the passion I recalled from Kroll years before. I knew, then, I owed it to Kroll to fulfill the original plan, a little book for rookie high school football coaches looking for an edge in how to succeed.

It wasn't until I fully retired from my second career that I was able to devote the time needed to this project. To do this right, I figured, I needed to understand the totality of Columbus High School football before comprehending Kroll's role in it. After all, Dons football did not begin, nor end, with Walt Kroll. The Kroll book will be a follow-up to this one.

And that's how this compendium came to be. It details each of the 489 games played in the 51-year football history of Marshfield's west side high school. In recapping each season I use the same structure: an overview followed by game-by-game highlights. I then end each annual essay with the seniors on that years' squad, leading scorers for the season, and players receiving All-Conference honors. To conclude that autumn's recap, conference standings are posted.

I tried to view each autumn's schedule as though it were my senior year. How would I want that year's team to be presented? Of course I do have a senior year, and as a member of the Class of 1972, our football season was 1971. Like all high school kids, the total width of the people I knew in high school covered a seven-year span. For me, these years were from the 1968-1974 Columbus football seasons. This "recency bias" in looking at my own years on Columbus Avenue enveloped those seniors when I was a freshman to the freshmen when I was a senior. Doing this research enlightened me well beyond my own 7-year window.

Viewing all 51 seasons at close range allowed me to eye the long-arc of history. Each decade had its ups and downs as far as football went. Discussions about the best teams of all time or best players of all time are endlessly debatable considering play started with eight-game seasons and ended with double-digit game seasons.

I got hooked on Dons football when my father took me to a Sunday afternoon game at Beell Stadium in 1961 against Edgewood. Other childhood highlights include being on hand for the 1965 season opener, the stunning 59-14 win over St. Paul Cretin and Bobby Koch's spectacular six-TD performance (he also tossed for one). Later that same year, my 11-year-old self was eating a hot dog from the Beell Stadium concession stand when the Dons stopped Pacelli one-foot short of the goal line on fourth down early in the third quarter. It was magical watching the Dons huddle a few yards from where I was standing near the goal posts. But it was even more remarkable, believe me, when Koch took a hand-off in the end zone and ran off-tackle for a 99-yard touchdown . . . I had the perfect angle to watch #48 vanish into the distance.

My playing days were limited to my freshmen year, the fall of 1968. We had 33 guys on a frosh team that went 7-1. I was the second-string QB and a defensive back. For the record, I was one-for-two in the passing department, my only completion a short roll-out to tight end Paul Clanton. But I did see varsity action. In the '68 home opener against Milwaukee Francis Jordan, our senior-laden team cruised to an early lead. Kroll, as was his trademark, allowed reserves to play late in these type of games. He wasn't worried about how the statistics would look if we gave up a late TD—he wanted game experience for the next iteration of Dons. On the second, and last, play of my Beell career, Francis Jordan scored on a 26-yard run. My "bell got rung" a couple of times that year. The last time, when I literally saw stars, was enough to convince me to cheer from the stands my remaining high school years. I wasn't headed to the NFL anyway being listed at 5-foot-even, 100-pounds that ninth-grade year.

After hearing coach Konieczny's uplifting update in 2017 about the total-person experience that is Columbus High School, things were slowly set in motion for what I thought would be the Kroll book. I had the goods (somewhere) after all.

The painful decision to drop football at Columbus was made in late spring 2001. Safety concerns for the young and limited number of players were reasons cited. In the intervening decades, young male Columbus athletes have transitioned into a fall soccer powerhouse and a perennial basketball contender.

Columbus High is now known as Columbus Catholic High School, and has been since 2003. Because all the games reported on here were under the Columbus mantle, I kept to that. Finally, it must be said again, whatever year you graduated in—subtract one—to find your years' football team. Football is a fall sport but, in central Wisconsin, sometimes that encompasses three of the four seasons—summer, fall, and winter.

I still find high school athletics the purest manifestation of sports on any level. Go out and support your local team!

Mike Varney
Milwaukee, Wisconsin

Fred Beell and His Stadium Legacy

Three generations of Columbus High School football were played at Beell Stadium in Marshfield. The field was named for Fred Beell, who emigrated from his native West Prussia in Germany at age 4 in 1880. He left Marshfield schools at 14 and went right to work at the Upham Mill. It was said that the squat 5'4" Beell could carry a dresser by himself, normally a two-man job. On August 5, 1902, he married Anna Scheuren of Colby. Beell developed into a professional freestyle wrestler of the first order. His first Marshfield appearance was at Adler's Opera House in February 1900, a three-falls-to-one win over Indiana champion Ed Adamson. Professional wrestling was a more raw, transactional business at the time. Gate receipts were determined by paid attendance and betting. In 1906 the 169-pound Marshfield wunderkind held both the middleweight and light heavyweight crowns. In a New Orleans matchup Beell took on 203-pound reigning heavyweight champ Frank Gotch from Humboldt, Iowa. He bested Gotch in the Big Easy on December 1, 1906. In doing so, Beell simultaneously held championships in three weight divisions.

It didn't last long. Gotch got a rematch, and took care of business in Kansas City 16 days later before 8,000 partisan spectators. The *Kansas City Star* newspaper observed that it was the largest purse Gotch ever wrestled for, and it was before a record-breaking crowd. Gotch remarked afterwards, "Beell can probably throw any other man in America, but never again will he be champion so long as I am in the game." The 5'11" north central Iowa native was correct. In seven more contests over the course of their lives, Gotch prevailed every time. Eleven years later, Gotch, the acclaimed "greatest wrestler of all time," died of kidney failure. He left behind a wife and 4-year-old son—and a brilliant 154-6 wrestling career.

Fred Beell held the world heavyweight wrestling championship for a total of 16 days—16 days more than most people. "I was certainly a short-term champion," Beell admitted. "I am not going to retire from the mat. I am still in the business to meet all comers." But holding all three titles at once—the first wrestler ever to do so—is why he was enshrined in the Wisconsin Athletic Hall of Fame. Beell remained a force in wrestling for many years. He was 5-3 overall against Adamson, the self-proclaimed Indiana champion. Beell's last match took place on the corner of Second and Central avenues in Marshfield in 1919. A veteran himself of the 1898 Spanish-American War, Beell performed in honor of returning Marshfield World War I soldiers from Company A of the Second Wisconsin Regiment. Fourteen years after his final athletic performance, Beell, 57, found himself as an auxiliary Marshfield police officer with 12 years on the job.

In the early morning hours of August 5, 1933, Beell and patrolman George Fyksen responded to a call at the Marshfield Brewery. Beell waited in the patrol car near the corner of Doege and Pine as Fyksen made a routine search. To everyone's surprise, Fyksen came upon a lookout for the burglary in progress. Fyksen fired two shots, wounding the burglar. The shots alerted Beell who, coming in from the other side, was riddled with four bullets by the fleeing bandits, who took off in Beell's car. Fred Beell immediately lost his life. The burglars switched cars several blocks north of St. Joseph's hospital, abandoning Beell's blood-stained police vehicle. They had with them $1,550 in federal government revenue stamps. The next day a shallow grave along a Minnesota roadside near Anoka revealed the fatally wounded burglar, Edward "Speed" Gabriel. It took four years before two others, "Sleepy Joe" Hogan and Elmer Dingman, were sent to prison for Beell's death. The other accomplice was never arrested for the killing.

Marshfield's football stadium dedication occured on September 27, 1941, before a crowd of 2,800. There was much pageantry, with Fred C. Rhyner serving as master of ceremonies. Sam E. Winch, the "M" Club's oldest active member, presented the game ball to officials. Winch played on the 1898 and 1899 Tiger teams. Marshfield defeated Wisconsin Rapids 14-7 in that first game. Weeks later, on November 12, 1941, the Marshfield Board of Education named its new football stadium to honor Fred Beell. He remains the only Marshfield police officer to give his life in the line of duty.

Fred Beell | Y103 | North Wood County Historical Society collection

1950 – 1959

1950: All Underclassmen

The inaugural Columbus High School football season was book-ended with victories—an opening 19-0 triumph over visiting Abbotsford and two road wins to close out the campaign. The Columbus 11 played with all underclassmen and finished the year 3-5. Coach Marty Crowe was brought in from Eau Claire St. Patrick High School (now Regis) to set Columbus football history in motion. Bob Mendyke recorded the first-ever TD on a 31-yard end-around scamper four minutes into the opener against Abbotsford. Mendyke was subbing at QB for the injured Paul Umhoefer. In CHS's second game Spencer dominated the line of scrimmage at Beell Stadium, and came away with a 7-0 win. Vic Carpenter's short third quarter TD run was all the Red Rockets needed on Wednesday night. Jim Sauter added the extra point for the visitors.

CHS ran into a McDonell buzzsaw in Chippewa Falls the following Sunday afternoon. A capacity crowd watched the Macks manhandle Columbus 35-0 on five touchdowns and a safety. The next game was cancelled when Pittsville Maryheart star Jack Hackman contracted polio days before the game. Marshfield sports fans fondly remember Hackman as the voice of the Tigers and Dons on WDLB radio. Thirteen days after the McDonell loss, sophomore QB Paul Umhoefer made his CHS debut on a rain-soaked field in Stanley. He threw for both Marshfield scores but it wasn't enough as Columbus fell 21-14.

Wabasha (Minn.) St. Felix provided the opposition for CHS's initial homecoming. At the pep rally on the Cleveland Street campus, Father Hugh Deeney announced that the Columbus team would be known as the Crows, the winning entry in a student contest. The new school pep song, composed by principal Sister Mary Eugene, was sung for the first time at the spirited gathering adjacent to St. John's Church. Indian-summer weather greeted 1,500 spectators for the Sunday afternoon gala. St. Felix downed the Crows 22-13 in an entertaining game. Perhaps one of the oddest touchdowns in Columbus history occurred in this fifth-ever contest. Jerry Schirpke recovered his own free kick after a safety and ran 40 yards for a score in the losing effort. The Crows could not overcome six lost fumbles. Coach Crowe noted John Kampine's outstanding line play. QB Paul Umhoefer connected on 15 passes, a school record that still stands.

Another large crowd was on hand the following Sunday afternoon in Rochester, Minnesota. Lourdes High School's Terry McCabe, rated one of the best high school running backs in the Gopher State that year, did not disappoint, scoring on runs of 10 and 15 yards in a 24-0 shutout. In the next-to-last game of the year in St. Paul, Columbus trailed St. Agnes 6-0 with three minutes remaining before halftime, a sixth straight loss clearly in sight. The annals of amazing Columbus football feats began in the 180 seconds before intermission. Columbus erupted for 20 points prior to the midway whistle sounding. Before the upstart Marshfield gridders departed Minnesota's capital city that day, they had secured an improbable 61-7 win. In the 489 Columbus High School football games ever played, those 61 points were eclipsed only once. Jim Moscinski scored five touchdowns and passed for another in the rout.

The Crows concluded their initial grid campaign with an 18-12 win over St. Mary's in Menasha. Crowe was ecstatic with the passing of Umhoefer and the defensive line play of Don Weinfurtner and Doug Schmidt in what he called the best game Columbus played all year. The local paper, the *Marshfield News-Herald*, recounted the winning touchdown for readers: "Umhoefer passed to Wilkins, who handed off to Moscinski for the remaining distance to the end zone. It was the most perfectly executed play engineered by Columbus all season." Playing a full varsity schedule with no seniors, the Crows ended their first season on a positive note. Jim Moscinski led the scoring parade with 50 points, followed by Jerry Wilkins with 21 and Bob Mendyke with 19.

1951: First Winning Record

The autumn of 1951 brought Columbus its first winning mark. The Crows won all four of their home games at Beell Stadium but lost three of four away, leaving them 5-3. *Marshfield News-Herald*, in previewing the team, said, "The fans can expect plenty of aerial fireworks and a lot of deception." Coach Marty Crowe brought in Wally Wallschlaeger as his assistant to take care of the defense. John Kampine and Don Cherf served as co-captains for the team. On the season, the Crows outscored their opponents 196-106 and finished with a three-game win streak that saw them outscore the opposition 124-6. Two of those wins came on back-to-back days to close out the season on an 80-6 scoring splurge. Jim Moscinski, a great open-field runner from Stevens Point, had five punt returns for touchdowns. All were from 50 yards or more. His total was topped only once (in 1996) in the 51 years of Columbus High School football. The Crows also perfected the timing necessary to make the hook-and-ladder pass-play work.

The Crows opened the season with a Friday afternoon game at Mosinee. Nine hundred fans braved intermittent showers to watch Mosinee win both the line of scrimmage battle and the game, 20-7. Nine days later the Crows traveled to Little Chute for a Sunday afternoon encounter with St. John's and one of the best backs in Wisconsin, Jim Hammen. But it was Don Van Handel who scored for the Flying Dutchmen on a 67-yard run 30 seconds into the game. Hammen did manage to tally 27 points in the 39-13 St. John's win. Crowe said the Flying Dutchmen were "the best team we've faced." He also lauded the defensive play of CHS's Jim Hederer. Great defensive play by Elmer Schreiner and Doug Schmidt allowed the Crows to topple St. Agnes the next Sunday afternoon at Beell Stadium. Columbus did not punt at all. Refusing to punt was a unique Crowe trademark. In contrast, only four plays separated Jim Moscinski's two punt-return TDs in the home opener. The 26-14 win over the St. Paul school brought the Crows to 1-2 on the season.

The local paper described the 26-0 home win over Beaver Dam's Wayland Academy the following Saturday night as the best performance yet by a Columbus team. Jim Moscinski scored all four Crow touchdowns, including another punt return. Great line play, both offensively and defensively, made the difference for the Marshfield contingent. Columbus journeyed to Prairie du Chien the following Saturday afternoon and played even with Campion for three quarters. The Red Knights erupted for 20 fourth quarter points, triumphing 27-0. Bob Schreindl had an excellent performance for Columbus in the loss. The following Sunday afternoon, Columbus recorded its first homecoming win before 400 fans who sat through a steady drizzle. The Crows dismantled Rochester (Minn.) Lourdes 44-0 while rolling up nearly 400 yards of offense and yielding a scant 29 yards. Beell Stadium was a mud hole due to heavy weekend rains. Crowe had adjusted his offense coming into the game, having his quarterback line up deep behind center. This allowed Paul Umhoefer more time to spot his receivers. Today, this is known as the shotgun formation. But not in 1951. Umhoefer tossed three TD passes with a wet ball in what the *News-Herald* called "one of the greatest passing exhibitions ever seen at Beell Stadium." Three of the passing TDs were of the hook-and-ladder, catch-and-pitch variety.

The Dons thrashed Menasha St. Mary's 33-6 the following Saturday night at Beell. Bob Schreindl ran for 108 yards and Jim Moscinski returned a punt for a touchdown in the win. Just hours later, the Crows boarded a bus for their season finale at Wabasha (Minn.) St. Felix. The Sunday afternoon encounter near the Mississippi River saw the Dons win going away, 47-0. Bob "Muzzy" Schreindl capped his career with 25 carries and 282 rushing yards in the consecutive-day games. Paul Umhoefer connected 14 times for 233 yards, including a 60-yard TD aerial to Moscinski to conclude the season's scoring.

Seven seniors finished their Columbus careers: Don Cherf, John Kampine, Jerry Schirpke, Cy Schlagenhaft, Doug Schmidt, Bob Schreindl, and Jerry Wilkins. Jim Moscinski again led the Crows in scoring with 92 of the team's 196 points. Rounding out the list were Schreindl (31), Wilkins (29), and Ron LeBlanc (20). Kampine became the first football player from a Marshfield school to be named to the All-State team at the end of the season. The straight-A student was selected at guard. His physical strength and intimidating size also anchored the middle of Columbus's five-man defensive front. Crowe said, "The gates were closed that way the day he took over." Kampine went on to a distinguished career as a doctor in the Milwaukee area. This season turned out to be Crowe's last season at Columbus. In a surprising August 1952 announcement, Crowe said he was moving on to Austin (Minn.) St. Augustine High School. The move left little time to find a new coach. Columbus decided to go with Crowe's assistant, Wally Wallschlaeger, in 1952.

1952: Best Losing Season Ever

The 1952 team was tough. Many of the players were in their third year of playing varsity football, as Columbus had no seniors in the 1950 season. The Crows finished with a 3-4-1 mark. Wally Wallschlaeger took the reins as coach after the sudden departure of Marty Crowe, who headed to Minnesota to lead Austin's St. Augustine (later known as Pacelli). All four Columbus losses were to formidable foes: Prairie du Chien Campion, La Crosse Central, Little Chute St. John's, and Green Bay Central Catholic. How good were the Crows? Despite the setbacks, Columbus outscored opponents 93-84.

The Crows cruised to a 38-0 win over Abbotsford in the season opener at Beell before 600 spectators. Defensive stalwarts Bernie Dick, Elmer Schreiner, and Jim Laffey held the Ramblers to 38 total yards. Three separate players each tossed a touchdown pass. Senior Jim Moscinski had 211 total yards (140 running and 71 receiving). The *News-Herald* reported on his spectacular 31-yard TD run: "Starting to his left, he found himself trapped, pivoted away from one man, reversed his field and swivel-hipped his way through the entire Abbotsford team." The next game, a Sunday afternoon home affair against Campion, was a deflating 12-6 loss. Campion came from behind on a world-class fake by their cool-headed junior QB Frank Leahy, Jr. (his dad was then the coach at the University of Notre Dame). It was the toughest football program loss up until then.

Eighty-five degree weather greeted 2,000 fans the following Sunday afternoon at Gosse Field in Fond du Lac. Pat Esselman sparked the Crows to a 25-13 win over St. Mary's Springs. Columbus built a 25-0 lead before yielding any points. Jim Moscinski scored three of the four CHS TDs. The following Friday night in La Crosse, eight Columbus turnovers—six interceptions and two lost fumbles—spelled doom. Central parlayed Columbus' generosity into a 14-7 win. It was a game that CHS should have won. A throng of 1,800 people showed up for the homecoming game against the Dutchmen of St. John's on a Sunday afternoon. The undefeated invaders from the Fox River Valley had not allowed a point all season. They were the best team Columbus faced all year and pitched a 19-0 shutout against the Crows. Ron Weinfurtner played a stellar defensive game in the loss. But, overall, it was a lackluster performance by the home team. Jack O'Reilly, freshman halfback, made his first appearance for the Crows.

Jim Moscinski, the first great Columbus player with a nose for the end zone, blazed by Mosinee defenders on a 50-yard TD run but saw his brilliant career come to a premature end. He dislocated his right elbow on a failed extra-point run before 300 shivering fans. Jerry Cherwinka added a third-frame TD, and Columbus hung on for a 12-6 win. The Papermakers were on the CHS 11-yard line when the final whistle blew. John "Jack" Kondzela and Joe Schlagenhaft were praised for their outstanding defensive line play. The last two CHS games were on the road, at Menasha and Green Bay. In the Saturday night game against St. Mary's, the Crows were burned on one of their old stand-by trick plays, the catch-and-lateral, tying the game at 6-6. That's where things ended up before the 500 spectators at Butte des Morts Field who watched Pat Esselman's spiraling punts give Zephyr returners fits all night. The Crows were marching to score when the game ended. In Green Bay to close out the season, the Central Catholic Cadets posted their fourth straight shutout with a 14-0 win against Columbus. Five CHS turnovers did not help. The Crows were literally stopped in their tracks. Only seven of their 20 running plays yielded positive yardage. They had a negative 26 yards. Three players were ejected for rough play: two Cadets and one Crow. Central Catholic would eventually transform into Premontre High School.

Seventeen seniors suited up for the last time in Green Bay: Jerry Cherwinka, Dan David, Russ David, Bernie Dick, Pat Esselman, Don Fischer, Vic Goldbach, John Hayward, Jim Hederer, Jack Kondzela, Jim Moscinski, Roman Schaefer, Elmer Schreiner, Paul Umhoefer, Ron Weinfurtner, Orman Welch, and Ken Wunsch. Moscinski scored 54 of the 93 points scored that year, with Pat Esselman adding 14 and Jerry Cherwinka 13.

1953: Dons Born During Winless Campaign

Coach Earl Perkins' first year at the helm was short on positive highlights. The Crows, as they were known at the start of the season, became the Dons by season's end. Regardless of their name, they would be winless at 0-8. Perhaps Columbus overscheduled this year. The team scored only 14 points all season, suffering five straight shutouts to begin 1953. The fourth one, a 53-0 loss to La Crosse Central, stands as the worst defeat in Columbus High School football history. CHS managed to reach Red Raider territory twice. It was Central's first win of the year and they left Marshfield sitting at 1-2 on the year.

The next week brought Menasha St. Mary's High School to Beell Stadium for the annual homecoming game. The Sunday afternoon affair proved historic. The Columbus 11 appeared as a totally different team from the one that had shown up the previous week. The Marshfield squad played their best football of the season. And they truly were a different team, of sorts. When the Zephyrs struck for the game's only score on the last play of the first half, it was against the Columbus Dons, not the Columbus Crows. On the Monday of homecoming week, the Columbus student body had voted to change the team name. Principal Rev. Richard Rossiter announced the winner Tuesday morning, October 6, 1953. "Dons" had been selected, Rossiter announced. Other names considered were Middies, Sailors, Crusaders, and Mariners. The original Crows label had been selected more than three years earlier when CHS first opened its doors. It was a tribute to the school's first football coach, Marty Crowe. Dick Schuerer's 22-yard touchdown reception allowed St. Mary's to escape Beell with a hard-earned 6-0 win on a perfect autumn afternoon. Since that game, all Columbus High School athletic teams have competed as the Dons.

Backing up to the start of the season, new Columbus head coach Earl Perkins made his debut at Mauston on a Sunday afternoon. The inexperienced Crows committed four turnovers in a 20-0 loss to Madonna. Ronnie Braem, however, made some impressive defensive stops for the Marshfield boys. Clarence Blattler also recovered a Madonna fumble for the black-and-white. The following Saturday afternoon in Praire du Chien, Campion senior QB Frank Leahy Jr. torched the Crows. He passed for two TDs, ran for another, and kicked three extra points in a 27-0 Campion win. The interior linemen manhandled the Columbus line. The Crows fumbled seven times, losing three of them. The Knights also swiped three CHS passes. Of the 41 players listed on Campion's roster, only four hailed from Wisconsin. The next Sunday afternoon St. Mary's Springs blanked the Crows 33-0 at Beell. Bob Sheridan ran for three Fond du Lac scores. Again, turnovers hurt. This time the four gifts came packaged as three lost fumbles and an interception. Both teams came into the game with 0-2 records.

Including the 14-0 loss to Green Bay Central Catholic at the end of the 1952 season, the consecutive shutout tally against Columbus reached six before Clarence Blattler connected with Ron Wipfli on a 22-yard TD toss in the fourth quarter of the St. John's Military Academy game. The Cadets immediately responded on the first play after the ensuing kick-off with a 63-yard Herbie Clark jaunt to up the score to 14-6. The military academy later tackled Blattler in the end zone for a safety to emerge with a 16-6 win in Delafield. The Dons traveled to Minahan Stadium in DePere to face St. Norbert the following Friday night. The Squires scored 26 first-half points and coasted to a 26-6 victory, upping their season mark to 5-1. The Dons remained winless, plagued again by fumbles. The CHS scoring drive featured four straight first downs that culminated in Blattler's 4-yard fourth-quarter score. The season finale took place at Beell Stadium on All Saints Day. Former Packer star Ted Fritsch, from nearby Spencer, coached the powerful Green Bay Catholic Central squad. The Cadets finished their season at 5-2 with a convincing 38-2 win. All the Cadets who suited up for the game saw action. The Dons' Gayle Van Ert tackled Dick Funk in the end zone for a CHS safety late in the fourth quarter for the only Columbus points in the mismatch.

Seven seniors concluded their Crow/Don careers: Dan Behrens, Bill Biechler, Clarence Blattler, John Dick, Chuck Radlinger, Gayle Van Ert, and Bernie Zimmerman. Blattler and Ron Wipfli each scored six points, followed by Van Ert with two. That was it for the scoring. Any time a team in any sport suffers through a winless season it is a tough ordeal. The players practice just as hard as in any other year. The young men develop just as much character, perhaps even more. They learn how to take it on the chin. The lifelong lessons that sports afford participants are not lost; in fact, they may be enhanced. In just four years, Columbus experienced the first of two winless seasons in school history. Hats off to the players who stuck it out.

1954: First Games vs. Long-Time Foes

While the Dons suffered their third consecutive losing season in 1954, they managed to score more points in the season opener than they did the entire previous season. The high notes lay at the start and finish. The year's final tally was 2-5-1, with wins coming in the opening and closing games of the season. Injuries can play a large part in a small high school's prospects for any year. This was one such year for the Marshfield lads. Columbus High School also began two relationships in the fall of 1954 that still exist today: with Wausau Newman and Wisconsin Rapids Assumption high schools, both newly opened and nearby. The Dons played a rugged schedule that included Campion Academy and Fox Valley Catholic Conference (FVCC) powerhouses Fond du Lac St. Mary's Springs, DePere St. Norbert, and Menasha St. Mary's. All 1954 games were played on Sunday afternoons.

The navy-and-white snapped their nine-game losing streak in the season opener at Beell Stadium, sending the Cowboys of Madonna back to Mauston after a hard-fought 19-0 win. The defense set up all the scores. The first came after a Jerry Ledger fumble recovery, the second after a Ray Braem recovery, and the third after a Don Komis interception. Jack O'Reilly's 12 points that day were two shy of the team total from the previous autumn. Ron Wipfli recorded the first extra-point kick in program history. It was also the first win for second-year coach Earl Perkins. A large crowd was on hand for the Campion Academy game the next Sunday in Marshfield. Campion played without Craig Mahar and Jack Lawler, their star backs. Poor tackling, which got worse as the game progressed, hurt Columbus in the 20-0 loss. QB Don Komis passed for 70 yards and recovered a third-quarter fumble from his Campion counterpart Jimmy Johnson.

The next Sunday Bob Sheridan, a 150-pound scatback, ran and passed St. Mary's Springs to a 21-0 victory in Fond du Lac. The Saints dominated their bigger, slower Marshfield rivals. This was a sharp Springs team. The Dons failed to generate any offense all day. Bob Pilsner was removed from the game in the fourth quarter due to a possible broken nose. The only Don threats were Pilsner and Jack O'Reilly. The first-ever game with Newman High School was played in a literal sea of mud at Wausau's Thom Field. The gridiron had been primed with a Central States Professional League game between the Wausau Muskies and the Detroit Tars immediately before. Five plays in, no player was recognizable with the field a quagmire between the 30-yard lines. Newman earned an 18-7 win over the Dons with Dave Stieber's hard running. The *News-Herald* noted that NHS freshman Don Brzezinski had "terrific possibilities." An 11-yard Ron Wipfli second quarter scamper gave the Dons a 7-6 halftime lead. However, Brzezinski and Stieber each collected second-half rushing touchdowns for the Pioneers, as they were originally known. Newman's only pass completion of the day put them ahead 6-0.

The hard-charging St. Norbert line blocked three CHS punts on homecoming the next Sunday en route to demolishing the Dons 31-0. It would prove to be the worst Columbus homecoming loss in program history. The Knights took the opening kick-off and scored six plays later. The score remained 6-0 at the intermission. The big, rugged DePere gridders took charge with 25 second-half points, led by bruising fullback Lloyd Jansky. St. Norbert also held the Dons to 10 total yards of offense. They left Marshfield 5-0 on the season. Linus Wittman and George Wenzel did manage to recover fumbles for Columbus. The local paper referred to the team as the "crippled Dons." Three regulars were out. The Dons traveled to Menasha the following week to face the 3-1 St. Mary's squad. They suffered their fifth straight loss, 32-0, their 14th setback in the past 15 games. Columbus entered this game with six regulars out with injury and lost a couple more during the game. It got so bad that Jack O'Reilly was forced to punt on first down because CHS didn't have enough backs to run their offense. Don Komis was lost for the season due to a concussion received in this game. O'Reilly ran for 67 yards on the first play from scrimmage. That early moment ended up being the one CHS highlight in another lopsided affair.

Victims of two straight shutouts, the Dons achieved their own back-to-back blank slates to finish out the year. The Pittsville Maryheart game at Beell Stadium the following Sunday ended in a 0-0 draw. All the serious scoring threats occurred in the first half, which concluded with the Dons poised to score. It was the last home game of the year as the November 6 home tilt with Delafield St. John's was cancelled. The tie snapped a five-game Columbus losing streak. In the last game against another new central Wisconsin high school, Assumption, speedy Jack O'Reilly picked off a Royals pass early in the first quarter and sped 45 yards, untouched, for the only score. Assumption may have won the statistical battle but the Dons won the game 6-0. Marshfield is on the northern border of Wood County. Wisconsin Rapids is on the far south side of Wood County. The county seat is in Rapids, and the regional University of Wisconsin extension campus is in Marshfield. The two schools have maintained a natural rivalry over the years, sometimes more heated than other times.

Eleven Columbus seniors had the satisfaction of winning their last high school game: Jerry Adler, Paul Adler, Art Baierl, Charles Blattler, Bill Cliver, Paul Goldbach, Don Komis, Bob Pilsner, Ron Wipfli, Paul Wolf, and Jim Zahradka. The scoring parade, such as it can be in a 32-point aggregate, consisted of a trio led by Jack O'Reilly (19), followed by Ron Wipfli (7) and Jerry Ledger (6).

1955: New Coach Turns the Corner

Prairie du Chien Campion Academy is a long 156-mile road trip from Marshfield. For new coach Joe Milokna it served as the site of his CHS debut. The Knights were inhospitable, scoring in every quarter and drubbing the Dons 35-0. On the front line Campion linemen outweighed CHS linemen 25 pounds per man. It made a difference. A week later the friendly surroundings of Beell Stadium proved no antidote as Columbus fell to Chippewa Falls McDonell 31-0. Ron Braem and Russ Truhlar anchored the defense. Jerry Ledger was injured during the game and out for the rest of the year. Milokna inserted freshmen and sophomores at the end to give them game experience. The next Sunday afternoon senior fullback Bernie Schlagenhaft scored the first points of the year for the Dons in a home tilt against the Newman Pioneers. Only two minutes remained when he plowed over from the 2-yard line. The TD was set up by a 29-yard Aaron Dix-to-Vic Vakoc reception. But Newman held on for a 13-7 win.

Even though Columbus got schooled 34-14 in DePere's Minahan Stadium the following Friday night, the St. Norbert game was their best effort of the year. The navy-and-white moved the ball between the 30-yard lines before the bigger, tougher Squires stiffened their defense. Dave Schlagenhaft's fumble recovery aided CHS's first touchdown. The Dons lost for the fifth straight time when Menasha St. Mary's breezed to a 37-7 win at Beell. With the score 31-7 at intermission, Milokna decided to play his freshman and sophomore reserves in the second half. That baptism unveiled their raw talent. The underclassmen outplayed the Zephyr regulars when they came back into the game with four minutes left. Having won only two of their previous 22 encounters, the Dons closed the season with victories against their fellow Wood County teams, Pittsville Maryheart and Wisconsin Rapids Assumption.

The Dons spoiled Maryheart's homecoming with a convincing 20-6 victory, piling up 271 yards along the way. Offensive tackle Ron Braem played a tremendous game but penalties and lost fumbles plagued the Dons. More than any other game, this one pointed Columbus football in the right direction. Milokna played all who suited up on this cold, wet, windy Sunday afternoon. Columbus saved its homecoming game for the season finale against the 5-1-1 Assumption Royals. The upstart Dons snatched a 13-6 upset win with inspired play on another gray day in late October. Dons defensive linemen bottled up the AHS attack, and Aaron Dix picked off two Royal passes. Russ Truhlar, a freshman, played stellar defense

13

with both a blocked punt and a fumble recovery in the shocking end-of-season triumph.

Finishing with a 2-5 mark, the Dons suffered their fourth consecutive losing campaign. It would never again happen in program history. These were the darkest days as far as losing seasons. However, the seniors applied the best salve to the situation with two triumphs to close out the season and their CHS football careers. Those eight seniors were Ron Braem, Gene Greenwald, Dave Holland, Jack O'Reilly, Bernie Schlagenhaft, Dave Schlagenhaft, Linus Wittman, and Jim Wunsch. O'Reilly led the team in scoring with 17 points. Aaron Dix and Greenwald each scored a pair of touchdowns for 12 points apiece. The only other Dons to brighten the scoreboard were Schlagenhaft (7), Vik Vakoc (6), and Holland (1).

1956: CWCC Era Begins

The Central Wisconsin Catholic Conference (CWCC) began play this year with four teams: Columbus, Wausau Newman, Wisconsin Rapids Assumption, and Chippewa Falls McDonell. Conference play would continue for the next 44 years before ending after the 1999-2000 school year. This was also the year the Dons put behind them their worst stretch in program history, four straight losing seasons. Coach Joe Milokna's 4-4 mark in his sophomore season affirmed that his steady guidance of the football program was working.

The Dons opened with two Saturday night affairs in Marshfield's Beell Stadium. Thorp quarterback Don Soderberg was the difference in the first. He rallied Thorp late in the fourth quarter with a 15-yard TD pass to give the Cardinals a slim 12-7 win. Soderberg passed for 215 yards. Many Columbians remember Soderberg as a math teacher, assistant football coach, and head basketball coach at 710 S. Columbus Avenue from August 1966 through May 1971. Thorp was coached by Marshfield native Ray Gripentrog, a fan of Marty Crowe's quirky methods. Three Cardinal TDs were called back due to penalties. In the second evening tilt, Colby outlasted Columbus in a 6-0 defensive battle. Russ Truhlar made a fantastic third quarter interception, weaving his way to the Colby 35-yard line. Bob Baer's recovery of a Colby fumble gave Columbus life with two minutes left. On the next play, QB Aaron Dix hit lanky Vic Vakoc, who made a great catch after getting behind the Hornets defenders. Unfortunately, Vakoc lost his balance and stumbled down on the 22-yard line. Elroy Diethman was Colby's workhorse this night, gaining 116 yards in 19 carries, including a 5-yard TD run in the second quarter.

The remainder of the 1956 games took place on Sunday afternoons. Columbus played the first-ever CWCC game the next week at the Chippewa Falls Fairgrounds, grinding out a 19-12 win over McDonell. Two second half Charlie Schlagenhaft TD runs, of 27 and 55 yards, made the difference. Both teams entered the contest with 0-2 records. For the Dons it was the 50th game in school history, leaving them with a 16-32-2 ledger. The *Chippewa Herald-Telegram* praised the play of Schlagenhaft, saying, "The big Columbus fullback was outstanding for the visitors on both offense and defense." The Dons initiated their six-year run of playing Ashland DePadua with a 35-12 win at Beell. Dick Grall and Russ Truhlar both ran for a pair of touchdowns. Truhlar found the end zone for a third time when he raced 52 yards with an interception in the fourth quarter. Milokna continued his practice of allowing as many reserves as possible to see action.

It was balmy in Wausau the following Sunday. Shedding their Pioneer nickname from earlier years, the newly christened Newman Cardinals sustained a 15-play opening touchdown drive. Don Brzezinski, Newman's stellar 195-pound fullback, capped the effort with a two-yard plunge and finished the day with 85 yards on 19 carries. Brzezinski also caught Dick Grall from behind at the Newman 8-yard line to save a touchdown after the Columbus senior had sped 44 yards. Don Offer's fumble recovery with two minutes remaining gave the Dons one last chance to even the score. Columbus came up inches short on fourth down at the NHS 24-yard line. Brzezinski's TD stood up in the hard fought, well played 6-0 Cardinals win at Thom Field. Columbus remained winless against Newman in its first three tries. The Cardinals would finish the year 7-1 and take the first CWCC football crown. The Dons put it all together the next week in Wisconsin Rapids, playing their best game of the season, a gratifying 25-6 triumph over Assumption. The Dons welcomed back Jerry Ledger from the injured ranks and he immediately made his presence felt. The interior line opened up huge holes all afternoon. The Witter Field turf overflowed with spectacular plays, especially on receptions. Vic Vakoc made a spectacular one-handed interception while dropping back in coverage. It was the best performance by a Columbus team in years.

Little Chute St. John's deflated homecoming festivities at Columbus the following week with a 21-12 win. It was the second time in the short CHS history that the Dutchmen marred homecoming. Aaron Dix connected with Russ Truhlar on a 55-yard aerial that narrowed the halftime gap to 14-6. Bob Baer's 9-yard fourth quarter TD run proved too little too late for the navy-and-white. The finale came next. It was played at the Juneau County Fairgrounds in Mauston. The Dons amassed 357 yards on offense and breezed to a 26-7 victory over Madonna. The Cowboys managed to score against Dons reserves in the waning minutes. The win allowed Columbus to put their losing-season streak in the rearview mirror.

The nine seniors leading CHS football to greater heights in 1956 were Bob Baer, Francis Blattler, Bernie Eilers, Dick Grall, Jerry Ledger, Tom Netzer, Don Offer, Chuck Ruder, and Charlie Schlagenhaft. The season saw the emergence of the second great running back in CHS history, sophomore speedster Russ Truhlar. He led the Dons in scoring with 38 points. Schlagenhaft (18 points) and Grall (16 points) were next. Junior quarterbacks Aaron Dix and Jim Heinzen each scored 12 points. Five Dons were named to the inaugural 11-person CWCC All-Conference team: end Vic Vakoc, running back Charlie Schlagenhaft, guard Bernie Eilers, center Chuck Fellenz, and Truhlar.

1956 CWCC Standings	W	L	TP	OPP
Wausau Newman	3	0	63	12
Marshfield Columbus	2	1	44	24
Wis. Rapids Assumption	1	2	33	49
Chippewa Falls McDonell	0	3	24	79

1957: First Championship Season

Was there ever a better time for Columbus High School football than 1957? Was there ever a better time for the fortunes of sports fans in Wisconsin? The entire State of Wisconsin was giddy with delight when the Milwaukee Braves turned back the New York Yankees in game seven of the World Series. Lew Burdette hurled his third Series win to bring home the championship—at Yankee Stadium, no less. They turned the trick on Thursday, October 10. Three days after this historic feat, the Dons claimed their own legacy with a 34-7 homecoming victory over the Assumption Royals at Beell Stadium. It brought the school's first-ever Central Wisconsin Catholic Conference (CWCC) title to Marshfield.

The season began with a pair of wins against Thorp and Colby, sweet revenge against teams that had defeated Columbus the previous season. Junior halfback Russ Truhlar sparked the season-opening 18-6 win over Thorp in Marshfield. After the Cardinals evened things 6-6 in the second quarter, the Dons defense toughened in the second half. On a rare Friday afternoon game in the town that inspired a cheese, the Dons routed Colby 38-6. Spectators enjoyed a beautiful, sunny autumn day. Columbus scored on all four of its first-half possessions, giving them a 25-0 lead at intermission. Truhlar scored three times in the first two stanzas with one of the scores set up on a blocked punt by Tom Hoff. The Hornets were done in by speedy CHS running backs and Aaron Dix's pinpoint passing. The school's long-time football rivalry with Stevens Point Pacelli began on September 21 on a Saturday night at Beell. Truhlar ran free for three touchdowns in a 26-6 romp. The navy-and-white linemen outplayed and outcharged their bigger Pacelli frontmen. It would not be the last time that smaller, quicker Columbus players keyed a Dons victory.

The nearby shores of Lake Superior welcomed the Dons the next Friday night in Ashland. The Cardinals of DePadua High School proved inconsiderate hosts as they outplayed the Dons and kept play on their half of the field most of the game. But this injury-plagued affair turned on a Truhlar 85-yard kick-off return TD, which opened the second half. The Dons departed with a narrow 6-0 triumph.

The Braves' World Series victory came between the Newman and Assumption games. The Dons got their first-ever win over Newman, in four tries, on a Marshfield Saturday night. Aaron Dix's early fourth quarter touchdown run from punt formation on fourth-and-10 extended the CHS lead to 18-7. Dix, an all-purpose athlete, also intercepted two Newman passes in the game's final five minutes to secure the win. After their celebrated 34-7 Assumption win, Columbus journeyed to the Northern District Fairgrounds in Chippewa Falls the following Sunday afternoon, where they pummeled McDonell 35-0 with almost flawless execution. Even with Dons reserves playing at the end, the Macks never crossed the midfield stripe. After only one season, McDonell had decided to leave the CWCC so this was a non-conference game. A flu epidemic throughout central Wisconsin cancelled the final game of the year against Mauston Madonna. Madonna couldn't field a team and the Dons had seven of 11 starters out sick the Friday before the scheduled Sunday kick-off.

The Dons were a juggernaut this season. They averaged 290 yards a game on offense while yielding only 100. Their 7-0 record proved historic as well. No prior Marshfield team had ever gone unde- feated. In 1957 high school football success and Marshfield were not synonymous. The public school, McKinley High, finished the 1932 year undefeated but posted three ties, marring their 4-0-3 mark. The Big Four backfield of the 1927 McKinley Tigers team led their teammates to greatest-of-all-time Marshfield high school football status to that date. They scored 238 points, surrendered 19, and won the always-tough Wisconsin River Valley Conference outright. The orange-and-black's 6-6 tie with Stevens Point tinged their 7-0-1 season tally just a tad. The three Big Four seniors all went on to play collegiately: Arnie Seidl at Notre Dame, Johnny Schlict at River Falls, and Mac McCorrison at Ripon. Bill Millar was the lone junior. McKinley High School, on the corner of Fifth and Oak, burned down in 1936 and was replaced on that site by Washington Elementary School. A new Marshfield Senior High School emerged on Palmetto Avenue after the blaze. Beell Stadium is adjacent to this complex.

Eleven Dons seniors had their last high school football game canceled on them: John Christner, Richard Curran, Larry Dick, Aaron Dix, Charles Fellenz, Edward Froeba, Jim Heinzen, Tom

Hoff, Earl Mike Kraemer, Earl Schlagenhaft, and Vic Vakoc. Junior Russ Truhlar scored 75 of the team's 175 points. Aaron Dix concluded his brilliant Columbus career with 26 points, followed by sophomore Pat O'Reilly (21) and sure-handed Tom Hoff (14). Five Dons were selected for All-Conference honors: quarterback Aaron Dix, tackle Vic Vakoc, end Tom Hoff, guard Larry Dick, and halfback Russ Truhlar. Vakoc and Truhlar were further honored as All-Diocesan picks for the La Crosse Diocese.

1957 CWCC Standings	W	L	TP	OPP
Marshfield Columbus	3	0	78	20
Stevens Point Pacelli	1	2	25	61
Wausau Newman	1	2	47	37
Wis. Rapids Assumption	1	2	27	59

1958: Streaking Dons Roar Forward

Columbus finished the 1958 campaign 8-0 and pushed their win streak to 16 games, while also claiming their second consecutive CWCC title, all under a new coach. Gordy Clay, 24, inherited a good situation on Columbus Avenue and kept it on track after his predecessor, Joe Milokna, took his skills to the West Coast at newly opened Myrtle Creek (Oregon) High School. Clay had the Dons run the straight-T formation between the tackles to perfection. Their passing game, when used, was also highly efficient. Quarterback Doug Koenig made good on 57% of his pass attempts and gave up only one interception the entire season. With their grind-it-out offense churning first down after first down, the Dons rarely permitted opponents to hold the ball. The navy-and-white defense allowed 32 plays per game to be run against them. When opponents did run, Pat O'Reilly was likely to be around. He contributed 11 tackles per game. Most of the 45 varsity players were in the 150-to 170-pound range. The only 200-pounder on the team was Phil Macht at 253. Twenty freshmen reported for play as well.

The Dons opened with a 12-0 win over Colby at Beell Stadium. Pat O'Reilly opened the season's scoring on a well-executed 25-yard halfback option pass from all-everything Russ Truhlar in the first quarter. A Tim Jirschele fumble recovery set up the second CHS touchdown, a 2-yard O'Reilly burst. The Dons moved the ball freely throughout the game. The following Friday night, the Dons achieved their third shutout in a row (going back to the 1957 season) with a 21-0 whitewash of Pacelli in Stevens Point. The Cardinals never advanced further than their own 45-yard line. Dons linemen shoved the big, burly Pacelli trenchmen wherever they wanted. Truhlar scored 20 of the Dons' 21 points. Don Gust had his best game ever, and even the third-string players were marching for a TD when the game ended. Future Wisconsin public official Bill Bablitch, who would serve on Wisconsin's Supreme Court from 1983 to 2003, was in the Pacelli backfield.

The DePadua Cardinals traveled from Ashland the following Saturday night and went 66 yards in only four plays to score the first time they had the ball. The northland team was a mirror image of the Columbus 11—small and swift. The Cardinals also scored the game's last touchdown on the last play of the game against CHS fourth-string players. Everything in between, however, belonged to the Dons in a 37-14 triumph. Sophomore QB Pat Johnson came in for the injured Doug Koenig and scored twice. Truhlar shined again. The *Marshfield News-Herald* observed, "Russ Truhlar is pound-for-pound as good a runner as you will find anywhere." The next Saturday in Wausau, the Dons marched 64 yards in 17 plays for an opening drive TD. Dons linemen, outweighed 20 pounds per man, again out-charged their opponents in a 19-6 victory. Columbus used ball control for superb clock management. The navy-and-white ran 66 plays compared to only 29 for Newman. Of 700 spectators on hand, 100 were Columbus backers who watched the Dons win their 12th straight.

A championship team rises to the occasion. QB Doug Koenig connected with Don Gust for a 41-yard gain on the final drive of the next game in Wisconsin Rapids. Gust fumbled at the end of the play, but Wendelin David was there to recover for the Dons on the 18-yard line. Trailing Assumption 6-0 with just 90 seconds to play, the Dons faced a fourth-and-7 situation from the 15. Koenig's end-zone pass to Russ Truhlar in the shadows of the goal posts succeeded, and his jump-pass to Tom Pankratz added the most important extra-point in Dons' history to that stage, securing a one-point victory. The last-minute heroics spoiled the Royals' homecoming game at Witter Field. The two acknowledged CWCC heavyweights had contrasting styles of play, the Royals relying on their passing attack and the Dons executing a ball-control run attack.

Both teams flipped their scripts on this Sunday when AHS showcased a superior run game and the Dons flexed their aerial muscle. The Royals had yet to beat Columbus in five tries. Truhlar, the 150-pound scatback, played the game on a bad ankle. The *Wisconsin Rapids Tribune* cited the stellar defensive play of Phil Macht, Dan Hughes, and Pat O'Reilly. On offense the paper noted the exceptional efforts of Gust, Truhlar, and Koenig.

The Columbus homecoming game was a rarity on several fronts. First, the small Dons team came in bigger than McDonell. Second, the 0-6 Macks came to Beell with only 16 players after 14 were lost for disciplinary (scholastic) reasons mid-week. Third, the Dons recorded the third most homecoming points ever to be scored in their history with a 51-7 win. The Dons were quite banged up themselves with Russ Truhlar (ankle), Mike Biechler (broken arm), Ron Heiting (knee), and Dave Sabrowsky nursing injuries. McDonell coach Al Jirele's gimmick-play offense extended to kickoffs. After the Macks' only score, Paul Adler recovered McDonell's onside kick attempt. Don Gust scored three times for the Dons in the runaway win.

Mauston Madonna was 5-2-1 when they visited Beell Stadium. Not a bad showing for a school with only 65 boys, 35 of whom were suited up for this encounter. A steady drizzle slimmed the crowd to 350. They saw Don Gust, Pat O'Reilly, and Russ Truhlar run for over 200 combined yards in a 20-6 Columbus win. The Cowboys scored on the next-to-last, or penultimate, play of the game. Columbus concluded its season at Beell hosting a 6-2 Thorp team coached by Ray Gripentrog with his wide-open brand of football. The Dons prevailed 26-7, concluding back-to-back unbeaten seasons on Dad's Night at the stadium.

Eleven seniors went out on a 16-game win streak: Mike Biechler, Tom Bradley, Wendelin David, Ron Heiting, Dan Henninger, Tim Jirschele, Doug Koenig, Tom Kopf, Phil Macht, Bob Multerer, and Russ Truhlar. For the third year in a row, Truhlar led the Dons in scoring. His 78 markers brought his career total to 191. Don Gust tallied 38 points, Pat O'Reilly added 32, and Koenig scored 19 to round out the scoring leaders. Four Dons were selected for the 11-man All-Conference team: Truhlar, O'Reilly, center Leo Fellenz, and guard Mike Biechler. Fellenz, a junior, was also third team All-State at center. The diminutive but tough-as-nails Truhlar was named second team All-State at halfback. He played mostly defense in his freshman year. He started all four years for the Dons.

1958 CWCC Standings	W	L	TP	OPP
Marshfield Columbus	3	0	47	12
Wis. Rapids Assumption	2	1	91	20
Wausau Newman	1	2	26	64
Stevens Point Pacelli	0	3	14	82

1959: Losses to Winners

The Dons saw their remarkable 17-game winning streak snapped in the second game of the season. Menasha St. Mary's administered the 28-27 setback at Beell Stadium. The other 1959 losses were to a pair of one-loss teams, Assumption (6-1-1) and Thorp (8-1). Never again in program history would the Dons string together as many victories. The 1959 campaign opened on a Friday afternoon in Colby, with the Dons winning 25-6. The first CHS drive of the season was a 12-play, 68-yard effort, culminating in a 2-yard Bob Keller run. After Chuck Aschenbrenner's 67-yard TD gallop in the second quarter, Paul Adler tacked on the extra-point kick to make it 13-0. It was the second successful placement kick in school history.

The St. Mary's game was a showdown between two schools coming off the best records in their respective histories. The Dons led 20-7 in the third quarter after Ralph Jensen connected with Aschenbrenner on a 52-yard TD pass. The Dons had dominated play up to then when the Zephyrs, and specifically Norman Brown, turned the momentum. Brown rallied his teammates with touchdown runs of 25, 20, and 62 yards. Place-kicker Pete Snyder booted points after every score. Brown had also raced for a 71-yard six-pointer on the first play from scrimmage. All told, Brown, a 170-pound speedster, picked up 225 yards in 13 carries to administer the Dons their first loss since 1956. Columbus' All-Diocesan halfback Pat O'Reilly was lost to injury in the third quarter. Don Gust proved to be a workhorse but it was not enough to offset Brown's spectacular performance.

The Dons rebounded with a 21-0 triumph over DePadua in Ashland. A steady downpour meant ankle-deep water in some spots. Columbus played with four regulars out of action: Pat O'Reilly (groin), Dave Sabrowsky (hip), Pete Behrens (ankle), and Jerry Brown (hip). The Columbus defense rose to the occasion and set up all three Dons scores in the mud. Bob Kraemer blocked two DePadua punts. The furthest penetration was to the Columbus 30-yard line. The following Saturday night, the Dons rallied for two fourth quarter scores in Mauston to defeat Madonna 26-7. Bob Kraemer blocked another punt—his third in two games—to set up the game's first touchdown. Madonna had a big line and a fast backfield. Speedy Jimmy Kelly was a thorn all night long on both sides of the ball. A late Jim Wein interception for CHS ended matters in the hard-fought game.

The Assumption match-up in Marshfield had all the markings of a league championship game. Pat Daly's 35-yard pass to Fritz Cummings just before halftime made it 6-0. Cummings was hit hard at the 5-yard line but managed to stumble into the end zone for the score. Royals fullback Bill Nimtz slashed over right tackle for the extra point to make it 7-0. Don Gust scored in the third frame and tied it up with an extra-point run. However, an illegal procedure penalty was called on the point-after attempt and the Dons had to try again for the extra marker, this time from the 7-yard line. Jensen's pass attempt was intercepted, leaving the score 7-6. Assumption's run defense forced the Dons to the air early and CHS QB Ralph

Jensen responded with a 144-yard performance. The final minutes of the game had everyone on the edge of their seats. A dozen penalties were called between the teams in the waning minutes, which kept the clock from moving forward and the frenzied fans from leaving. Still trailing 7-6, the Dons advanced from their 23-yard line to Assumption's 13-yard line. On fourth down Jensen tossed a screen pass to Gust. Assumption tackle Jim Jacunski sniffed it out, though, and dumped him for a 3-yard loss. Assumption held on to the ball as the clock ran out. It was Assumption's first win over Columbus in six tries and extended their own win streak to eight.

The Newman game the next Saturday night was a good all-around high school football contest. The Cardinals rallied twice to gain a 13-13 tie in the high-spirited affair. The Wausau team turned the tables on Columbus, controlling the clock by running twice as many plays. Tim Tranetzke and Ron Onopa picked up 177 yards and 88 yards for the Cardinals, who were driving for the go-ahead points when the game ended. The Dons welcomed a fully recovered Pat O'Reilly back into the lineup against Newman. The hard-tackling Dons created mayhem for Pacelli on homecoming the next Sunday afternoon and came away with a 20-7 win. Pacelli fumbled seven times. Columbus recovered them all. Dave Sabrowsky, the defensive captain for Columbus, led the way. CHS used 31 players in their fourth win of the year. With Don Gust out with an arm infection, Pat O'Reilly stepped up and energized the Dons offense. Columbus improved its overall mark against the red-clad Cardinals to 3-0. The *Stevens Point Journal* described O'Reilly as "not too big, but fast, slippery, and hard-running."

The season finale at Thorp was played in slick, muddy conditions. While Thorp prevailed 25-12, Ralph Jensen swiped an enemy pass on the third play, propelling CHS to a seven-play, 63-yard scoring drive. The big play in the series was a Jensen lateral to junior Ron Maurer for 49 yards. Maurer had his best game yet in a Dons uniform. He opened and closed the scoring, with a 6-yard pass from Jensen and an interception on an errant Thorp pass, sloshing 85 yards for a TD to end the season's scoring. Maurer's long interception return was equaled once, in 1977. Eighty-five yards remains the longest TD interception return in CHS grid history.

Fourteen seniors concluded their careers in the Thorp quagmire: Paul Adler, Pete Behrens, Dick Bell, Jerry Brown, Leo Fellenz, Mert Fischer, Don Gust, Ralph Jensen, Bob Kraemer, David Mech, Pat O'Reilly, Dave Sabrowsky, Norm Wittman, and Dale Wolf. Gust led the year's scoring with 48 points, followed by Chuck Aschenbrenner (26), O'Reilly (20), and Maurer (18). Both O'Reilly (halfback) and Fellenz (center) repeated as selections to the All-Conference team. O'Reilly's pick was especially noteworthy because he missed games due to injury.

1959 CWCC Standings	W	L	T	TP	OPP
Wis. Rapids Assumption	2	0	1	40	19
Marshfield Columbus	1	1	1	26	81
Wausau Newman	0	0	3	39	39
Stevens Point Pacelli	0	2	1	20	53

1960 – 1969

1960: Roller Coaster Season

This would be the last year the name "Central Wisconsin Catholic Conference" would truly fit, as all four members were actually located in the middle part of the state. In years forward, teams from western and southwestern Wisconsin would make the conference name a head-scratcher. With the exception of the McDonell loss following a defeat at Assumption, the Dons fell into a lose/win pattern and finished with a 3-5 mark. But when the Dons fell, they fell hard. To Regis, 33-0. To Assumption, 42-7. To Pacelli, 33-6.

The Dons opened the season at home against a talented Eau Claire Regis team. It was the first of many gridiron encounters with the Ramblers over the years. On this Saturday night there was no dispute which was the better team. Regis drilled Columbus 33-0. The Ramblers were led by their excellent ball-handling QB Jim Nispel. The RHS defense scored 14 points, including Steve Stolp's swipe of a CHS pitchout. He raced 35 yards after his well-timed theft. Paul Wunsch gave Columbus fans something to cheer about late in the game with nifty runs of 22 and 36 yards. Jim Weister, a promising sophomore, gained 10 yards on his first carry. Columbus ground out a 20-0 home win over Colby a week later. The Dons amassed 261 yards rushing with Jim Wein's 106 leading the way. Weister had a 21-yard TD run. The Hornets played only 15 guys in the Beell loss. For the first time the Dons embraced the idea of kicking for extra points. Future CHS star Chuck Koch, a freshman, got his first against Colby, one of four he would record in the season.

The next Sunday afternoon game in Menasha was played in a steady rain. The Dons scored on a 70-yard drive the first time they got the ball against St. Mary's and that would be it for the day. The Zephyrs defense improved throughout the game, forcing four Columbus turnovers and holding CHS to one first down in the last two quarters at Butte des Morts Field. Coach Ralph McClone inserted the doubtful-to-play Bob Jensen in the second quarter and he sparked the 12-7 Zephyr win with 111 yards in 18 carries. The following Saturday night Larry Meress almost took the opening kick-off against DePadua for a touchdown at Beell. He got tripped up after toting it 40 yards to the Bruins' 45-yard line. The Dons rode a 12-0 halftime lead to an 18-6 victory. Their superior depth (45 players vs. 22 for the Ashlanders) was a factor late in the game. Chuck Aschenbrenner emerged as a threat to go all the way at any time for the Dons. Meress scored the last points on a 52-yard reverse TD run in the third quarter.

In Wisconsin Rapids the next Saturday night, a near-capacity crowd filled Witter Field to see the Dons take on Assumption for the AHS homecoming game. Royals halfback Jerry Bach had the game of his life in an easy 42-7 Assumption win. The CHS defense collapsed in the second half, with Assumption turning four miscues into four touchdowns. It was Assumption's best backfield in their short history. Both QB Pat Daly and the speedy Bach would be named to the All-Diocesan team, and Bach would top all 1960 CWCC ground gainers. It was the worst CWCC defeat in Columbus history to that point. Next, McDonell eked out a 6-0 win at the Fairgrounds in Chippewa Falls on Saturday night. Larry Thiel's 10-yard run in the fourth quarter accounted for the scoring in a hard-hitting defensive battle. The Dons made a game of it after losing four first quarter fumbles. Danny Hughes' punt block in the third quarter gave the Dons great field position at McDonell's 27-yard line. Even the outstanding defensive play of Tom Heinzen wasn't enough for the Dons. On the final play of the game CHS advanced the ball to the 15-yard line on an 18-yard pass but ran out of time.

The Dons resumed their win-loss pattern with a 13-6 homecoming win over Newman before the largest crowd ever assembled for a Columbus home game the following Sunday. The game was not as close as the score indicated on this brilliant autumn afternoon. Newman scored first but the Dons came right back to tie it. The Columbus defense responded, never allowing the Cardinals to cross the 50-yard line the rest of the day. It was CHS's day. Jack Morzinski kicked off to the Cardinals and recovered the Newman returner's fumble. Pat Johnson's 3-yard run in the third quarter were the points that made the difference. Pacelli's convincing 33-6 win in Stevens Point the next Sunday afternoon was its first-ever victory over Columbus. With 30 mph winds blowing out of the north, Columbus decided to go with the wind in the first quarter. It backfired. Pacelli went headstrong into those winds on runs of 13, 17, and 15 yards by halfback Bill Nugent. PHS dominated from the get-go. Nugent led the Cardinals with 72 rushing yards but other teammates did the scoring. The Dons managed to score with 20 seconds left. It was Pacelli's first CWCC win in over three years. For coach Dick Dargis and his Cardinals, the 33 points were the most ever by a Pacelli squad. The October 23 game closed out the 1960 campaign. Sixteen days later John Fitzgerald Kennedy was elected the nation's first Catholic president.

The 13 seniors on the 1960 squad were Chuck Aschenbrenner, Dan Hughes, Charles Johnson, Pat Johnson, Frank Kleinheinz, Ron Maurer, Jack Morzinski, John Scheuer, Terry Siemers, Mike Wallschlaeger, Jim Wein, Dennis Wiltgen, and Dick Woodkey. With only 71 points to show for the season, the scoring tally was closer than ever. Wein had a baker's dozen of 13, narrowly edging the 12 apiece scored by Johnson and Warren Rhyner. There was a five-way tie for third place among those who crossed the goal line once that season. Junior Russ Adler was the lone Columbus player named to the CWCC All-Conference team.

1960 CWCC Standings	W	L	T	TP	OPP
Wis. Rapids Assumption	3	0	0	90	20
Marshfield Columbus	1	2	0	26	81
Stevens Point Pacelli	1	2	0	39	40
Wausau Newman	1	2	0	32	46

1961: Close Losses Mar Perfection

Despite a 6-2 record, the 1961 team was one of the school's strongest ever. Both losses were one-score affairs. All six wins were convincing. The team had tremendous balance, depth, and a devastating defense led by Corky Wilczewski, Ken Allington, and Russ Adler. The offense averaged more than 300 yards per game. The menacing backfield of Mr. Inside, Warren Rhyner, and Mr. Outside, the elusive Larry Meress, proved problematic for opposing defenses. Sophomore QB Chuck Koch connected on the school's first-ever field goal, adding yet another dimension to his well-rounded game.

The Dons dominated Regis in the season opener at Carson Park in Eau Claire but fell 6-0. A good-sized crowd witnessed 140-pound Regis senior scatback Dick Adler pick up a punted ball that was about to roll dead at his own 20-yard line and bolt 80 yards for the game's only score in the third quarter. Columbus ran 56 plays to only 33 for the Ramblers. Warren Rhyner ran 21 times for 82 yards, the better part of the CHS offense. Ninety-five-degree temperatures in Ashland greeted the Dons the next Saturday afternoon on the shores of Lake Superior. Columbus dominated DePadua from start to finish. After jumping to a 26-0 halftime advantage, the Dons played their reserves in the second half and departed the northern reaches with a 26-0 win. Five DePadua players suffered game injuries that put them in the hospital for two nights. For the sixth year in a row the Dons faced Colby in an early season match-up and for the fifth time the Dons won. Columbus blew the Friday afternoon game wide open in the fourth quarter with four touchdowns to land a 47-13 victory. The Dons picked up over 400 yards in offense. Many of coach Gordy Clay's reserves saw action in the one-sided affair.

Columbus established football relations with Madison's Edgewood High School in 1961. The Dons were fired up for Edgewood's visit to Beell Stadium and played with inspiration. The defense held the Crusaders in check. Jim Weister's two TD gallops of 83 and 56 yards sealed a 25-13 Columbus win. As in the previous three years, the following Assumption game was played for the CWCC crown. Officials moved it to Monday night at Beell Stadium because of a Saturday deluge in Marshfield. Even though the CHS line wasn't as big as Edgewood's or Assumption's, it benefited from playing together for two years. The real difference, though, was AHS quarterback Pat Danno and his command of the Assumption offensive attack. The Royals prevailed 27-20, but the Dons were 20 yards from paydirt when the final whistle blew. Stalwarts for CHS were Corky Wilczewski on defense and Warren Rhyner on offense. It was the quintessential high school football game.

Against Newman, Larry Meress proved menacing on the pitchout play all night. Paul Wunsch's fumble recovery set up CHS's second score of the game, a 29-yard pass from Chuck Koch to Mike Weber. Trailing 19-0, Newman came to life during the fourth quarter of the homecoming game after affairs had been decided. Columbus came away with a 19-13 win. The following Sunday afternoon saw the largest Columbus homecoming gathering watch the Columbus defense put on a clinic, yielding only 35 yards to McDonell in a 23-0 win. Larry Meress and Warren Rhyner amassed nearly 270 yards of offense between them for the Dons, and Koch kicked the first field goal in school history late in the fourth quarter, a 32-yard boot that the *News-Herald* said "had a lot left on it when it split the uprights." McDonell was added as the fifth CWCC member in 1961. Columbus dominated the season-ending game against Pacelli at home. The *Stevens Point Journal* described Rhyner's 44-yard TD run to give CHS a 26-0 lead as "the finest run of the night, the hard-running fullback shaking off tacklers all the way to the goal line." Defensive standouts for the navy-and-white were Russ Adler and Ken Allington.

Secure with a 27-0 advantage, the Dons sent in an All-Senior lineup that had everyone playing out of position. Center Tom Heinzen scored on a pass reception and other linemen got a chance to run the ball. Meanwhile, Pacelli scored the last two touchdowns in the 33-13 CHS win.

The 12 seniors were a stellar bunch. Mike Weber's switch from quarterback to wide receiver to better the team epitomized the group. Besides Weber, the seniors were Russ Adler, Ken Allington, Ron Beaver, Jack David, Dennis Desbrow, Tom Heinzen, John Henning, Larry Meress, Warren Rhyner, Jerry Wilczewski, and Paul Wunsch. Rhyner's 11 touchdowns paced all scorers with 66 points. He was followed by Meress (43), Koch (29), junior speedster Jim Weister (24), and Mike Weber (13). The versatile Weber made All-Conference in his first year playing end. The dangerous backfield duo of Meress and Rhyner were also CWCC All-Conference picks.

1961 CWCC Standings	W	L	T	TP	OPP
Wis. Rapids Assumption	4	0	0	94	34
Marshfield Columbus	3	1	0	95	53
Chippewa Falls McDonell	2	2	0	46	43
Stevens Point Pacelli	0	3	1	27	94
Wausau Newman	0	3	1	40	78

1962: First Pacelli-for-Title Game

Many fans of CHS football savored the battles of conference unbeatens from Columbus and Pacelli high schools, with the CWCC crown on the line. The season-ending faceoffs between Columbus and Pacelli had a 14-year run from 1977 to 1990. But the first one occurred in 1962, and it was the toughest Columbus loss of the year, a sign of things to come. The season opened on a Saturday evening with a new electric scoreboard on display at Beell Stadium. The Dons manhandled Mosinee 33-2 in a steady downpour. The game featured a pair of long touchdowns—Jack Morzinski's 50-yard interception return and Mike Dumas' 75-yard TD reception from Chuck Koch. On the extra-point attempt before halftime, an alert Koch grabbed a low, skidding snap, took two steps to his right, and drop-kicked the point after to make it 27-0. The last CHS touchdown was set up by a Pete Mancl fumble recovery. Dons reserves played most of the second half.

A new Catholic high school, Lourdes Academy of Oshkosh, controlled their first game against CHS, thanks partly to a pair of classy backs, Celichowski and Grable. The Dons fell to the bigger Knights 19-7 in their second game of the year the following Saturday night in Marshfield. A week later they traveled to historic Breese Stevens Stadium in Madison and were outmanned in a 19-13 loss to Edgewood. The win pushed the Crusaders' mark to 3-0. Bruising 235-pound fullback Tom Teff created havoc for the Dons in the first half. But the Dons made halftime adjustments and Teff ended with 80 yards on the night. Whoever wrote the book on how tides shift quickly in high school football must have seen Columbus play Assumption in Wisconsin Rapids. Chuck Koch's 59-yard TD weave through the Royals defense just before halftime turned the game upside down. Trailing 14-0 before Koch's jaunt, the Dons went on to topple Assumption 27-14, their first win over their Wood County rivals in four years. Coach Gordy Clay's move of Bill Bymers from the line to fullback also proved integral to the win. Bymers' speed and raw power enabled the Dons to convert four fourth-and-short situations into first downs. Assumption ran 29 plays for 214 yards in the first half but eked out only 8 yards on eight plays in the second half.

The largest turnout of the season witnessed Chuck Koch's pinpoint accuracy in the Dons' 25-0 homecoming win over Newman on the next Saturday night. Mike Dumas was fast emerging as both a superb receiver and Koch's favorite target. Newman ran the ball well at the end against CHS reserves. The Cardinals' no-huddle offense perplexed the young Dons. But it was the sixth homecoming win in a row for Columbus. At the Fairgrounds in Chippewa Falls the next week, the Dons trailed the McDonell Macks 21-19 with just under a half-minute to go. What happened next is one for the ages. QB Chuck Koch, playing with a sore arm and hurting every time he passed, attempted what today is called a Hail Mary pass. On his own 45-yard line, Koch took the snap and threaded a perfect spiral into the end zone. Three Macks defenders were covering junior Mike Dumas but the six-one end had a step on them. With his back to the ball, Dumas made a spectacular over-the-shoulder catch of a perfectly thrown ball. With the scoreboard now reading Columbus 25, McDonell 19, Macks fans slowly realized the glitter of homecoming events would take on a different sheen. Twenty-one seconds remained on the scoreboard after the "Miracle at McDonell." The fairytale ending overshadowed Jim Weister's sensational second-quarter, 48-yard jaunt on a hook-and-ladder play.

The Pacelli match-up at Goerke Field in Stevens Point didn't quite live up to its billing. The Cardinals double-teamed Mike Dumas, who had gotten at least one reception in every game. Pacelli's big, swift line just got stronger as the game progressed. The Cardinals were deserving of their first CWCC crown and defeated

Columbus 28-12. There is no doubt the Dons came into the season finale against Campion banged up from the Pacelli game, and the Red Knights took advantage, annihilating them 51-0 at Beell Stadium. The truth is, Campion annihilated everyone that year. It was their last game as an independent. The next fall they would be the newest member of the Central Wisconsin Catholic Conference.

Eight seniors capped their Columbus careers against Campion: Dennis Blum, Bill Bymers, Rick Merkel, Pat Nealis, Denny Regele, Paul Ruder, Ken Weigel, and Jim Weister. Chuck Koch led all Dons in scoring with 46 points, followed by Bymers (36), Weister (24), and Mike Dumas (18). Dumas, Koch, and Bymers were selected for All-Conference honors. Dumas and Koch, both juniors, were unanimous picks by the coaches.

1962 CWCC Standings	W	L	TP	OPP
Stevens Point Pacelli	4	0	75	31
Marshfield Columbus	3	1	89	63
Wis. Rapids Assumption	2	2	75	60
Wausau Newman	1	3	24	65
Chippewa Falls McDonell	0	4	46	90

1963: The Amazing Koch Brothers

There was no doubt which of the six teams was best in the CWCC in 1963. To claim the crown, undefeated newcomer Campion Academy drubbed CHS 39-0 on a misty, muddy day in Prairie du Chien. But the Koch brothers—not the ones who would become famous in business and politics—paced the Dons en route to a 4-1 second-place finish. All-Diocesan quarterback Chuck Koch, a senior, was joined in the backfield by a pair of sophomore running backs, his younger brother Bobby and pile-driving bruiser Lloyd Hoffman. Coach Gordy Clay moved Bobby from fullback to halfback just before the first game to make room for Hoffman.

In the season opener to dedicate Mosinee High School's new football field, the Dons bolted to a 27-0 lead after three quarters and cruised to a 27-13 win. The Koch brothers scored 21 that Saturday afternoon. Chuck Koch displayed his CWCC 100-yard dash champion speed on an 80-yard TD run. The Dons humbled the Lourdes Academy Knights in Oshkosh the following Saturday afternoon, 36-0. The Koch tandem tallied 20 points, including a spectacular 64-yard tote by Bobby that saw him twist, turn, and hurdle over two players to reach the end zone. Against Pacelli, the hard-core nucleus of talented Columbus sophomores continued to show their abilities, winning 25-0. All-CWCC end Mike Dumas scored twice: on a 24-yard halfback-option toss from Bobby Koch and a nifty 50-yard swipe of a Cardinals pass.

The three-hour trip to Hoffman Memorial Field in Prairie du Chien proved no more satisfying for the Dons than any of their previous six contests against the Red Knights. The Dons had only one touchdown to show over all of those encounters. Coach L.G. Friedrichs and his Campion team overwhelmed conference competition in 1963 by scoring 215 points and yielding a scant 7 in their five CWCC encounters. At Wausau the following Saturday night, Newman and Columbus headed into the halftime break knotted at 13-13. Lloyd Hoffman injured his knee just before the whistle. Bobby Koch, who didn't have a carry in the first half, helped the Dons control the ball in the second half. With 20 unanswered points, the Dons departed with a convincing 33-13 victory. The Kochs scored 15. The talented brothers scored all 13 of the team's points in a slim 13-6 homecoming win over Assumption on Columbus Day evening. The Dons broke the goal line on their opening drive and again with six minutes left. Columbus halted a Royals rally at the end to preserve the victory. Dan Hoffman stood out on defense, even stealing the ball from an Assumption player on one occasion. In the penultimate game of the year, played in a heavy Beell Stadium fog, the Dons blanked McDonell 20-0. Players could not see each other across the field at game's end. The Macks managed to cross midfield just twice. The Koch brothers accounted for all scoring.

A bruised and battered Columbus 11 hobbled into the season finale at Beell Stadium against coach Earl Wilke's talented Edgewood Crusaders. CHS had four players out with injuries, and would lose two more (tackle Bob Fischer and guard Tom Knauf) during the contest. In his 35th year at Madison, Wilke boasted a 38-man traveling squad. His Crusaders overcame an early 7-0 CHS lead (on a 52-yard pass from Chuck to Bobby Koch). Though the Dons dominated play in the second quarter, a Tom Teff touchdown for Edgewood before half shifted the momentum. Even Jerry Morzinski's 77-yard kickoff return to the Edgewood 11-yard line late in the game didn't alter the flow. Edgewood prevailed 28-7. It was a tough-luck ending to an otherwise stellar 6-2 season.

For these 13 seniors the game marked their last appearance as players at Beell Stadium: Terry Behrens, Glenn Brost, Mike Dumas, Tom Green, Dan Hoffman, Chuck Koch, Gerry Langreck, Pete Mancl, Tom Merkel, John Miller, Jerry Morzinski, John Nesser, and Pete Weinfurtner. Chuck and Bob Koch accounted for 103 of the team's 161 points, with Bob scoring nine TDs for 54 points and Chuck adding 49 points. Mike Dumas and Lloyd Hoffman each scored four touchdowns for 24 points each. Chuck Koch booted 40 extra points and a field goal in his brilliant four-year kicking career. He went on to kick collegiately for the University of South Dakota. The season turned out to be coach Gordy Clay's sixth, and final, guiding the Dons. With a newly earned master's degree in counseling from UW-Stout, the 31-year-old Clay decided to transfer to Menomonie High School with his wife Joan and their two small children. He compiled a 31-16-1 mark in Marshfield. Mike Dumas and Chuck Koch were the only repeaters on the All-Conference team. Koch was one of four unanimous picks.

1963 CWCC Standings	W	L	TP	OPP
Prairie du Chien Campion	5	0	215	7
Marshfield Columbus	4	1	91	59
Wis. Rapids Assumption	3	2	102	61
Chippewa Falls McDonell	2	3	24	100
Stevens Point Pacelli	1	4	32	110
Wausau Newman	0	5	27	154

1964: The Walt Kroll Era Begins

Columbus High School Principal Father Dan Kelly hired Glenwood City-raised Walt Kroll as Gordy Clay's replacement. Kroll, a University of Minnesota graduate, had been head track coach at Milwaukee Lincoln High School and assisted a well-entrenched Comet football coach. The first points of the Kroll era came on a 3-yard plunge by Lloyd Hoffman, set up by a Denny Goeres fumble recovery. It occurred in the early going of a 26-7 sun-splashed home win over Mosinee. Tom Knauf and Dave Kraus also recovered fumbles for the victorious Dons in the season opener.

Bob Koch scored two second-half touchdowns the following Saturday night when Columbus blanked Newman 14-0 at Beell Stadium. The first half was played in a steady downpour on a field already softened by drizzle the previous day. It was a true mud bowl when the teams went to the locker room locked at 0-0. CHS took the second half kick-off and marched 66 yards in 13 plays to take the lead. Two stellar defensive plays by Ray Mancl in the fourth quarter swung the momentum to Columbus. Kroll admitted in later years that part of the lure in coming to Columbus was the talent-laden class of 1966. It did not take long for two of those juniors to emerge, the one-two backfield punch of halfback Bobby Koch and fullback Lloyd Hoffman.

After the Dons got off to a 2-0 start, they ran into a 3-0 Wisconsin Rapids Assumption team. The annual game was becoming a heated rivalry between the two Wood County schools, usually with championship implications. An early Tom Knauf fumble recovery led to Eddie Fischer's 43-yard TD gallop on the next play. The extra-point pass attempt failed. Columbus held on to a slim 6-0 lead until the fourth quarter when Assumption QB Bill Korbol scampered in from 11 yards out on a keeper. Korbol's boot put the Royals ahead with 6:15 remaining. CHS had the ball on Assumption's 5-yard line at the end of the game but could not score on three tries from there. The Dons definitely had their chances at Witter Field but could not capitalize and fell to the Royals 7-6 in a defensive battle.

McDonell came to a windy Beell Stadium the following Saturday. The Macks played like they wanted the game more and emerged with a 14-0 shutout. Columbus had difficulty passing in the windy conditions and tossed three interceptions. Many other passes were dropped by CHS receivers. Next game, Columbus scored its first-ever athletic victory over Regis, 14-6 in Eau Claire. The Koch-Hoffman rushing duo punished the Ramblers by picking up 275 yards, with Koch scoring the touchdowns and Hoffman adding the extra points on runs. Koch had a highlight reel-worthy 36-yard TD run midway through the fourth quarter. The hard-charging Dons line won the interior battle as the game progressed. Previous to 1964, the Dons had lost twice to Regis in football and 11 straight times on the basketball hardwood. On the following Saturday night, the Campion Red Knights doused some Columbus homecoming spirit with a convincing 25-12 victory. It would be the most points the defense-minded Columbus squad would give up all year. It was a brutal high school battle filled with vicious tackling. Two of the toughest Dons, Lloyd Hoffman and Tom Knauf, were sidelined for a spell due to the savage play. Interestingly, the Dons scored 12 points before they logged a first down.

Columbus ruined Pacelli's homecoming the following week in a commanding 20-0 performance, with Koch scoring three times. Koch turned heads with some sensational plays. His one-handed goal-line interception of a fourth down pass thwarted Pacelli's best scoring opportunity. Koch returned it 20 yards. When the junior speedster hit the corner on his last TD run, he carried several Cardinals with him for 5 yards before breaking free for a 54-yard run for the final score in the game. In the last game of the year, the Dons outplayed Edgewood at Warner Park in Madison but lost, 13-12. With Columbus down 13-6 in the fourth frame, the Dons marched back into contention with a 40-yard Dave Weber kickoff return. Ten plays later Dave Kraus charged over from the 1-yard line to make it 13-12. For the second time in the game, the extra-point run failed. The stop allowed the Crusaders to finish the season undefeated—for the tenth time in Edgewood history. Ed Fischer was tenacious on defense for Columbus.

Seven seniors said farewell to their Dons playing days: Dan Carsten, Larry Eckes, Denny Goeres, Jim Gruber, Gerry Loos, Jim Ohlsen, and Tom Scheuer. Juniors Bob Koch and Lloyd Hoffman were selected as All-CWCC picks. Koch had nearly half of the team's points, scoring 51. He was followed by Hoffman (16), Ed Fischer (13), and Dave Weber (12).

1964 CWCC Standings	W	L	T	TP	OPP
Prairie du Chien Campion	5	1	0	125	33
Wis. Rapids Assumption	5	1	0	113	46
Eau Claire Regis	3	3	0	74	101
Marshfield Columbus	3	3	0	66	52
Chippewa Falls McDonell	2	3	1	37	84
Stevens Point Pacelli	1	4	1	57	99
Wausau Newman	1	5	0	64	121

1965: Almost Perfect

In the most spectacular opening game in Columbus football history, the Dons dismantled a highly regarded St. Paul Cretin team, 59-14. Bob Koch scored six touchdowns, a school record that still stands, and threw for another on the Sunday afternoon before Labor Day. The Dons rolled up 507 yards of offense, behind the blocking of linemen Tom Knauf, Tom Wittman, Ken Scheuer, and Eddie Fischer. A perennial Minnesota high school powerhouse, Cretin had lost only five times in the previous nine years before entering Beell Stadium. Koch's singular performance against top-shelf competition, including 292 yards rushing, led Bob Stevenson of the *Marshfield News-Herald* to remark that it was "perhaps the greatest one-man performance in the history of Beell Stadium."

Aquinas entered the conference in 1965, and 3,000 turned out at Memorial Field in La Crosse to watch their first CWCC tilt. The Dons prevailed 13-2 with fullback Lloyd Hoffman grinding out crucial first downs in the second half. It was the first time in 13 years the Blugolds dropped their season opener. The conference had expanded to eight teams and would remain that size for 10 years. Blugolds coach John Michuta, in his 25th year, had been coached at Notre Dame by Elmer Layden, one of the famed "Four Horsemen."

Some Columbus football observers consider the third game of the season against Assumption among the toughest defeats ever. Both teams were loaded with talent. The game was played in a downpour at Beell Stadium. The Royals proved to be the better mudders, prevailing 19-7. It was impossible to distinguish jersey numbers by the end of the first quarter. The Dons fumbled 15 times, losing four of them. Bob Koch was held to 46 yards. The *News-Herald* praised Assumption's Steve Krumrei as someone "who doesn't know what it means to quit." Krumrei had 109 rushing yards and was aided by the blocking of sturdy fullback Bob Hyland, who as of 2024 was still adding to his total as the winningest coach in Wisconsin high school football history at Fond du Lac St. Mary's Springs.

The Dons rebounded with a resounding 44-0 Pacelli homecoming win the following week. Koch ran for 304 yards. One of his touchdowns was a 99-yard off-tackle burst that remains the team's longest run from scrimmage. The Dons lost hard-hitting linebacker Ed Fischer to a broken elbow in this encounter. Sophomore Terry Mancl answered coach Walt Kroll's "next up" call to fill in for the spirited senior. The *Wisconsin State Journal* reported that the Dons "stunned Edgewood" and called Koch "the sensational speedster" after he rushed for 257 yards and Columbus ended the Crusaders' 13-game winning streak in Madison. Koch's 70-yard fake punt TD run with 20 seconds before the half allowed the Dons to take an emotional 18-6 lead into the locker room. Lloyd Hoffman added a second half touchdown to make the final margin of victory 25-6. Edgewood would finish the season 7-1-1.

In Wausau the following Saturday afternoon, QB Dave Weber's 62-yard TD pass to Buster Sexton 14 seconds before halftime put an exclamation point on two solid quarters. Even though Koch was double- and triple-teamed, he emerged with 178 rushing yards. The Dons breezed to a 40-21 win over Newman. In the final quarter Kroll gave valuable playing experience to the reserves and freshmen. Columbus finally got a win over Campion, and in Prairie du Chien, no less. The 21-6 triumph left CHS trailing 1-8 in the all-time series. Columbus set the tone with a 70-yard opening touchdown drive. The last touchdown sealed the win for the navy-and-white. It was a 97-yard punt return by Koch that remains the longest in the team's chronicles. Regis came into Beell Stadium for the next-to-last game of the year. The Ramblers controlled the ball for the first five minutes. When Columbus finally got the ball, Koch ran 65 yards for a touchdown. He ended the night with 195 yards. The Dons evened the series with the Ramblers at 2-2 with a convincing 28-7 win. In the season finale, the Dons pummeled McDonell 34-13 in Chippewa Falls. Four busloads of Columbus fans roared their approval at the fairgrounds as the Dons finished 8-1, their best mark since their undefeated 1958 season.

These 11 seniors ended their CHS careers playing on one of the most-remembered Columbus teams: Greg Capes, Ed Fischer, Lloyd Hoffman, Tom Knauf, Bob Koch, Steve Koenig, Dave Langreck, Ray Mancl, Don Pueschner, Dave Weber, and Tom Wittman. Koch became the first Dons player to record over 100 points in a season, tallying 132 on 22 touchdowns. The team's 271 points were the most ever scored by a Columbus team to that point. Lloyd Hoffman contributed 46 and Dave Weber 32. Knauf, Hoffman, and Koch were all selected for the All-Conference team. Koch's singularly spectacular nine-game season (22 touchdowns, 1,698 yards rushing, 11.6 yards per carry) led to All-State and Parade Magazine All-American honors.

Koch played in college at the University of South Dakota (USD). His career was cut short by injuries but not before he and his 1968 Coyote teammates made their mark in coach Joe Salem's third year at the helm. The only blemish on their 9-1 record was a loss to decades-long powerhouse North Dakota State. In 2018 the entire 1968 team was inducted into the USD Athletics Hall of Fame. The place-kicker on that decorated Coyotes team was none other than Bob's older brother, Chuck Koch. The *Sioux Falls Argus-Leader* newspaper referred to Bobby Koch as the "Coyote Dazzler." In less than two years of varsity play in college, he set USD records for single-season scoring (102 points), longest run from scrimmage (89 yards), and longest touchdown reception (80 yards). He also returned four kicks for touchdowns: kick-offs of 94 and 92 yards and punts of 70 and 65 yards. Later in life, when asked about his best players ever, Kroll often remarked that there was "the great one" and then the others. Few players wore Koch's #48 in Kroll's remaining decades on Marshfield's west side.

1965 CWCC Standings	W	L	T	TP	OPP
Wis. Rapids Assumption	7	0	0	127	74
Marshfield Columbus	6	1	0	187	68
La Crosse Aquinas	4	2	1	145	88
Chippewa Falls McDonell	4	3	0	55	111
Eau Claire Regis	3	3	1	90	144
Prairie du Chien Campion	2	5	0	85	140
Wausau Newman	1	6	0	99	183
Stevens Point Pacelli	0	7	0	73	178

1966: Steady Improvement

After a shaky start, the Dons made a full recovery, going 5-4 on the year and 5-2 in the CWCC. But in their first two encounters, they got spanked as they would never be spanked again in the Walt Kroll era. Superior Central drubbed the Dons 40-13 in the season opener. It was the northern-most game played in Dons history. Superior's two 1965 losses to Minnesota powerhouses Edina and Bloomington probably cost the northerners the previous year's mythical Wisconsin prep championship. Against Columbus, Superior speedster Packy Paquette scored four TDs. Roger Goldbach, a transfer from Marshfield Senior High, was the Dons' workhorse in the loss. This time around, it was the Dons who scored a couple of consolation touchdowns at game's end.

The following Saturday afternoon at Beell, the Dons were humbled 48-7 by the Kenosha St. Joseph Lancers. It was the most points ever scored on a Kroll team. St. Joe's sparkling halfback Mike Vernezze got the Lancers on the board on the second play. He finished with three touchdowns and 161 rushing yards on 10 carries. The Dons managed to move the ball between the 20-yard lines but did not threaten to score. Poor tackling, along with having only ten players on the field six times, hurt CHS. The early season setbacks proved to be fruitful learning experiences for the young team. The third game, a 32-12 win over Pacelli in Point, saw the

Dons return two punts for touchdowns. Dan Maurer took the first one 60 yards in the second quarter. One frame later Buster Sexton returned a punt 55 yards for six points. Tom Tobin spearheaded the tough CHS defense. It was the first time in four years that the Cardinals managed to score against the Dons. Sexton's brilliant 34-yard end-around touchdown run 16 seconds before halftime added emotional heft to the Columbus intermission break.

Homecoming pitted the Dons against the ninth-ranked team in the state, La Crosse Aquinas. The first Blugold TD came gift wrapped as the Dons yielded a misplayed punt to the visitors on the two-yard line. Columbus settled down and gave the Blugolds all they could handle. Two late Aquinas TDs in the final six minutes made the 26-6 loss appear worse than it was. Six-three defensive end Roger Goldbach played tough all day for the navy-and-white. Aquinas would finish the year ranked eighth in the state.

Columbus had Newman down 28-6 late in the fourth quarter when the Cardinals struck like lightning—two touchdowns in 44 seconds—against the Dons freshmen unit. Danny Maurer's 31-yard runback of the opening kick set the tone for the night at Beell. The ensuing 10-play TD drive finished with a 4-yard Roger Goldbach run. The Dons used the tackle-eligible play to perfection three times in critical situations. Bob Vobora ran over three Cardinals on the first connection, resulting in a 32-yard TD. Even though Columbus dominated, the 28-20 final score made it appear a much closer contest. Goldbach injured his knee in the match. He was out for the remainder of the season.

For the second year in a row Campion fell to the Dons, this time in Marshfield, 33-13. The Red Knights scored first but the Dons immediately countered with a nifty Buster Sexton 39-yard end-around. Team captain Ed Frary recovered a Campion fumble on the first play of the second half. Later in the same period Jim Haselberger returned an interception 45 yards to the 2-yard line. Terry Mancl took it over from there. He led the 266-yard team ground effort with 101 yards and two rushing touchdowns. The next Saturday night Columbus controlled play in the first half in Eau Claire but Regis turned the tables in the second half, building a 20-0 lead. With four minutes remaining, CHS QB Paul Mancl lofted a screen pass to Sid Seidl for a 23-yard score. Bill Rhyner recovered the onside kick at the Columbus 44-yard line, which had Ramblers fans squirming in their seats. Paul Mancl marched the Dons down the field and scored on a 2-yard QB sneak with 1:38 left. John Kleiber snatched Mancl's all-important extra-point pass to tighten things up at 20-13. Columbus' second onside kick within three minutes fell into Regis arms, ending chances for a come-from-behind win. The Ramblers hung on for the victory.

Terry Mancl's extra-point run in the third quarter of the McDonell game proved to be the decisive point in a 7-6 fumble-plagued win the next Saturday night in Marshfield. The point-after followed an impressive 11-play, 65-yard opening third quarter drive. Tom Seidl ran 18 yards on a reverse for CHS. Sophomore Paul Blum did a good job playing for the injured Dan Maurer. McDonell's Krhin brothers, Gene and Dan, gave the Dons fits all night. The Dons lost Buster Sexton to a knee injury when a Macks defender piled on after the whistle had blown.

The season finale against Assumption was played before a good-sized crowd in Wisconsin Rapids. The Royals were undefeated and ranked fifth in the state. The Dons were battered with injuries and had four starters unable to play, forcing them to start seven sophomores. They used ball control to try to thwart Assumption. The Dons ran 48 first-half plays to 16 for the Royals in sub-freezing temperatures. A third quarter bounce of the football saw a Royals fumble taken in stride by speedy Tom "Sid" Seidl for a 68-yard score. The Dons hung on for an improbable 14-7 win that cost the Royals outright claim to the CWCC title. Bob Stevenson of the *Marshfield News-Herald* wrote, "In 16 years of football, Columbus has won some big games, and some Columbus team may have played as well, but no victory was ever bigger, and no Columbus team ever played better than the 1966 aggregation that was at least a three-touchdown underdog going into a game against a team that outweighed it almost 30 pounds to the man in the line." The fired up Dons had achieved one of the most memorable wins in program history. The unexpected win also snapped Assumption's two-season unbeaten streak. The Royals finished the year ranked tenth among large schools in Wisconsin.

The eight seniors on the CHS roster for the Assumption upset were Jake Dick, Ray Durst, Ed Frary, Roger Goldbach, Dave Kraus, Walt Sexton, Tom Tobin, and Bob Vobora. The Dons had seven players score in double digits on their way to 153 team points. Roger Goldbach led with 32 points, followed by Terry Mancl with 24 and Paul Mancl, Buster Sexton, and Tom Seidl with 18 each. John Kleiber tallied 16 and Willy Wilcott notched 12 points. Center Dave Kraus was the lone CHS pick on the All-Conference team. Like most other conferences at the time, the CWCC selected only an offensive team.

1966 CWCC Standings	W	L	TP	OPP
La Crosse Aquinas	6	1	279	46
Wis. Rapids Assumption	6	1	195	80
Marshfield Columbus	5	2	133	104
Eau Claire Regis	4	3	168	131
Prairie du Chien Campion	4	3	164	156
Chippewa Falls McDonell	2	5	81	186
Wausau Newman	1	6	111	200
Stevens Point Pacelli	0	7	56	275

1967: Third Best in Wisconsin

Columbus concluded its best season to date, going 9-0 and ranking third in Wisconsin's final big school poll. It wasn't just that the varsity squad went undefeated, so did the junior varsity and freshman teams. They finished with unblemished 5-0 and 8-0 marks, respectively. Coach Walt Kroll's 1967 football program at Columbus High School compiled an impeccable 22-0 record. The Dons opened the campaign against the same two teams that shredded them in 1966—but with opposite results this time.

Columbus stunned Superior Senior High 39-0 at Beell Stadium. Prep football fans came to see Superior's all-state QB candidate Paul Hammerbach but walked away talking about the marvelous play of Columbus QB Bill Draxler. Bob Stevenson, writing for the *Marshfield News-Herald*, called Bill Draxler's five-touchdown pass performance "a passing exhibition that ranks as probably the finest ever put on by a Marshfield prep player." In the first half of his first varsity start, Draxler threw four TDs, including a 34-yarder to Paul Mancl on the Dons' first offensive play of the year. He finished the day seven of 12 for 197 yards. His five TD tosses broke the school single-game record. It would never be topped. Paul Mancl, who Kroll shifted from QB to halfback for his junior season, snatched the ball from a Superior defender for the last touchdown of the day. It was Mancl's third TD reception in the game.

The following week Columbus battled both gale-like winds off Lake Michigan and St. Joseph High School. The northeasterly winds blasted into Kenosha's Lakefront Stadium, playing havoc with both teams. The Bob Carbone-led Lancers dominated play in the first half and held a 7-0 halftime advantage. The Dons, playing against the wind in the first and fourth quarters, managed to score 14 unanswered second-half points for a 14-7 win. Sid Seidl's 34-yard TD run on a reverse in the third quarter reset the Dons. The Saturday afternoon affair was ill-fit for football and the Dons were glad to make the long bus ride home with their second win in as many games. The following Friday night an enthusiastic Columbus team lit up Memorial Stadium in La Crosse. Willy Wilcott dumped Aquinas' Dave Weiland for a 5-yard loss on a goal-line play just before halftime. The stop further energized a Columbus team already ablaze with energy. Tom Schuetz recovered a Blugold fumble in the third quarter that proved fortuitous. On the next play Dan Maurer scored on a draw for the Dons. Columbus took a well-earned 33-12 win over Aquinas. Kroll always believed that to win the CWCC crown, the Dons had to beat Aquinas.

The swift Dons clobbered Newman's lumbering Cardinals 46-6 the following Saturday night in Wausau. Columbus wasted no time, scoring on their first drive, an 11-play, 68-yard effort capped by Terry Mancl's 1-yard plunge. The Dons executed their draw play to perfection several times. Dan Maurer helped spoil Newman's homecoming with 149 yards on the ground en route to scoring two touchdowns. The elusive Maurer also picked off two passes and had a 90-yard kickoff return called back. Many on-target passes were dropped by Dons receivers. Even in defeat, Newman's Mark Duginske showed why he was regarded as one of the best receivers in the state. The Dons earned a 12-7 win over Campion the next Saturday afternoon in Prairie du Chien near the confluence of the Wisconsin and Mississippi rivers. Campion established control immediately by running 21 first-quarter plays compared to five for Columbus. A Sid Seidl end-zone interception at the start of the second frame sparked the Dons. They embarked on a soul-destroying, 13-play, 80-yard march that kept the ball away from the Red Knights. Terry Mancl carried it over from the 1-yard line. The final CHS score was set up on a smartly executed Bill Draxler-to-Paul Mancl screen pass. Maurer took it from there.

Regis and Columbus played in mud at Beell the next week. It reminded many game goers of the fateful Assumption-Columbus game from two years earlier. Columbus adjusted to the field conditions and never fumbled. The Dons played nearly flawless football in the second half and emerged with a 16-0 triumph. Kroll said Maurer "ran with a great deal of authority and determination." Also coming in for praise were defensive tackle Paul Sinn and replacement punter Curt Kaiser, who kept Regis in their own territory much of the game. Sophomore reserve defensive back Dave Drach nabbed three interceptions against the Ramblers.

As usual, Ray Gripentrog invoked his Marshfield and Marty Crowe connections to inspire McDonell in Chippewa Falls on Friday night, the 13th of October. The Dons were paced by the running of Terry Mancl and Dan Maurer. Paul Mancl's booming punts kept McDonell deep in their own territory most of the third quarter. When the Macks scored with 1:21 left in the game, it tightened the score to 19-13. McDonell's Jack Kelly recovered his team's onside kick at the Columbus 40-yard line to make things interesting. The Dons sighed relief when McDonell yielded the ball on downs with 37 seconds left.

A harvest moon brought Assumption to Beell for another CWCC title showdown. Both teams were undefeated in league play. The Royals were the biggest and fastest team Columbus had seen all year. The undefeated Dons were ranked fifth among large schools in

Wisconsin. The game proved to be a hard-hitting defensive classic yielding a 14-7 Columbus win. Assumption featured offensive multi-threat Tom Duval and a defense that keyed on Terry Mancl all night. The Royals scored first but the Dons responded to the late first quarter score with a seven-play, 75-yard scoring drive. In the end Assumption had no answer for Columbus' speed. Sid Seidl, the state 440 dash champion, twice turned the corner for touchdowns. CHS dominated the second half, holding Assumption to 16 total yards and no first downs. Kroll called it "one of the greatest wins at Columbus. Assumption has a fine football team and a great coach and gentleman in Don Penza. We enjoy our rivalry with the Royals. It was a team victory over a strong foe."

In the season finale in Marshfield the Dons scored in every quarter, blanking Pacelli 41-0. The ferocity of the game reverberated throughout Beell Stadium. The Cardinals were the biggest team CHS faced all year and employed an eight-man front at the outset. Tom Coleman's key block sprung Sid Seidl's 43-yard TD jaunt just before halftime to give CHS a 20-0 lead. The *Marshfield News-Herald* recapped the Dons' 9-0 year as "the most glorious in their history." Columbus achieved all of it with a largely underclass team.

The seven seniors who donned their game uniforms for the last time in the Pacelli rout were Gerard "Giggs" Mancl, Terry Mancl, Dan Maurer, Tom Schuetz, Ken Scheuer, Tom "Sid" Seidl, and Paul Sinn. Maurer led all Dons scorers with 72 points, followed by Seidl with 51 and Terry Mancl with 33. Paul Mancl scored 24 points, and Paul "Willy" Wilcott and Bill Draxler had 14 each. All-Conference honors were accorded halfback Danny Maurer and offensive tackle Paul Sinn. Kroll had petitioned the conference on several occasions, unsuccessfully, to add a defensive unit to the CWCC's end-of-year honors list. He was unhappy that two of Columbus' best defensive players ever—Paul Mancl and Willy Wilcott—were overlooked. Both juniors played defense predominantly. In the final statewide high school football poll for large schools, the Dons ranked third, behind Milwaukee Boys Tech and Madison La Follette. It was their highest ranking ever.

1967 CWCC Standings	W	L	TP	OPP
Marshfield Columbus	7	0	181	45
Wis.Rapids Assumption	6	1	127	53
Prairie du Chien Campion	4	3	122	104
La Crosse Aquinas	3	4	160	113
Chippewa Falls McDonell	2	5	73	114
Eau Claire Regis	2	5	80	93
Stevens Point Pacelli	2	5	65	183
Wausau Newman	2	5	81	184

1968: Sensational Seniors

The Dons opened the season at home against Milwaukee Francis Jordan under their new coach Phil Datka. After building a 39-0 lead by halftime, the regulars were pulled one play into the second half. Sixty-nine Dons saw action, down through the sixth-string. The Dons' second-string freshman squad was on the field at game's end. Columbus rolled to their 12th consecutive win with a light-hearted 51-22 triumph on a perfect early September Saturday night. The only downside was the loss of Willy Wilcott to injury in the second quarter. The next Saturday night, and for the second week in a row, the Dons held back in a game where the score could have been much higher, emerging with a 41-0 win over Newman. Juniors Dave Drach and Ray Scheuer accounted for 28 of the 41 points. Bill Draxler lit up the sky with three TD passes and 223 yards passing. Paul Mancl nabbed five of those passes for 101 yards.

Averaging over 400 yards per game on offense, the Campion Red Knights came to Beell Stadium with a 2-0 mark the following Saturday. But Ray Scheuer picked off a Campion pass in the second quarter and raced 55 yards. It was the game's only score. The 6-0 win was earned by a superior defense, despite being outweighed 25 pounds per man on the line. Defensive end Perry Kaiser's sacks spearheaded the Dons defense. Paul Mancl had a highlight-reel, one-handed interception grab as well. The following Saturday in

Eau Claire, the Dons saw their 14-game win streak come to a halt, falling 19-12 to Regis. Miscues aided Regis. A block of a CHS punt by the Ramblers with seven minutes left in the game turned the tide. Coach Tony Fiore had his Regis players sky high for this game. Wiry senior halfback and team captain Dan Pedersen led their attack with 86 yards on 25 carries. Regis stopped the Columbus wide-running game, a trademark of their impressive three-season win streak. On homecoming Columbus rebounded with a 33-0 win over McDonell on a rainy Saturday night. Dave Drach scored four touchdowns, including two on interception returns (of 55 and 35 yards). The latter TD was aided by defensive end Perry Kaiser's rush, causing a wobbly pass.

Times change. In 1967 Don Penza was Assumption's football coach. But in 1968 he had moved on as mayor of Wisconsin Rapids. The annual nail-biter between the two Wood County rivals morphed into an easy 52-14 Dons win in the Rapids. Jim Morzinski's 30-yard TD reception just before intermission made it 26-0. Columbus churned out 505 yards of offense and took a 10-5 lead in the all-time series. The following Saturday night in Stevens Point, the Dons dominated Pacelli in a 27-0 shutout. They ran 74 plays, the Cardinals just 42. Columbus showcased backfield depth with five runners gaining at least 30 yards. Pacelli's Mike Zimmerman was the CWCC's leading rusher coming into the game but the Dons limited him to 16 yards. The game highlight was Bill "Sudsy" Seidl's brilliant leaping TD catch in the third quarter.

The seniors of the class of 1969, many now in their third year of varsity action, closed out their conference careers with a 19-6 win over Aquinas in Marshfield. It was a hard-hitting, well-played high school football game with only one penalty infraction. Paul Mancl— an all-purpose threat as a runner, receiver, passer, and punter—had another sparkling performance for the navy-and-white. Coach Walt Kroll said it was the team's finest game of the year. The season finale was a non-conference affair with always-tough Dubuque (Iowa) Wahlert. The Golden Eagles shut down the Dons ground game in the second half on their way to a convincing 33-13 victory. Seven turnovers did not help. At the time Wahlert was said to be the tenth largest Catholic high school in the country.

The 1968 team finished their season at 7-2. The 13 seniors were Jeff Binder, Paul Blum, Mike Colby, Tom Coleman, Bill Draxler, Alan Hartl, Jim Haselberger, Fritz Hastreiter, Paul Mancl, Jim Morzinski, Jim Sexton, Mark Smith, and Willy Wilcott. Six Dons claimed seven spots on the 1968 All-CWCC squad. It was the first year selections were made for both offense and defense. Five-nine, 160-pound Jim Haselberger was named to both units, at guard and linebacker. Other CHS picks were QB Bill Draxler, halfback Paul Mancl, offensive end Jim Morzinski, defensive middle guard Ed Smrecek, and defensive back Dave Drach.

1968 CWCC Standings	W	L	TP	OPP
Eau Claire Regis	7	0	161	30
Marshfield Columbus	6	1	190	39
La Crosse Aquinas	5	2	155	82
Prairie du Chien Campion	4	3	77	56
Chippewa Falls McDonell	3	4	80	99
Stevens Point Pacelli	2	5	104	160
Wisc. Rapids Assumption	1	6	82	191
Wausau Newman	0	7	18	210

1969: Tough Start, Brilliant Finish

The new season brought changes to Wisconsin high school football. Running or passing after a touchdown now counted for two points; kicking the PAT remained as one point. The year also saw the introduction of high school playoff football at the end of the season. The Wisconsin Independent Schools Athletic Association (WISAA) would name four schools to vie for the first-ever independent state football championship. It would take the public school association, the WIAA, seven years to catch on to this good idea. Columbus started slowly but finished with a four-win conference flourish outscoring the opposition 108-26. It enabled the Dons to achieve an overall 5-4 mark and a 4-3 CWCC record.

Two Wisconsin football powerhouses met at Beell Stadium in an opening-game dream match-up. In their past 25 games George Chyrst's Edgewood Crusaders were 23-2 and coach Walt Kroll's Columbus Dons were 21-4. The Dons dominated the first half until the Madison school found their weakness—pass defense—and exploited it for a 22-6 win. CHS receivers also dropped a couple of sure-TD passes. Columbus rebounded the following Friday night, rolling to a 20-6 win at Plymouth after trailing 6-0 at the half. Jeff Rasmussen and Dave Drach each had over 100 yards rushing, with both hitting their stride in the second half. Early in the fourth quarter QB Steve Varney's fourth-down tackle-eligible pass to Chuck Vobora came up a yard shy of the goal line. Plymouth signal-caller Clark Kaufmann tried passing from his own end zone but the ball was batted into the air. Dons defensive end John Adler came down with it for a rare end-zone TD interception.

Campion torched Columbus 36-12 in Prairie du Chien the next Saturday afternoon. The Red Knights already had notched wins over Milwaukee Marquette and Racine St. Catherine's. While this was a bigger Columbus team than most, Campion was even bigger. The Dons threatened three times inside the 20-yard line in the first quarter and came away empty-handed. Greg McMoore ran wild for Campion, getting 184 yards on eight carries. The only Columbus highlight was a third-quarter 62-yard TD pass from Varney to Bill "Sudsy" Seidl.

"It is not often Columbus loses a game it should have won, but it happened Saturday night," the *News-Herald* stated after a bitter 20-18 home loss to Regis. Columbus dominated play until 4:51 in the third quarter. A controversial TD caused a momentum switch that the Dons were unable to overcome. Defensive back Ray Scheuer jarred an end-zone pass loose but the official, screened from the play by both the receiver and defender, said the Regis receiver held it long enough to have possession. The touchdown stood and brought the Ramblers to within four points at 18-14. The Dons, a notoriously poor extra-point team over the years, had fate catch up with them as they failed to convert on any of their three post-touchdown tries. All three Rambler scores came on fourth-down passes.

The Dons were blanked for the first time in 40 games at Chippewa Falls the following week in a true defensive battle. Jeff Pulver's 27-yard McDonell field goal with four minutes left in this rugged contest allowed the Macks to escape with a 3-0 victory. Sophomore QB Jim Stangl filled in for the injured Steve Varney but it was John Adler's booming punts and good downfield coverage that kept the Macks in the hole throughout much of the game. Kroll said, "McDonell is the best team we've played all year." Columbus got back on the right track with a 30-6 homecoming win over Assumption the following Saturday night. Jeff Rasmussen dashed 50 yards, untouched, on CHS's first play from scrimmage. The junior fullback added two more scores and rushed for 117 yards. The formidable Dons defense nabbed four interceptions and limited the Royals to 26 yards rushing.

Rasmussen had another outstanding game in a 20-6 home win over Pacelli. He ran for 127 yards on 29 carries. Pacelli managed to dominate the first half of play even though the Dons held a 12-6 lead at intermission. Steve Varney's fourth-quarter insurance TD run sealed the win. The Dons won their next game at La Crosse by forcing seven Aquinas turnovers. They stopped the Blugolds 24-6 and held their ace halfback, Jim Harding, to 33 yards. Steve McMillan, a Senior High transfer playing his final year at Columbus, played his best game. His crushing performance at linebacker led the team's defensive gem. He also scored two TDs. Columbus closed the season with a 34-8 romp over Newman in Wausau. Coming into the game Newman had the leading quarterback in the CWCC, Clark Woznicki. But the Dons intercepted him five times, tossed him for a safety, and blocked one of his punts. Meanwhile, McMillan finished his short CHS career with a 42-carry, 204-yard rushing performance. The 42 totes remains a program record. Jim Stangl grabbed two interceptions with the other three tallied by Ed Smrecek, Seidl, and McMillan. Greg Higgins blocked a punt that set up McMillan's fourth and final touchdown of the night.

For these 15 seniors it was their last chance to suit up for the Dons: Dave Drach, Tim Fehrenbach, Kurt Koenig, Steve McMillan, Bob Merkel, Jim Niehaus, Jim Perner, Randy Pokallus, Scheuer, Greg Scheppler, Dave Schindhelm, Paul Schlagenhaft, Seidl,

Smrecek, and Varney. McMillan led all scorers with 48 points. Junior Jeff Rasmussen was not far behind at 38, followed by Seidl with 26, junior John Adler with 14, and Ray Scheuer and Steve Varney with 12 each. Three Dons were named All-Conference at four positions. Junior Bob Rose was selected as a tackle on both offense and defense. McMillan was chosen at linebacker and Seidl at defensive back.

1969 CWCC Standings	W	L	T	TP	OPP
Chippewa Falls McDonell	6	0	1	74	42
Prairie du Chien Campion	6	1	0	206	70
Eau Claire Regis	5	2	0	108	85
Marshfield Columbus	4	3	0	138	85
La Crosse Aquinas	2	5	0	108	139
Wausau Newman	2	5	0	110	138
Wis. Rapids Assumption	2	5	0	98	142
Stevens Point Pacelli	0	6	1	18	159

1970 – 1979

1970: Four Consecutive Shutouts

The 1970 team finished 6-1 in the conference, second behind a great Aquinas team. All the blemishes on their 6-2-1 overall record were to top-shelf opposition. The last time Columbus had traveled to Madison to play Edgewood, in 1965, Warner Park hosted Crusaders home games. This time, Edgewood played its home contests at Mansfield Stadium on Madison Memorial High School's west-side campus. About 1,500 excited fans were on hand for the opener, including 69 Crusaders suited up for varsity football action. In four years under coach George Chryst, Edgewood had lost only four games. After holding the Dons to a three-and-out on their first possession, the Crusaders scored when Rusty Marshall went 52 yards for a touchdown on their first play from scrimmage. With two minutes left in the quarter, Edgewood led 20-0. Although the Dons gathered their wits and played even football statistically the rest of the way, Edgewood hung on for a 20-13 win.

The next Saturday night, Milwaukee City Conference power Rufus King came to Beell. The Generals had tied for the city crown the year before, holding opponents to less than 100 yards per game. The teams played to a 0-0 tie on a wet, but not rain-soaked, field. The Dons recovered two King fumbles on the 1-yard line, one by Greg Higgins and the other by John Adler with two minutes left. Columbus managed to get into King territory only twice the entire game. Defense was key for both teams. With seconds remaining, King's Bill Stewart attempted what could have been a game-winning field goal from the 40-yard line. When it fell short, Greg Higgins of the Dons alertly returned it all the way back to the King 45-yard line to end the game. King went on to an 8-0-1 season and finished tenth in the final statewide poll, with QB Bill Stewart and tackle Lonzo Edwards being selected first-team All-State.

Carson Park in Eau Claire hosted a game of contrasting halves the following week. Regis tossed around CHS in the first half and the Dons shoved the Ramblers about, even more so, in the second half. The turning point came in the third quarter. John Adler of Columbus got off a high 35-yard punt. When Jack Felmlee tried to make an over-the-shoulder catch, the ball struck his shoulder pads and bounced toward the Columbus goal line. Chuck Vobora recovered for the Dons on the 10-yard line. Gary Heiting ran for 9 yards before Jeff Rasmussen blasted over for the TD. The Dons won 6-0. "Rarely has a Columbus team worked so feverishly to protect a six-point lead," reported the *News-Herald*. "The Dons did it best by simply refusing to let Regis have the ball."

The Dons followed with their third straight shutout, a 24-0 win, against McDonell on a homecoming field that was wet from the previous night's rain. "It was the quickness and the alertness, the pursuit and the hard hitting of the defense that told the story," the *News-Herald* observed. Effective ball control didn't hurt either as the Dons ran 70 plays to just 42 for the Macks. Freshman place-kicker Steve Seidl also emerged in this game, kicking a 30-yard field goal. It was only the second field goal in Dons history and their first since 1961.

Columbus continued their punishing, clock-eating, ball-control ways at Wisconsin Rapids against Assumption, prevailing 21-0. Jeff Rasmussen's leg injury limited his play to defense. The Royals didn't get into CHS territory until 4:52 was left in the game. The Dons defense set a school record with a fourth consecutive shut-out. Along with the last three scoreless quarters of the Edgewood game, it brought their consecutive scoreless-quarter streak to 19. Assumption was under the tutelage of first-year coach Dick Basham, who had helped out with the Notre Dame freshman team the year before while pursuing a master's degree in South Bend.

Pacelli was sky high for their homecoming game on a brisk, sunny Saturday afternoon in Stevens Point. The Dons' scoreless string of quarters ended at 20 when PHS scored on a halfback option pass from Tom Cashin to Fritz Menzel in the second quarter. Cashin, their three-year star speedster, was held to 30 yards rushing. In the third quarter, Dale Fischer blocked Larry Sowka's punt, allowing Bob Rose to recover it at the Pacelli 19-yard line. Gary Heiting ran for the decisive go-ahead TD four plays later to make it 13-7. The Dons hung on for the win.

When undefeated Aquinas invaded Beell Stadium, they were ranked fourth in the state. The Blugolds averaged nearly 400 yards per game thanks to a large line anchored by two 225-pound tackles.

The Dons scored on the opening drive, going 67 yards on the ground. Coach Walt Kroll said Jeff Morzinski and Gary Heiting "are developing into two of the best rushers we've ever had," calling them collision backs, not home run hitters. Columbus dominated play in the first half and led 7-6 at intermission. "We should have scored a couple more touchdowns in the first half," Kroll said. "We made some key mistakes and you can't do that against a good team." Aquinas dominated the second half. An 80-yard Mike Hammes punt-return TD proved to be the backbreaker for the Dons. The Blugolds wore down the Dons and returned to La Crosse with a 36-14 win and a 7-0 record. Aquinas defensive back Jim Sackmaster would be named All-State at the conclusion of the season.

Coach Russ Grundy's Newman Cardinals came to Beell Stadium the next week with a 5-1-1 mark. The muddy field did not stop the Dons from amassing 240 yards on the ground and bolting to a 32-0 lead. Newman's initial first down came with 3:35 left in the third quarter. The Dons stopped Newman's three stars, who were conference leaders coming into the game: Barry Green, the top rusher at 6-plus yards per carry; QB Clark Woznicki, first in passing yards and TD passes; and end Mike Brzezinski, top in reception yards. Columbus held Green to 24 yards, intercepted Woznicki three times, and allowed Brzezinski only one 12-yard catch. The Dons finished with their reserves in the 32-20 win.

The Dons played their season finale at home against Campion, opening it with an onside kick. Gary Heiting recovered his own kick on the Campion 43-yard line and the Dons set sail for the evening. For the second week in a row Morzinski and Heiting each ground out more than 100 yards apiece. The pair almost accomplished the feat in two other games as well. Campion did not get its initial first down until the second minute of the fourth quarter. The Dons picked off five Red Knight passes—three by Jim Stangl and two by Bill Uthmeier. Columbus almost matched the CWCC four-game shutout mark of the 1968 team but were thwarted by Campion's 94-yard TD interception return on the last play of the season. The final score was 36-8.

Ten seniors bid farewell to Dons football: John Adler, Jim Dehn, Dale Fischer, Greg Higgins, Steve Koller, Gary Mech, Steve Meress,

Jeff Rasmussen, Bob Rose, and Chuck Vobora. Jeff Morzinski's 60 points led all Dons scorers. Rasmussen contributed 30 points and Gary Heiting 24. Freshman kicker Steve Seidl booted 21, and Adler added 12. Three Dons were selected for All-Conference honors. Rose repeated at both offensive and defensive tackle, Adler was named at defensive end, and Gary Mech was chosen at linebacker.

1970 CWCC Standings	W	L	T	TP	OPP
La Crosse Aquinas	7	0	0	268	44
Marshfield Columbus	6	1	0	146	71
Wausau Newman	4	2	1	160	98
Eau Claire Regis	3	3	1	105	84
Chippewa Falls McDonell	3	4	0	54	142
Prairie du Chien Campion	2	5	0	49	206
Stevens Point Pacelli	1	6	0	32	129
Wis. Rapids Assumption	1	6	0	52	92

1971: Injuries Dampen Season

Injuries to key players took the Dons from being a pre-season title contender to the first losing team under coach Walt Kroll. Center Jerome Perner and two way star Gary Heiting suffered season-ending injuries in the first and second games. Linebacker Jim Hastreiter was lost for four games midway through the season, and Jeff Morzinski was hampered by a deep thigh bruise that saw him miss one game but slowed his play in several others. Things started out fine on the southern border in Monroe in the season opener. The Dons bolted for all 20 of their points in the second quarter against the Cheesemakers in a 20-0 win. Ed Sheahen collected the first two of his CHS record-setting nine TD receptions, and Jeff Morzinski had his fourth straight 100-yard rushing game (carrying over from the previous season). But the loss of senior center Jerome Perner would be felt throughout the year. Next, the Dons outplayed Edgewood for three quarters in their Beell debut. When the Crusaders scored with 18 seconds left in the third quarter, the tide turned. The Crusaders rode the arm of QB Dave Geier and his short passes to a 15-3 victory. Gary Heiting suffered his injury on the last play of the first quarter.

The Dons lost a 19-14 heartbreaker at McDonell. After Bill Uthmeier ran for a two-point conversion, they held a 14-13 lead with three minutes left in the game It looked as if Ed Sheahen's two touchdown receptions would sustain the Dons. But with 19 seconds remaining, the Macks went ahead on a fourth-and-19 play. Assumption's 33-0 whitewash of Columbus at Beell Stadium the following Saturday was historic. Between 1955 and 1998, the Dons and Royals would face each other 22 times in Marshfield. But this game would be the only time the Royals would shut out the Dons on the CHS field. Assumption coach Dick Basham had his Royals on an undefeated track in only his second season.

The Dons said farewell to Don Soderberg when he decided to take his coaching and scouting skills to Stevens Point Pacelli after the class of 1971 graduated in May. He had been at Columbus High five years. The move meant the Dons faced Soderberg from across the field when Pacelli trekked to Beell for the CHS homecoming game. Missed tackles plagued the Dons defense all night. The Cardinals left Marshfield with their first win in nine years in the series, a 21-6 triumph. Ed Sheahen snared another TD pass in the loss. A 22-6 setback followed on a brisk Saturday night in La Crosse, bringing the losing streak to five. Not since Columbus lost its first five games in 1955 had they endured a spell like this. Aquinas jumped to a 14-0 lead before Ed Sheahen found Bill Uthmeier on a 28-yard option pass before halftime, narrowing the gap to 14-6. Kroll cited Uthmeier's tenacity and sensational defense in the hard-hitting contest. This campaign also marked Aquinas coaching legend John Michuta's 31st and final season guiding Blugold gridders.

The Dons got back on the winning track the following Saturday night at Thom Field in Wausau, outlasting Newman 28-14. Newman's Duane Griff scored on a pair of second-quarter reverses from his wingback position, throwing an early scare into the Dons. On the last play before halftime, Ed "Eddie Bear" Sheahen "made probably the finest catch of his career in the corner of the end zone," according to the *Marshfield News-Herald*. "Everybody but the official who was right on top of the play figured he didn't have possession when he went out of bounds with the ball." That play changed the momentum of the game. The Dons dominated the second half with outstanding ball control, running 74 plays to Newman's 43. They also welcomed back Jim "Heimer" Hastreiter, who had missed four games with an injury. The crafty, compact linebacker had numerous quarterback sacks and also ran for 46 yards. Morzinski churned out 111 yards and Jim Stangl ran for 83, including a 31-yard TD, as the Dons ground out 251 yards.

Columbus made history with their 30-6 drubbing of Campion in Prairie du Chien. No other Dons team had ever scored that many points at Hoffman Memorial Field. In fact, the first four times Columbus visited Campion they rode back to Marshfield without having scored a point. The Dons took a 17-0 halftime lead on a Morzinski run, a Sheahen reception, and a Steve Seidl field goal. Senior QB Jim Stangl connected two more times with Sheahen for second-half TD passes of 44 and 15 yards.

The home season finale also was historic. The game was cut short after three periods with Regis leading 6-0 and getting the win. The game started in a warm, light drizzle. Then the rains came. With 50-mile-an-hour winds blowing, the rain fell in sheets. The second quarter was just a few minutes old when officials halted the game at Beell Stadium. Both teams took cover in nearby junior high locker rooms. After a 20-minute wait and no let up in sight, play resumed. Because of the unbelievable weather conditions, coaches Tony Fiore of Regis and Walt Kroll of Columbus agreed to play straight through halftime and call it quits at the end of the third quarter. Rather than punt into gale-like winds, the Dons decided to go for it on fourth down from their own 10-yard line. They failed and the Ramblers took over. Three plays later John Rice scored for Regis with 1:27 left in the second quarter. The *News-Herald* described it as "the worst conditions imaginable for a football game."

The Dons finished the season 3-6 overall, 2-5 in the conference. It would not be Kroll's worst team record-wise but no other Dons team ever sustained five conference losses. Fourteen seniors saw their careers come to an end: Dick Hannum, Bob Hannum, Gary Hartnett, Gary Heiting, Steve Herkert, Dan Huber, Pat Ledden, Jeff Morzinski, Jerome Perner, Ed Sheahen, Jim Stangl, Fred Trudeau, Bill Uthmeier, and Paul Wenzel. In a nod to his steadfast services over the years, Kroll named manager Randy Kraemer as the 15th senior saying farewell to the program. Sheahen scored over half of the team's 107 points on nine TD receptions. Morzinski tallied 24 points and sophomore kicker Steve Seidl booted 15. Uthmeier's eight points and Stangl's solo touchdown rounded out the year's scoring. Three Dons were selected for All-Conference honors. Sheahen was a unanimous pick at end, shattering two CWCC receiving marks (receptions and yards receiving) and tying the TD reception mark. Morzinski was selected at halfback despite his injuries, and Uthmeier was named at linebacker.

1971 CWCC Standings	W	L	TP	OPP
Stevens Point Pacelli	7	0	129	44
Wis. Rapids Assumption	6	1	180	58
Eau Claire Regis	5	2	129	68
La Crosse Aquinas	3	4	128	87
Wausau Newman	3	4	106	136
Marshfield Columbus	2	5	84	121
Chippewa Falls McDonell	1	6	56	191
Prairie du Chien Campion	1	6	85	192

1972: A Tale of Two Seasons

The first four games were on the road and the Dons lost them all. Returning to Beell Stadium provided the balm this team needed. They won all four home encounters, scoring an eye-popping 114 points while surrendering a scant 12. Halfback Jim Hastreiter especially enjoyed the comforts of home, picking up 404 yards in the four Beell games. A late season 26-14 loss at Regis meant a second straight losing season. But the season finale at home against

McDonell turned into one of the best senior send-offs ever. When the Dons opened the season in Antigo, it marked the earliest start to a Columbus football season. The Red Robins were again loaded with talent and easily dispatched the Dons 34-0. Antigo would finish the 1972 season ranked as the top team in the state. Jim Hastreiter gave notice as an emerging star on both offense and defense. Tackle Pat Krier, a newcomer to football, played in his first high school game. Sophomores Bob Dickman, Brian Fehrenbach, and Steve Burr all got their varsity baptisms in the contest.

At Dynie Mansfield Stadium in Madison, new Edgewood coach Joel Maturi guided the Crusaders to a 21-14 win. The difference was a late-game blocked punt, which was recovered by John Kornell for a touchdown in the far reaches of the end zone. Ron "Sonny" Swenson returned punts for 53 and 21 yards. The *News-Herald* noted that sophomore halfback Steve Burr "appears headed for great things." Columbus faced Assumption next. Pete Pavloski had become the first Assumption alum to come back and coach at his alma mater. His and coach Walt Kroll's teams waged a fierce defensive battle for three quarters before the Dons faded in the fourth. Assumption won 27-0. Dan Waters ran for 128 yards for the Royals. Assumption placed eight players on the All-CWCC team at the end of the season. At Pacelli the following week, the Cardinals owned the first half and the Dons the second half. Few games could match this one for excitement. Pacelli's front wall outweighed the Dons' by 20 pounds to the man. The game was decided for good when Dave Draxler's end-zone pass to Dave Jaye sailed high with 14 seconds left. PHS prevailed 10-7. Pacelli would finish sixth in the final state big school poll with an 8-1 mark. The Cards also would be one of four teams chosen for the WISAA championship playoffs.

Having watched some of the state's best teams operate from close quarters, the Dons put it all together in their home opener, a 35-0 win over Aquinas. It snapped a five-game CHS losing streak going back to the previous season. The first Blugolds drive stalled at the Columbus 25-yard line. It would be Aquinas' deepest penetration of the night. When the Dons scored on an 11-play, 60-yard drive in the second quarter, it was only the second time all year that they had a lead. Ron Swenson's 53-yard run set up the third CHS TD. "It was the best game we've played at Beell Stadium in five years," Kroll said. It would be the most points ever scored against Aquinas in Marshfield. The 35-point differential was also the biggest ever in the 32-game rivalry that ran 1965 through 1996.

In the first quarter of the homecoming game, Ron Swenson recovered a Newman fumble from a punt at the Cardinal 28. The Dons capitalized, with Jim Smrecek scoring on a 5-yard run with nine minutes gone in the game. The TD supplied all the points the Dons would need for the 6-0 win over Newman, which nearly rallied. Newman was driving to the Columbus 16-yard line in search of a score when the game ended. Pat Krier was injured in the action and lost for the season. The Dons defense had put together 10 quarters of scoreless football heading into the Campion game at Beell Stadium. The navy-and-white extended the streak to 13 quarters before yielding a late fourth-quarter touchdown in a convincing 27-6 win. The victory upped the all-time series record with the Red Knights to 7-9, making them one of the few teams the Dons didn't hold an advantage on. The 13 scoreless quarters are even more impressive because nine of the starters on defense were underclassmen, including five sophomores. The *News-Herald* said Dave Draxler "was on the money most of the evening, but his receiving corps had a hard time hanging onto the ball." The elusive Hastreiter had his best game, running the ball for 148 yards.

Regis' big line greeted the Dons at Carson Park in Eau Claire the following Saturday night. Beset by injuries, the Ramblers were trying out 145-pound scatback John Giammona at QB. The Ramblers dominated the Dons in the first half with a new-found ground game. Their 63-yard, 11-play opening TD drive set the pace. The field was slippery and Regis adjusted to the conditions better than Columbus. Steve Burr's 70-yard second-half kickoff return put the ball on the Regis 6-yard line, setting up Hastreiter's score a few plays later. Paul Roessler was the Regis star in the 26-14 Ramblers win, getting 130 total yards, 104 running and 26 receiving. Roessler also had three interceptions. The last game of the year was a 46-6 romp over McDonell in Marshfield. The Dons jumped to a 26-0 lead before the Macks scored in the first half. McDonell was 1-7 coming in and 0-6 in the conference. It was not one of their better teams. The Dons charged out of the gate, scoring on Dave Draxler's 57-yard TD pass to Ron Swenson on the second play from scrimmage. Shortly afterward, a Steve Burr block set Swenson free down the sideline for an 82-yard punt-return touchdown. It was the most points a Dons team had scored since beating Assumption 52-14 in 1968. The Dons were playing all freshmen when the game ended.

Columbus finished the season 4-5 overall and 4-3 in the CWCC. It would be the only time in the Kroll era that back-to-back losing seasons occurred. Ten seniors played their last high school game in the McDonell rout: Paul Buttke, Jim Hastreiter, Rick Henrichs, Dave Jaye, Rick Knauf, Pat Krier, Don Oppman, Jim Smrecek, Ron Swenson, and Joe Tracy. Hastreiter and Swenson shared scoring honors, each recording six touchdowns (36 points). Smrecek added 18 points and Steve Seidl booted 13 extra points. QB Dave Draxler contributed 10. No Dons were picked for All-CWCC honors.

1972 CWCC Standings	W	L	TP	OPP
Stevens Point Pacelli	7	0	191	72
Wis. Rapids Assumption	6	1	254	35
Eau Claire Regis	5	2	138	137
Marshfield Columbus	4	3	135	75
La Crosse Aquinas	3	4	76	179
Wausau Newman	2	5	66	76
Prairie du Chien Campion	1	6	52	192
Chippewa Falls McDonell	0	7	33	179

1973: A Return to Winning Ways

The 1973 team had balance. Led by skillful ends, powerful runners, heady linemen, a determined defense, and the accurate Dave Draxler at QB, the Dons did not disappoint. They finished the season 5-3-1 overall and 4-2-1 in conference. The kicking game was covered by four-year veteran Steve Seidl handling extra points and field goals and Bob Dickman booming 37 punts for a 35.9 conference average. Much of the team's success came from a stellar group of junior-class athletes.

Menominee, a perennial powerhouse from the Upper Peninsula of Michigan, came to Marshfield for the home opener. The Indians took a 20-18 lead with 3:06 remaining but the Dons surged back. Brian Fehrenbach returned the ensuing kickoff 34 yards. The winning 14-yard TD came when Draxler rolled to his right and connected with Seidl, who made an outstanding catch in the back of the end zone for the 24-20 win. Earlier, in the third quarter, Fehrenbach had a 67-yard punt return, aided by several great blocks. The junior speedster went untouched for the TD. The biggest injury for Columbus occurred when coach Walt Kroll suffered a triple-fracture of his right arm near the wrist as he was backing up near the sidelines and slipped, hitting his hand on a drainage ditch. Team physician Dr. Robert Haight attended to Kroll immediately.

The next game featured a "battle of the quarterbacks"—Jim Schneider of Edgewood vs. Dave Draxler of Columbus. The game was played in a steady rain. The Dons didn't put as much pressure on Schneider as EHS did on Draxler. That proved fatal as the game's decisive factor was the inability of the Dons to stop the Crusaders' short passing game. The Dons only controlled the second quarter and it hurt when CHS couldn't score from the 1-yard line on two tries at the end of the first half. Tim Martinelli played a magnificent game for Edgewood, nabbing nine catches for 101 yards in the 14-0 Crusader win. Martinelli's mother had died two days earlier, and he and his teammates had attended her funeral that morning in Madison before heading north to Marshfield.

The 7-7 Pacelli standoff the next Saturday at Beell would be the last tie in school history. Overtime play would determine outright game winners from the 1974 season onward. Pacelli rode into town with a 14-game conference winning streak. They had not lost a conference game since assistant coach and mastermind Don Soderberg arrived in Stevens Point from Marshfield. The Cards had fallen, however, to Milwaukee Pius XI in the WISAA state championship game the previous fall. Against Pacelli, the Dons were unable to score despite dominating play for more than three quarters. A 7-yard pass from Dave Draxler to Steve Burr got CHS on the board with under six minutes left. Steve Seidl's PAT kick was perfect, upping the margin to 7-0. Pacelli got on track, though, picking up over half of their total yards in the minutes that remained. Pacelli scored on a 10-yard pass with two minutes left, leaving the Dons with a slim 7-6 lead. PHS head coach Bob Raczek wanted to go for the tie. His assistant Soderberg lobbied for a two-point try and the win. Greg Schulist split the uprights to tie the game. The Cardinals managed to stop Columbus and were driving for a potential game-winning Schulist field goal when called for holding. This bone-jarring, defensive affair was marred by 90 yards in penalties against the Dons.

An Aquinas homecoming game the following Saturday night found the Blugolds fired up for home battle. Aquinas scored in the second quarter to take an 8-0 lead. A fabulous punting exchange followed between Bob Dickman of Columbus and Tim Meyer of Aquinas. They gave the Memorial Field crowd something to ooh-and-ahh about with their 45-yard boomers. Brian Fehrenbach managed to take a later Meyer punt 47 yards to the Aquinas 30. From there, Dickman gathered in a 22-yard Draxler rocket for the only Dons score. Draxler and Dickman also teamed up for the PAT pass, evening the score at 8-8 before the Dons allowed two late Aquinas TDs and fell 20-8. The Blugold PAT kick attempts were their first tries in 22 years. Wausau's Thom Field provided the salve the Dons needed the following Saturday evening when the Dons humbled Newman 27-0. Needing a shake-up, Kroll moved junior Tom Draxler from guard to halfback during the week. Clarence Hartl's 43-yard interception return to the Newman 3-yard line set up the first Dons TD. Brian Fehrenbach's punt return to the Newman 42 set up the second touchdown, along with a 27-yard pass play, Dave Draxler to Tom Draxler. Newman crossed the 50-yard line only once in their homecoming game. With their 14th win in a row over the Cardinals, the Dons rode past Rib Mountain on the way home with an all-time 16-3 mark against Newman.

Prairie du Chien was not as friendly the following Saturday afternoon, with Campion triumphing 18-14. The Red Knights defense was tough, holding Steve Burr and his "hit, spin, and roll" style of running to 63 yards. The previous week this same defense held shifty Dan Waters to 56 yards against Assumption. A 22-yard TD strike from Draxler to Dickman narrowed the score with four minutes left. The Dons recovered their onside kick attempt but Draxler got sacked three times in a row by Campion's Mike Fichter to end Columbus' come-from-behind hopes. It was the last time Columbus would play in Wisconsin's second oldest city. The following week, Brian Fehrenbach electrified a large Columbus homecoming crowd on a 67-yard TD punt return early in the second quarter. His ballet down the sideline set the pace for the Dons' 26-6 win over Regis on a brilliant October afternoon. For the second consecutive week Bob Dickman caught two Draxler TD passes. The Dons put forth a great defensive effort all day long, with Roger Trudeau and Tom Draxler picking off errant passes. The *News-Herald* singled out Draxler: "Time after time (he) knifed through to drop Rambler ball carriers at or behind the line of scrimmage."

In Chippewa Falls the following week, Fehrenbach again started the Dons' scoring, going all the way on a 57-yard punt return. Later in the first quarter he gathered in a 14-yard pass from Dave Draxler to make it 14-0. Tom Draxler ran an interception back 26 yards in the second quarter to give the Dons a comfortable 20-0 halftime advantage. A tough Dons defense allowed the Macks past midfield only once. Dons reserves played the last four minutes and did okay against the McDonell regulars in the 45-7 win.

Assumption traveled the 31 miles to Marshfield the following Saturday night with a #1 statewide ranking among medium-sized schools. And rightfully so. The Royals had amassed 197 points and yielded a minuscule 18 on their way to a perfect 8-0 mark. Kroll called this Assumption team "the finest ever assembled in the CWCC." As in the game against AHS eight years and 38 days earlier, this one was played in the rain at Beell Stadium. But Dons signal-caller Dave Draxler played like it wasn't raining. The Royals were not content with an 8-7 lead. With the ball on the Columbus 46-yard line and 40 seconds remaining before halftime, Assumption took to the air. Bob Dickman intercepted Tom Brey's pass and returned it to the Royals' 26-yard line. Dickman followed that feat with a sensational grab of Dave Draxler's 26-yard scoring pass. Tom Draxler's two-point run made it 15-7 before the horn sounded, sending the teams into dry locker rooms. The Draxler brothers each played their best games for the Dons in this major 22-14 season-ending upset. Assumption would finish the year 10-1 and win the WISAA state championship with a 12-10 victory over Milwaukee Marquette and Dick Basham at Lambeau Field.

Six Dons seniors ended their careers with the Assumption stunner: Don Apfel, Tony Blattler, Dave Draxler, Clarence Hartl, Steve Seidl, and Roger Trudeau. Leading the Dons in scoring were juniors Bob Dickman with 44 points and Steve Burr and Brian Fehrenbach with 30 each. Dave Draxler tallied 20 points and Steve Seidl added 16 on one TD and 10 extra point kicks. Junior Tom Draxler scored 14 points. Four Dons were picked for All-CWCC honors. Junior guard Jerry Weinfurtner and senior quarterback Dave Draxler were selected on offense. Linebacker Steve Burr and defensive back Brian Fehrenbach, both juniors, were named on defense.

1973 CWCC Standings	W	L	T	TP	OPP
Wis. Rapids Assumption	6	1	0	211	40
La Crosse Aquinas	5	1	1	110	60
Marshfield Columbus	4	2	1	143	65
Stevens Point Pacelli	4	2	1	132	109
Eau Claire Regis	3	4	0	124	58
Prairie du Chien Campion	2	4	1	79	142
Chippewa Falls McDonell	2	5	0	65	176
Wausau Newman	0	7	0	65	181

1974: The First Playoff Appearance

In Columbus' first 14 years of football, the teams played eight-game seasons. Over the next nine years, from 1965 to 1973, they played nine-game campaigns. In their 24th year, the 1974 Dons proved to be the perfect bridge between past single-digit grid seasons and the new reality of WISAA playoff football with its possibility of extended double-digit seasons. The Dons finished 8-4 but this team was unique in many ways. Consider these distinguishing characteristics:

- First Wisconsin high school team to play 12 games in a season
- Earliest and latest calendar games in Dons history
- First CHS team to play in the state of Michigan
- First CHS team to play in overtime
- Most points in a game (68) by a Dons team
- More points in a season (293) than any previous Dons team
- More field goals (4) than any Columbus squad
- Perfection on 28 of 28 extra-point attempts
- Final year competing in the eight-team CWCC
- Share of the CWCC championship in a five-way tie (never to occur again)
- Ranking as the conference's #1 team offensively and defensively
- First CHS team to make the WISAA playoffs
- First CHS team to play in a state championship game

The August 30 opener was at historic Walter Blesch Field in Menominee, Michigan, across the river from its twinned city of Marinette, Wisconsin. The Dons dominated the rain-soaked affair behind Stratford transfer Joel Weigel's two first-half TD runs. They won 23-12. Senior stalwart Steve Burr led the Dons ground attack with 125 yards. It was the 200th game in the school's football history. In Madison the following Friday night, Edgewood continued to be a formidable foe and bested the Dons, 15-8. Columbus took an 8-7 lead in the third quarter when Brian Fehrenbach made a sensational 23-yard TD catch and the thrower, Dean Dix, followed with a two-point PAT run. Fehrenbach literally took the ball away from two defenders on the 5-yard line and roared into the end zone for the score. Unfortunately for CHS, Steve Burr injured his foot before halftime and sat out the rest of the game. The star of the game was 155-pound Crusaders halfback Pat Gentilli. His 175 yards gave him over 300 yards in his two outings.

In the Dons' home opener the following Saturday night, Tom Skemp of Aquinas shocked everybody when he sped 85 yards for a touchdown on the opening kickoff. The Dons rallied from a 14-0 fourth-quarter deficit on two TD passes from Dean Dix to Brian Fehrenbach, forcing overtime. With Burr still injured, Joel Weigel did yeoman's work in picking up 166 yards in 30 carries. Junior Ricky Coleman also emerged as another running threat. But the Blugolds prevailed in OT, taking a 22-14 victory back to La Crosse. The *News-Herald* reported, "Rarely, if ever, has Columbus dominated a game as it did this one and lost." Sitting at 1-2 in the young season, the Dons welcomed Newman to Marshfield the following Saturday and emerged with a 28-14 win despite poor tackling throughout the game. Six Cardinals turnovers did not help the Wausau 11. Rick Coleman's two second-half touchdown runs sealed the Dons victory. Newman's Mike Krienke scored all the NHS points and took game-high rushing honors with 145 yards.

Dean Dix had the game of his life at Beell Stadium the following Friday night, tossing five first-half TD passes and running for another score in a 68-0 rout of Campion. Dix's feat tied Bill Draxler's performance in 1967. All 56 Dons in uniform played. For longtime Columbus fans it was reminiscent of the 51-0 pasting the Red Knights administered to the Dons at Beell in 1962, the Dons' second worst defeat in program history. This encounter proved to be the biggest CHS win ever. Perhaps the best news for Columbus was the sight of Tom Draxler appearing for one play. The senior leader was recovering from pre-season knee surgery. The following Saturday afternoon the Dons won the statistical battle at Regis on the Ramblers' homecoming but lost the game 14-7. It was the same fate that befell the Dons against Aquinas a few weeks earlier. Junior QB Dean Dix was taken off the field on a stretcher on the last play before halftime. Sophomore Bruce Norfleet quarterbacked the Dons in the second half and filled in admirably. Next, the Dons celebrated their own homecoming with a 45-7 shellacking of McDonell. Steve Burr ran with abandon for 144 yards in 24 carries. Tom Draxler, making a remarkable recovery from knee surgery, passed his first test against the Macks. Draxler had 42 total yards on offense and the game's only interception on defense. All 55 Dons who suited up saw action.

Columbus found the perfect blend of offense and defense at Wisconsin Rapids the following Saturday night and blanked Assumption 24-0. It was the fourth time the Dons rolled up 25 or more first downs in a game. They were aided by strong rushing performances by Rick Coleman (159 yards) and Steve Burr (125). Coleman also had 11 yards receiving for 170 total yards on the night. The Dons needed to beat Pacelli in Stevens Point the following Saturday night to force a five-way tie for the CWCC crown. A Pacelli win would have allowed the Cardinals to claim the title outright. Columbus jumped to a 14-0 lead when Dix found his favorite targets, Bob Dickman and Brian Fehrenbach, for touchdowns in the first quarter. Dickman played superbly in all facets of the game. He picked off two PHS passes, kicked two extra points and a field goal, contributed his TD reception, and, most important, as the punter pinned Pacelli deep in their own territory, making them start from inside the 13-yard line four times. His punts averaged 41 yards. The Dons held on for a 17-7 win—and a share of the title.

Coach Walt Kroll's penchant for scheduling tough teams never became more important than the end-of-season non-conference tilt at Milwaukee Marquette. Already saddled with three losses, the Dons could ill afford to stumble against a 7-1 school ranked ninth in the state. In addition, the Milwaukee school boasted six times as many enrolled boys as the Dons. It was a classic David-versus-Goliath scenario but Kroll boldly stated, "We are not awed by Marquette." Kroll admitted that even a win might not be enough for the Dons to get invited to the WISAA playoffs for the first time. However, the veteran coach also knew Columbus had an intangible asset: their fans. "We had more fans at Pacelli than they did, and we might have the same at Marquette," he said. A sensational 80-yard punt return TD by Brian Fehrenbach late in the third quarter broke the game open for the Dons and spelled doom for the heavily favored Hilltoppers. Kroll said afterward, "Brian Fehrenbach is the finest punt returner ever to play in the CWCC." Kroll, in his 11th year at Columbus, said the team's year-end defensive improvement was due to the play of Tom Umhoefer, Dave Panske, and Greg Herkert. Umhoefer's third-quarter 16-yard TD reception was the first catch of his career. It was the junior's first year playing football.

Reserve halfback Mark Meyers ran five straight times at the end of the game to take valuable time off the clock by picking up vital first downs for the Marshfield boys. The 28-13 win at 39th and St. Paul in Milwaukee allowed the Dons to finish their regular season with a 7-3 mark.

Strength of schedule and a stellar Marquette performance got the Dons into the WISAA playoffs. For the fourth week in a row, the Dons took to the road, this time to Hart Park in Wauwatosa to face undefeated Milwaukee Thomas More. Over 3,000 fans were on hand to watch the state's fourth-ranked team take on their central Wisconsin foe. The game was almost a miscarriage of justice. The Dons thoroughly outplayed the Cavaliers but almost lost. With 7:04 remaining, and down 7-3, Columbus put together an impressive 85-yard scoring drive. It ended with Mark Meyers' 1-yard TD plunge with just over three minutes left. Meyers, a junior, was pressed into service when starting fullback Joel Weigel injured his ankle early in the game. The Dons defense throttled coach Jim Haluska's Thomas More attack. Three CHS running backs ended up having more individual rushing yards than More did as a team: Burr (83), Meyers (70), and Coleman (60). A late Coleman touchdown run, when the Dons were trying to run out the clock, ballooned the winning tally to 17-7.

On Friday, nearly 6,000 fans were on hand at Titan Stadium in Oshkosh for the sixth WISAA state championship game. The Dons stunned Oshkosh Lourdes when they scored a touchdown on their first play from scrimmage, a 51-yard bomb from Dean Dix to Brian Fehrenbach. Dix scrambled in from 11 yards out later in the first quarter. With Bob Dickman's 28th consecutive extra point, the Dons led 14-0. Lourdes fought back, though, scoring all 15 of their points in the second quarter. The score stayed at 15-14 until 3:14 remained to play. Columbus drove the ball from their own 28 down to the Lourdes 3-yard line. Facing first-and-goal, Burr plowed to the 1-yard line. Lourdes stiffened and held Dons runners Burr and Mark Meyers to no gains on second and third downs—a fierce goal-line stand. The thrilling finish came down to an 18-yard field goal attempt. The *News-Herald* observed, "With the ball on the right hash mark Dickman had a difficult angle to kick from but the snap was good and he got plenty of foot into the ball and the kick looked good until it drifted off to the left and smacked the upright dead center. An inch to the right and it would have caromed through." It proved a quick end to one of the most successful seasons in Dons lore. The final minutes—a 72-yard Columbus drive under great pressure followed by a Lourdes goal-line stand for the ages, capped by an attempted game-winning field goal from a difficult angle—left fans buzzing. They knew they had just witnessed an epic battle between two evenly matched teams. Kroll, ever the wise man, had stated days before that "the game will be more meaningful to the players in 20 years."

Sixteen seniors gladly endured the five-game road schedule to end their careers vying for the Dons' first state championship: John Baltus, Steve Binder, Steve Burr, Rick Derge, Bob Dickman, Tom Draxler, Brian Fehrenbach, Kevin Gehler, Dan Gust, Vern Hagstrom, Steve Hughes, Jim Scheuer, Ken Smrecek, Joel Weigel, Jerry Weinfurtner, and Tom Weinfurtner. While 14 Dons scored during the season only six were in double figures: Fehrenbach with 68 points, Dickman with 58, Weigel with 44, wingback Rick Coleman with 36, Burr with 26, and Dean Dix with 20. All-CWCC honors were awarded to six Dons. Three were repeaters from the 1973 team. Weinfurtner was selected at guard, Burr at running back (he was named at linebacker in 1973), and Feherenbach at defensive back. This time Fehrenbach was a unanimous pick. Dickman made the All-CWCC team at end and Scheuer was picked at offensive tackle. All were seniors. The only junior from CHS to make the prestigious team was defensive lineman Greg Herkert. Three Dons also gained further CWCC honors. Dickman was top place-kicker, Burr was Back of the Year, and Kroll was Coach of the Year. Fehrenbach was also named second team All-State at offensive end.

1974 CWCC Standings	W	L	TP	OPP
Eau Claire Regis	5	2	112	67
La Crosse Aquinas	5	2	149	50
Marshfield Columbus	5	2	203	64
Stevens Point Pacelli	5	2	103	41
Wis. Rapids Assumption	5	2	111	75
Wausau Newman	2	5	117	149
Chippewa Falls McDonellm	1	6	26	155
Prairie du Chien Campion	0	7	44	264

1975: Platooning Starts

A tough-nosed defensive team, the Dons also knew how to put points on the board. The combination would prove lethal to most opponents in 1975. The Dons dashed out to 9-0 start and a #3 state ranking in the medium-sized school AP poll, with coach Walt Kroll crediting the success to the start of platooning at Columbus. "We have 22 players, plus alternates, who are responsible for our record and this has been our salvation, especially as the game wears on," he said. Aquinas upset Columbus in the last regular season game of the year in La Crosse, forcing the Dons to share the conference title with Assumption. But their 9-1 mark would allow them to be named one of four teams in the WISAA playoffs.

For the seventh year in a row, the Dons opened with an early game against Edgewood. The Crusaders came to Marshfield sporting an all-time 8-2 mark over the navy-and-white. On this night, though, the Dons left no doubt which team was better. They were in stronger shape, playing with separate offensive and defensive units for the first time in program history. The visitors tired and the Dons made two second-half TDs stand up for a 14-0 win. The next game, in Waterloo, Iowa, was the farthest from home any Columbus team ever ventured. Kroll's Dons dominated Waterloo East. Columbus took the second-half kickoff and surgically ran 20 plays before scoring. All 47 Dons on the trip saw action in racking up a 25-8 win. Roosevelt Field in Oconomowoc was the site of the next victory. CHS moved the ball but had trouble scoring. Sixty yards in first-half penalties didn't help. The Ed Rux-coached Racoons team took an 8-7 halftime lead. The Dons came out of the locker room and scored on a long-drive capped by Dean Dix's QB keeper and a Tom Stangl point-after kick. The school with five O's in its name never threatened after that score. The Dons returned home with a penalty-free second half and a 14-8 win.

Columbus attained its 16th consecutive win over Newman in Wausau the next week with a 23-6 triumph. Kroll credited his assistants—Jerry Koslowski, Alex Hilber, and Mike Flynn—with playing big roles in the team's fine start. He also noted the outstanding defensive play of Bruce Norfleet and Dale Pritzl in the Wausau game. Sophomore Denny Sternweis and junior Tom Stangl stepped up to fill in for injured senior teammates Jim Knauf and Mark Meyers. The Dons hosted Onalaska Luther for the first time the next Saturday. The 145-pound Wayne Zygarlicke ran the counter play to perfection, becoming only the fourth Dons player to rush for more than 200 yards. Kroll expected seniors to set the leadership tone each year. For this game he named Steve "Bear" Trudeau as team captain. Kroll said, "He is the most spirited and enthusiastic player we have. He personifies the spirit a good team must have." The Dons coasted to a 47-14 win. Luther found success facing the Dons sophomores and freshmen in the fourth quarter.

It was obvious that Regis came to play the next Saturday afternoon at Beell when they scored the first time they had the ball. The CHS homecoming game with Regis was a hard-hitting contest that became tense and emotional when Dean Dix was rammed into the front row of bleachers after almost breaking away on a punt return. (The stands were at least 20 feet from the playing field.) Later in the game Dix was sidelined with a painful hip-pointer. His replacement, Bruce Norfleet, threw a perfect ball to Joe Henrichs, who made a leaping catch between two Ramblers defenders for a 25-yard touchdown reception and the Dons only six-pointer of the day. Ken Kraus added two field goals. His last one, from 39 yards, set a school record. The powerful boot into a stiff wind cleared the bar by five yards and increased the lead to 13-7 with 5:22 left in the game. Regis quick-kicked on second down with just under five minutes left, hoping to get the ball back with better field position. However, fullback Mark Meyers ran on 10 of the following 12 plays, as the Dons strung together three first downs to run out the clock and secure the win. Greg Herkert and Norfleet anchored the defense that yielded little after the Ramblers initial burst.

The Dons had an easy time in Chippewa Falls the following Saturday as they beat McDonell 47-12. Mark Meyers' 8-yard TD burst before halftime came "with a tremendous display of power and second effort," said the *News-Herald*. Wayne Zygarlicke rushed for 107 yards and Meyers for 101. Nearly 140 of the Macks' 186 total yards came against Dons reserves. Assumption came to Beell Stadium the following Saturday ranked ninth in the Wisconsin medium-school poll. They had the leading ground-gainer in the CWCC in Bill Ritchay. The Dons were ranked second so this had the makings of a great high school football game. The Royals struck paydirt on their third play from scrimmage when QB Dave Lownik hit Bob Gruber in stride on a slant pattern near the Royals' 40. He was off to the races for a 79-yard score. The Dons came right back, though, and scored 10 points before the first quarter ended. Assumption could not run on the Dons, so they took to the air, connecting eight times in 41 tries. The Dons grabbed a 24-9 win by holding Ritchay to 12 yards on 11 carries.

Pacelli resembled the Dons: small and quick with excellent team speed. The Dons, however, controlled the tempo of the game with their varied running attack featuring bull runs, counter plays, and off-tackle slants. Tom Umhoefer, normally a defensive end, ran in a play on third down on the Dons' first possession of the game. QB Dean Dix rolled to his right and lofted a pass to Umhoefer, who made an excellent leaping catch in the corner of the end zone for the game's first score. That pass notwithstanding, Pacelli defenders did a great job covering Dons receivers. This was the first game in CHS history where the Dons kicked three field goals, helping them to a 23-7 win.

Columbus arrived in La Crosse undefeated at 9-0 and assured of no worse than a tie for the conference title. The navy-and-white struck first early in the second quarter on a short run by

Joe Henrichs. For only the second time all year, the point-after kick went awry. Kroll remarked that it was the best hitting game the Dons were involved in all season. Aquinas stopped Columbus when necessary, but the Dons were unable to stop the Blugolds. Fumbles, even though many were recovered, played havoc with the Dons' timing. CHS had several untimely 15-yard penalties as well. The most heartbreaking came in the final minutes while mounting a rally. Dix narrowly missed going all the way on a QB keeper, managing to get to the 8-yard line after a 49-yard pick-up. Again, penalties quashed the drive. "Their line just dominated ours," Kroll said. "They created their own breaks and then capitalized on them." The late Columbus revival came up short and Aquinas ended their own season playing spoiler with a 13-6 win over the Dons.

The Dons' second trip to the WISAA playoffs was staged at Beell Stadium, where they faced unbeaten Fond du Lac St. Mary's Springs. With 4,300 fans on hand, it was the largest crowd to ever witness a game at the 34-year-old stadium. It was also the largest gathering for a semi-final football game. Columbus thoroughly outplayed Springs in the first half, not allowing a first down until 13 seconds before intermission. The Dons scored on short runs by Henrichs and Meyers. The second TD was set up by a nifty 48-yard Scott Radlinger punt return to the opposition's 10-yard line. Whatever fifth-year Ledgers coach Bob Hyland said to his team in the locker room worked. The Fox Valley Catholic Conference champs came out inspired, willing themselves to a remarkable 20-14 victory. It was the most points the Dons yielded all year. Hyland was on target with his five-year plan to resurrect Springs football. After suffering through the first two seasons with only one win, the 15-3 mark of his teams in years four and five proved he was on the right path. The 1966 Assumption grad was remembered for his own games against Columbus, losing in his sophomore year but taking the 1964 and 1965 contests. He became an honorable mention Little All-American guard at North Dakota State. Hyland admitted, "Columbus executed better than any team we've played all year." (Springs would lose 28-6 to Marquette High for the WISAA title the following week.)

Columbus finished 9-2. While this team will be remembered as the one that initiated platoon football at CHS, it also should be noted the team kicked seven field goals, more than any other Columbus team, including a school record 39-yarder. This group had a penchant for returning punts to give the formidable offense good field position. Its Achilles' heel was untimely penalties. Eighteen seniors played their last game before a jam-packed Beell Stadium crowd: Jim Braem, Dean Dix, Mike Fait, Greg Herkert, Steve Huber, Jeff Jaye, Jim Knauf, Roy Krier, Ken Kraus, Pat Ley, Mark Meyers, Dave Panske, Mike Ploen, Dale Pritzl, Steve Trudeau, Tom Umhoefer, Perry Zukowski, and Wayne Zygarlicke. Top scorers were Joe Henrichs with 66 points and Tom Stangl with 40 points. Wayne Zygarlicke and Chuck Hagman each added 24. Dean Dix contributed 18 and strong-legged Ken Kraus booted 17. Al Nikolai's two touchdowns rounded out the year's scoreboard leaders. Seven Dons were awarded All-CWCC honors. On offense, guard Jeff Jaye, center Steve Huber, and fullback Mark Meyers were chosen. Defensive end Tom Umhoefer, defensive tackle Greg Herkert, and linebacker Bruce Norfleet were named to the defense unit. Ken Kraus made the team as the best place-kicker in the conference. All were seniors except Norfleet, a junior. Additionally, Meyers was selected as Back of the Year and Walt Kroll was voted Coach of the Year. Herkert was a repeat All-CWCC awardee.

1975 CWCC Standings	W	L	TP	OPP
Marshfield Columbus	5	1	136	54
Wis. Rapids Assumption	5	1	159	38
La Crosse Aquinas	4	2	110	92
Stevens Point Pacelli	4	2	115	57
Eau Claire Regis	2	4	80	87
Chippewa Falls McDonell	1	5	62	206
Wausau Newman	0	6	46	176

1976: The Most Exotic Schedule

The 1976 schedule had everything on it from a Minnesota state champion to Wisconsin's second-best team and an Iowa school with a rich athletic tradition. All were big schools. Of course, it also featured all the six other teams in the far-flung Central Wisconsin Catholic Conference (CWCC). And the Dons fared well, losing only to the Minnesota champs and by a field goal each in their other two losses. The Dons were unable to platoon their units in 1976. Ten players went both ways. Highlights included senior signal-caller Bruce Norfleet having about as good a game as any high schooler could at Assumption. There were also a Pacelli game for the ages (with a long delay for a play-under-review before plays under review were even dreamed about) and a fantastic flourish by Joe Henrichs to cap his Dons career in the season finale.

The season opened in Madison against Edgewood on August 27, the earliest start yet for the Dons. Just two minutes into the year, Henrichs put the navy-and-white on the scoreboard with a 20-yard run. Veteran place-kicker Tom Stangl added the point-after and it was 7-0 before fans had settled into Mansfield Stadium. All the scoring in this 13-0 Dons win occurred in the first nine minutes. Henrichs scored again on a draw play on their next possession. Denny Sternweis' punting kept the Crusaders at bay all evening. Motion penalties plagued CHS but the saving grace was the tough Dons defense. The *Wisconsin State Journal* noted the defense was led by tackles Al Nikolai and Denny Sternweis, linebacker Jake Gropp, and defensive back Bruce Norfleet. Swanson Field in La Crosse welcomed the Dons the following Friday night. Logan High was rebuilding under new coach Dan Meinert after a spectacular 1975 campaign (8-0, ranked #2 in Wisconsin). The Rangers' Tom Horton ran wild in this 17-13 Columbus victory, which was not as close as it sounded. The 5'9", 168-pound speedster gained 221 yards and ran for two long touchdowns. The Dons duo of Joe Henrichs and Tom Stangl countered with a combined 245 yards rushing. Seven illegal procedure penalties hurt CHS. Their final scoring drive was a classic, though. Starting on their own 26, Henrichs and Stangl punished Logan defenders time and again. Stangl pounded it over from 3 yards out to make it 17-6 as the third quarter ended.

The home opener was against Waterloo (Iowa) East, a school founded in 1874 and sporting a great athletic tradition. The Dons prevailed 13-8. "It was a real dog fight," said coach Walt Kroll. "Our defense was outstanding." Columbus had a vicious pass rush throughout most of the game. Like so many games, it was a game of halves—the Dons dominating the first half and the Trojans the second half. CHS took a 13-0 advantage into the locker room. East came out charged up and held the Dons to 10 yards in 20 plays in the final two quarters. Columbus picked off two East aerials in the last five minutes to preserve the win. St. Thomas Academy, an all-boys school of 900 in St. Paul, brought their 68-man squad and championship swagger to Beell the following Saturday night. The Cadets, coming off a 12-0 season, were the defending big-school state champions of Minnesota, a state where public and parochial schools competed in the same playoff system. Wisconsin public schools were about to compete for state championships at the end of the 1976 season for the first time. The Cadets scored the first two times they had the ball and dominated the first quarter of play. The teams played more or less evenly the final three stanzas. St. Thomas platooned players and that made a difference. The final score was 21-0, the first time in 31 games that the Dons had been shut out.

Columbus had a bad case of fumble-itis at Regis the next week, turning the ball over four times. A mix-up in the Columbus secondary allowed Mark Fisher to catch a pass over the middle with no one around him for a 65-yard score on the first play of the second quarter. Two CHS scores in the last 13 minutes of the game allowed the Dons to depart Carson Park with a narrow 13-7 win. But the final outcome was not truly known until a timely Steve Sydow sack of Ramblers QB Jeff Durkee. Three first-quarter touchdowns set a joyous tone for the homecoming game against McDonell the next Saturday afternoon. The second TD was set up by a 57-yard pass from Bruce Norfleet to Al Nikolai, with Tom Stangl running the final 9 yards to paydirt. Only 40 seconds separated that score from the next one, a Norfleet aerial to Chuck Hagman. In between, Jake Gropp recovered McDonell's fumbled kickoff return. Stangl took over as the Dons workhorse after Joe Henrichs twisted his ankle. Stangl responded with 127 yards in 25 carries. Most of the Macks' yardage came at the end against Columbus reserves in a crisp 33-7 victory. The following Saturday night, Columbus ruined Assumption's homecoming by scoring in every quarter for a 27-0 win. The sensational play of QB Bruce Norfleet turned heads. Norfleet was eight-for-eight for 176 passing yards and three touchdowns, one a spectacular 51-yard connection with Al Nikolai. At safety, Norfleet had two interceptions and a jarring TD-saving tackle on a fourth-down play at the 1-yard line. "It's been a long time since I've seen a high school quarterback have a game like that," Kroll said. He also praised the offensive line for the improved running game.

The tradition of fierce, championship-on-the-line battles with Pacelli may have started in earnest in 1976. With the Dons leading 14-6 with 1:50 left in the game, Denny Sternweis punted for the Dons. It went short, to the Dons' 44-yard line. Officials ruled that it hit a Pacelli player and awarded the ball to the Dons. The *Stevens Point Journal* reported, "The short punt landed among a crowd of players from both teams and the officials first indicated it had been touched by Pacelli's Pat Thompson and then recovered by Columbus. After several minutes of discussion, however, the officials ruled that the ball hit the leg of a Columbus player and Pacelli took possession." Nonetheless, three plays later the Cardinals were facing fourth-and-10 from the same 44-yard line. A 13-yard connection moved the ball to the 31 and secured an all-important first down. Pacelli picked up 4 yards but an illegal procedure penalty moved the ball back to the 32. Pacelli QB Paul Soik then hit Ken Hoerter for a 29-yard pick-up, down to the 3. Tim Redding was stopped for no gain and with time running out Soik threw a quick pass to Steve Laszewski over the middle for a score. Soik and Laszewski teamed up for the game-tying extra point pass, sending the game into overtime. Pacelli won the toss and decided to go on defense first. Soik intercepted a Norfleet pass in the flat to end the Dons' overtime scoring opportunity. Columbus stopped Pacelli in their first three tries but sophomore Dave Jajewski booted a 21-yard field goal on fourth down for the improbable 17-14 Pacelli win. The defeat took some glow off a spectacular Columbus performance.

Kroll said, "Norfleet had another great game. He passed for one TD, rushed for another, was involved in 23 tackles, nine primary and 14 assists, he intercepted one pass, broke up another, and caused and recovered one fumble." A rich rivalry was born at Goerke Field that night. Pacelli finished 10-0 and third in Wisconsin among medium-sized schools.

Aquinas came to Beell the next Saturday night with a pass-happy attack led by sophomore QB Bob Katchel, a left-hander. But it was their fierce defense that throttled the Dons running attack, holding Tom Stangl, the leading rusher in the CWCC, to 29 yards in 12 trips. Columbus was beaten off the ball all night long. Excellent coverage of their receivers by the Blugolds also hampered the navy-and-white. Ill-timed encroachment penalties did not help the Dons either in the 10-7 loss. Their season finale was at home against Newman, and the seniors ensured little time was wasted in taking a 13-0 lead, scoring the first two times they had the ball. Joe Henrichs ran for the first score, an 18-yard gallop, and caught an 18-yard pass for the second one. Henrichs concluded the game's scoring, and a stellar career, with a short run in the fourth quarter. He accounted for 203 yards and three touchdowns in the 19-0 win. His eruption allowed the Dons to finish as the #1 offensive team in the division. They were 7-3 overall and 4-2 in the conference. Even with a win in the Newman game, the Dons knew no WISAA playoff invite would be coming their way. "I sometimes think too much emphasis is placed on the playoffs," said Kroll. "There is a great deal more to high school football than the playoffs." Eleven seniors played their last game: Jake Gropp, Chuck Hagman, Tim Haight, Joe Henrichs, Bob Jensen, Mike Kraus, Mark Martin, Greg Lindner, Al Nikolai, Bruce Norfleet, and Tom Stangl. Scoring leaders were Henrichs with 48 and Stangl with 41, followed by Nikolai with 30 on five TD receptions, Norfleet with 18 on three TD runs, Hagman with 12, and Chris Zygarlicke with 6. Six Dons were awarded All-CWCC honors. Norfleet was the only repeater. On offense, end Al Nikolai, guard Mike Krause, QB Norfleet, and running back Tom Stangl were selected. On defense, Joe Henrichs was named at linebacker and Nikolai at defensive end. Nikolai was one of only two players league-wide named to both units. The Dons took both kicking picks with Stangl named best kicker and junior Denny Sternweis best punter. Norfleet was named Back of the Year and Kroll was selected as Coach of the Year—the third year in a row Columbus copped those awards. It also was the third year straight that a Dons player was selected as the league's best place-kicker. Kroll was miffed that Norfleet was by-passed at defensive back, saying, "He's the best tackler I've ever coached."

1976 CWCC Standings	W	L	TP	OPP
Stevens Point Pacelli	6	0	110	56
La Crosse Aquinas	4	2	67	42
Marshfield Columbus	4	2	113	41
Eau Claire Regis	3	3	65	47
Wis. Rapids Assumption	3	3	50	78
Wausau Newman	1	5	72	64
Chippewa Falls McDonell	0	6	40	189

1977: Fast Start, Fantastic Finish

The Dons returned to platooning, with one exception, and got immediate results with two shutouts. Columbus snapped the 22-game win streak of Caledonia, Minnesota, at Beell Stadium, compiling a 3-0 mark going into CWCC play. Heavy winds moved in and the Dons dropped four in a row. It was a mixed season for the Dons, who were 5-5 overall and 2-4 in league play.

The opener at Beell Stadium started with a tornado watch posted for the area. The Dons dominated Edgewood in the first half, holding the Crusaders to 24 yards rushing. With both teams running the ball it only took 35 minutes to play the first two quarters. CHS kept an upper hand in the second half but fumbles and untimely motion penalties hurt. A Marty Draxler interception set up the lone Dons score, a 5-yard Tom Huber run one minute into the fourth quarter. The Crusaders threatened late in the game, facing fourth-and-9 from the 14-yard line when a heavy downpour and high winds appeared out of nowhere. Fewer than five minutes remained. Edgewood managed only five yards on their fourth-down attempt, turning the ball over on downs. Both teams had to take shelter in the locker rooms. After a 50-minute delay, the coaches agreed to call the game due to torrential rains and wide-spread lightning in the area. The Dons were credited with a 6-0 win, the third year in a row they held the Madisonians scoreless.

La Crosse Logan pushed the Dons around at the outset of their game the next week at Beell. But the Dons' first pass completion of the year, a 26-yard "wounded duck" from Pat Connaughty to John Pritzl, resulted in the game's first touchdown. Scott Radlinger intercepted just before halftime enabling Tom Huber to score from 4 yards out with 18 seconds left. Chris Zygarlicke ran for two-point conversions after each score. Tim Dickrell added a 2-yard plunge, with Denny Sternweis booting the extra point for insurance in the fourth period. The Dons defeated the Rangers for the second year in a row, this time 23-0. Caledonia, the defending Minnesota Class B champions, brought their 22-game win streak to Marshfield next. The Warriors had both tradition and size going for them but they had never experienced a misdirection attack featuring counter plays, play-action passes, and a quick inside trapping game. Columbus held a 19-0 lead at the half. Caledonia fared better in the second half, gaining 133 yards and holding the Dons to 45. Caledonia scored with 1:41 left to narrow the gap to 19-14. But CHS held on, snapping the Warriors' string of wins. Coach Walt Kroll praised defensive end Bob Saverda for an outstanding performance.

The Dons were outplayed in all facets of the game the next Saturday night in Chippewa Falls and fell to McDonell 9-0. Not only was it the first CHS road game of the year, it was the first Macks victory over Columbus since 1971. The Dons didn't get their initial first down until nearly halftime. The only bright spot was the continued punt-return prowess of Scott Radlinger. Kroll also commended the leadership of Pat Connaughty, citing how vital it was to have that characteristic at the quarterback slot. The Dons lost a wild offensive battle in La Crosse the following Saturday night, 30-27. Not since 1959 had Columbus scored so many points and lost. The Dons took a 13-0 lead and headed into halftime nursing a 19-14 margin. But Aquinas went ahead 22-19 midway through the third quarter. With 8:31 left in the game Scott Radlinger turned the corner and sped 90 yards for the second-longest TD run in Columbus history. Dave Meyers caught a Pat Connaughty pass for the two-point conversion, putting the Dons up 27-22. In the closing minutes, though, the Blugolds drove 82 yards in eight plays, scoring with 1:03 left. It was a loss that was hard to swallow. The CHS defense recorded 10 tackles for losses in a game featuring spectacular offensive fireworks. Radlinger's 172 rushing yards were offset by the eight catches of Sam Sloggy of Aquinas for 150 yards.

Regis scored the first two times it had the ball the next Friday night on a wet field in Marshfield. Tim Bell went 15 yards, untouched, for the first Ramblers score. The agile 170-pound Regis QB threw a 24-yard strike to Kevin Pulkrabek, who was alone in the end zone, for the second first-quarter tally. The Dons managed 34 yards on 20 carries in the first half. In the closing minutes CHS QB Pat Connaughty found Tom Huber on a short pass that Huber turned into a 26-yard gain with some fancy running on the slippery field. Huber was downed at the 2 and Scott Radlinger took it over from there, tightening the game to 13-6 with 2:53 left. Kroll opted not to go for the onside kick but the Dons did get the ball back. They were 53 yards away with 31 seconds left. Time expired as Columbus was driving for another score. Fruth Field in Fond du Lac was not hospitable to Columbus the following Saturday afternoon, as St. Mary's Springs pounded the Dons 28-0. The bruising Ledgers ground game, spearheaded by burly, 215-pound Dave Tighe and six-two Rick Flanders, rushed for 244 yards. Gang-tackling, a staple of most Columbus teams, was absent. Columbus got past midfield twice. The Ledgers used their second stringers during the fourth quarter. Springs, now 5-1, had outscored their opponents 152-19 in their five wins.

The Dons put a stop to their four-game skid in Wausau Saturday night with a 22-8 triumph over Newman. The Cards took an 8-6 lead in the first quarter. It held up until Scott Radlinger timed his swipe of a Newman aerial perfectly and sped 85 yards to the end zone, tying the school record for longest interception. Paul Fehrenbach caught the two-point conversion to give the Dons a 14-8 advantage three minutes before half. Pat Connaughty's insurance TD run in the fourth frame sealed the win. It was a hard-hitting defensive battle. Newman was hampered by the absence of star QB Pete Chilsen, who was lost to knee surgery. Future Dons assistant coach Russ Grundy got off two punts for Newman, averaging 37 yards. It was the 18th straight time the Dons defeated Newman.

The 1977 homecoming game with Assumption was a battle royale. Both teams played solid, hard-nosed football. The punting game became increasingly important as the afternoon wore on. Dons punter Denny Sternweis launched spectacular boomers and the Royals'Tom McHugh showed consistent reliability. CHS's first TD came after a bad punt snap sailed over McHugh's head. The Dons took over on the Assumption 22-yard line. Pat Connaughty found Dave Meyers via the airwaves and he lugged it down to the 1, where Tim Dickrell put the Dons on the board with three minutes left in the first half. A strategic move by Royals coach John Swendrowski at halftime paid dividends. He moved split end Pat Cavanaugh to QB to get the Royals offense back on track. Cavanaugh had not played a down at quarterback all year. The defense tightened in the second half and limited CHS to two first downs and 39 yards. Momentum shifted on the last play of the third quarter with the Dons holding a 6-0 lead. Scott Radlinger fumbled a punt on the 10-yard line and Assumption recovered on the 6. One play later tailback Todd Joosten went over for a touchdown. With the reliable leg of Mike Ritchay, AHS took a 7-6 lead early in the final stanza. The Dons had trouble containing Joosten on wide sweeps all day. The Royals went to their workhorse nine out of 12 times in a clock-eating drive. Joosten's 1-yard lunge with 1:34 left clinched the 14-6 Assumption win.

The season finale against Pacelli in Marshfield was a classic defensive struggle with no team scoring until overtime. It was the start of a 14-year run where the two opponents would face each other in the last game of the year. The Dons were 1-4 in conference play while the Cards were 4-1 and looking for a second straight title. Columbus came into the game with a host of injuries, with more occurring during action. Kroll said, "Our defense was super, especially Gary Ruder, Steve Sydow, and Randy Nikolai." The teams exchanged field goals in the first overtime.

In the second, Pacelli went first from the 10-yard line and eventually connected on a 20-yard field goal to take a 6-3 lead. When the Dons got their chance from the 10 their star running back, Scott Radlinger, was injured on second down at the 4-yard line. His replacement, Brian Rasmussen, was called on to carry the ball next. It was only his second rush attempt all season. He swept around the right side for the winning points with key blocks thrown by Denny Sternweis, Dave Meyers, and Joe Koening. The stunning 9-6 win allowed McDonell to claim sole ownership of the conference crown. Kroll beamed afterwards, "This is the best win we have had in terms of players being hurt and the caliber of the opposition since we beat Assumption in the 1966 game."

Thirteen seniors claimed their last Dons game as a thrilling, two-overtime, title-denying victory: Pat Connaughty, Dave Daniel, Tim Dickrell, Marty Draxler, Steve Durst, Mark Greenwood, Mark Herkert, John Pritzl, Scott Radlinger, Gary Ruder, Tom Rupel, Denny Sternweis, and Steve Sydow. Chris Zygarlicke (34 points) and Radlinger (26) were the top scorers. Dickrell and Tom Huber each contributed 12 and Dave Meyers added 8. Radlinger was the lone CHS player selected for the All-CWCC team. He was one of five chosen on both the offensive and defensive units. The 165-pounder was a dangerous breakaway threat and the most exciting runner in the conference, averaging 6.1 yards. CWCC coaches noted Radlinger's willingness and ability to play while hurt. The senior was named at both running back and defensive back.

1977 CWCC Standings	W	L	TP	OPP
Chippewa Falls McDonell	5	1	102	54
La Crosse Aquinas	4	2	121	93
Stevens Point Pacelli	4	2	61	51
Wis. Rapids Assumption	4	2	92	58
Eau Claire Regis	2	4	81	74
Marshfield Columbus	2	4	70	80
Wausau Newman	0	6	52	169

1978: The Halfway Point

The 1978 Dons contingent didn't know it, but the exact halfway point in the history of Columbus High School football occurred on a Tuesday afternoon practice when the 2-0 Dons were preparing for a game at recently opened Apple Valley High School just south of the Twin Cities in Minnesota. Scheduling patterns were emerging: open against Edgewood, close against Pacelli. This was another tough defensive group with most playing both ways. The offense centered around the running duo of halfback Chris Zygarlicke and fullback Gary Skaya. David Fait and Paul Fehrenbach proved to be good targets for QB Tom Zukowski. CHS finished the season 5-5 overall and 3-3 in the CWCC.

Edgewood scored against the Dons for the first time in four years in the season kickoff at Madison. The Dons won 20-6 on the strength of two fourth-quarter touchdowns by Skaya and Zygarlicke. Skaya was playing in his first varsity game on this sweltering night. Zygarlicke torched the Crusaders with 167 yards on the ground. The difference, though, was the defense, allowing one Edgewood drive all night. Mark Knauf and Randy Nikolai led the charge. Overall it was a ragged contest, marred by turnovers and penalties. The Dons next travelled to Nekoosa to face coach Dick Hyland's Papermakers. Skaya scored three TDs in the 28-0 whitewash. *The Marshfield News-Herald* described his second touchdown this way: "He was hit twice at about the 10, broke free, was hit twice at the 5, broke free, and crashed into the end zone with two defenders hanging on." Senior workhorse Zygarlicke churned out 109 yards on 22 tries, his second consecutive game topping 100 yards.

Even though Apple Valley had only been open for three years, the Eagles already had laid claim to two conference championships and one trip to the Class A Minnesota playoffs. Coach Walt Kroll remarked that they took their football very seriously as evidenced by a 60-man varsity squad to go along with two full JV teams and two full freshman teams. The south suburban school didn't mess around against Columbus, marching 91 yards in 12 plays the first time they had the ball. The Dons countered with a drive into Apple Valley territory that faltered at the 34-yard line. It would be the only time all night the Dons would venture across midfield. While the Dons fell 18-0, Matt Rauh, the Apple Valley coach, said, "They really execute well, and we have nothing but admiration for their team."

After three CHS road games, Columbus hosted Dave Reinders and his Aquinas Blugold team for the home opener. Entering his 18th year at the helm, Reinders was the dean of all CWCC coaches. His always physical and well-coached teams proved problematic for the Dons. He came to town with five straight wins against Columbus. A 54-yard pass from Tom Zukowski to Paul Fehrenbach set up the game's first score. With the ball resting on the 6-yard line, fullback Gary Skaya was called on to get it into the end zone. Hit hard, he fumbled the ball forward, and an alert David Fait fell on it for a Columbus touchdown. The Dons dominated the first half and took a 7-0 lead into the locker room. The second half belonged to Aquinas. A Blugold block of a Frank Baltus punt turned the momentum toward Aquinas. Their physicality wore down the Dons. Afterward, Kroll cited the stellar play of QB Zukowski, end Paul Fehrenbach, and defensive halfback Larry Olsen in the 20-6 defeat.

Columbus caught some breaks the next Saturday night in Eau Claire against Regis. The Dons jumped to a 7-0 lead after scoring on their first drive of the game, a 12-play, 68-yard beauty. Regis QB Greg Mack later marched the Ramblers down the field and had Mark Califf all alone in the end zone for a sure score. But Califf dropped the ball. With time running out in the fourth quarter, the score knotted at 7-7, Califf went back to punt for Regis. He couldn't handle the low snap from center and the Dons took over on the Ramblers 20 with three minutes to play. Tom Zukowski immediately connected with David Fait for a 14-yard gain to move the ball to the 6-yard line. It was the only CHS completion in the game. Gary Skaya ran the final 6 yards, and Mike Rasmussen added the point-after kick. The Dons held on to a 14-7 advantage with 2:11 remaining in the hard-nosed contest where four Regis players had to be removed from the game. "I certainly hope they weren't hurt too seriously," Kroll said, "because we don't like to see injuries occur." DePere Pennings invaded Beell for a non-conference match the following Saturday evening. Three glowing CHS performances marked the game: 122 reception yards for Paul Fehrenbach,

110 rushing yards for Gary Skaya, and 149 passing yards for Tom Zukowski. But they weren't enough. The Squires came back from a 19-7 deficit with fewer than five minutes left to snatch a 20-19 victory from the Dons. The tying score came in the final 34 seconds on a 36-yard TD reception from Todd Wingrove to John Murphy. Scott Hoeft put his point-after kick through the uprights, giving the Squires a road victory.

The running tandem of Skaya and Zygarlicke exploded again, this time against Newman the following week. Skaya picked up 137 yards and Zygarlicke 125 in a lopsided 49-14 win. Skaya ran for four touchdowns and QB Tom Zukowski connected with David Fait and Paul Feherenbach for two more. Kroll complimented Pat Panske for exceptional defensive effort. After starting the 1978 season 4-0, Newman sat at 4-4. The last time Newman had notched a win over the Dons was in 1956. At 2-1 in the conference, the Dons went to Witter Field in Wisconsin Rapids to take on the 3-1 Royals of Assumption. The game came down to a late 24-yard field goal by Assumption's Mike Ritchay with 3:44 left for the 10-7 win. Before that the game had devolved into a punting contest between Frank Baltus of Columbus and Tom McHugh of Assumption. The Dons never did get their offense moving. The swarming Royals defense denied the Dons good field position all day. Recovered fumbles gave Columbus their best scoring opportunities.

Against McDonell at Beell the following Saturday night, Zygarlicke and Skaya again made their marks. Zygarlicke had 178 yards and three touchdowns and Skaya had two scores, giving the Dons a comfortable 32-6 advantage midway through the third stanza. The momentum shifted, though, when McDonell QB Dave See gave up on the run and went strictly to the air. It worked. Two touchdowns followed, and all of a sudden the Macks had narrowed the gap to 32-19. They recovered their onside kick with just over ten minutes left in the game but the Dons hung on for the win. In the next game, an undefeated Pacelli looked like the state's #1 WISAA team on their opening kickoff drive, going 60 yards in 14 plays. The 7-0 margin stood until Dave Fait hauled in a 32-yard strike from Dons QB Tom Zukowski to knot the finale at 7-7 before halftime. A third-quarter Dave Jajewski 22-yard field goal was vital for PHS.

Both teams traded fourth quarter touchdown runs. The Dons tried an onside kick with 1:50 left but it was recovered by Pacelli ace Brad Soderberg. The Cardinals preserved their perfect mark by running out the clock to secure a slim 17-14 win.

Fourteen CHS seniors closed out their careers: Mark Bloczynski, Paul Fehrenbach, Mark Knauf, Randy Nikolai, Pat Panske, Steve Radlinger, Brian Rasmussen, Mike Rasmussen, Bob Saverda, Jay Schlagenhaft, Joe Selner, Gary Skaya, Tom Zukowski, and Chris Zygarlicke. Skaya tallied 100 of the team's 190 points, only the second Dons player in history to reach 100 or more in a season. Other scoring leaders were Zygarlicke (36), David Fait (24), Fehrenbach (14), and freshmen kicker Dick Stevens (11). Zygarlicke was selected for both the offensive and defensive All-CWCC teams. On offense, the senior was named at running back and on defense he was chosen at linebacker. He was the only Dons player chosen.

1978 CWCC Standings	W	L	TP	OPP
Stevens Point Pacelli	6	0	152	20
Wis. Rapids Assumption	5	1	92	56
La Crosse Aquinas	4	2	183	72
Marshfield Columbus	3	3	123	87
Chippewa Falls McDonell	1	5	77	187
Eau Claire Regis	1	5	69	168
Wausau Newman	1	5	52	158

1979: Sizzle and Fade

The 1979 team got out of the gates better than any other Dons team in history, winning their first four games by a combined score of 151-27. Only the 1967 squad was close to this sensational start (4-0, 132-25). The rub was that the teams they beat were all winless. The early wins allowed for lots of playing time for many underclassmen. The experience would prove valuable the following year. It was also the first Dons team in four years to return a punt for a touchdown, which coach Walt Kroll considered the most exciting play in high school football. The scoring was front loaded this season. The Dons tallied only three touchdowns in their last five games, finishing 6-4 overall and 3-3 in the conference. They opened with an impressive 35-7 win over Edgewood in Marshfield. The August 25 start was the earliest ever. David Fait got the season off to a great beginning when he stole the ball from Andy Shulla, who thought he had an interception. The result: a CHS touchdown. Junior Jon Radlinger rushed for four TDs and 98 yards. Sophomore halfback Robby Wagner emerged as one to keep an eye on. The ability to platoon teams was a decided advantage for Columbus, with 42 players seeing action. The loss marked the 11th consecutive defeat for the once mighty Crusaders.

Good offensive line play enabled the Dons to score the last 20 points in a 20-6 win over Nekoosa. Halfback Rob Wagner displayed excellent open field running, collecting 49 yards on the initial Dons' score. Kroll singled out defensive end Larry Olsen for his stellar play. The Dons saw both Winnecone and the wishbone offense for the first time the following Saturday night in Marshfield. CHS glided to a 35-0 halftime advantage. Forty-four Dons took the field, with reserves playing most of the second half. Back-up QB Brian Morgan looked sharp, tossing two TDs. End Frank Baltus grabbed both of those, plus another from Tim Connaughty, for three TD receptions. Kroll cited defensive end Wally Schuetz for outstanding play in the 49-14 rout. Columbus also dominated Regis in a 47-0 romp at Beell. The Dons capitalized on scoring opportunities, including a safety by defensive end Larry Olsen. Many said it was the worst Regis team in history. The following Friday night, the Dons faltered at Minahan Stadium in DePere, falling to Abbott Pennings, 21-14. The Squires, coached by Don Violette, were 3-0 coming into their homecoming game. The Dons scored with 1:42 left to tighten the score to 21-14 but their ensuing onside kick failed. Despite the loss, Kroll thought the offensive line gave a good account of itself.

A long streak of 19 straight wins over Newman was in peril the next Saturday afternoon in Wausau. Fired up for their homecoming game, the Cardinals hit a 28-yard field goal in the second quarter that looked as if it might stand up for a 3-0 win. (Newman had already knocked off regional powerhouse D.C. Everest.) But the Dons got a break when Newman punter Pete Baumann ran the ball late in the game on a fourth-down play near midfield. He lost 2 yards and the Dons took over on the Newman 48-yard line. Eleven plays later Jon Radlinger ran it in from 2 yards out with 13 seconds left on the game clock. The Dons escaped Thom Field with a last-minute 7-3 win. "The key during the drive was the fourth-and-6 play where Radlinger ran the quick trap," Kroll said. "It was just a super win for us and a great drive." Paul Hughes put pressure on Newman punters all game long. Kroll also praised the efforts of defensive end Larry Olsen and defensive halfbacks Jeff Weister and Rob Wagner. The good crowd on hand for the Saturday afternoon homecoming game against Assumption was treated to a well-played game by both teams. All of the touchdowns were scored in the game's first eight minutes. The Royals' Ken Prokash had his biggest game ever at quarterback. Rather than pitch the ball, he kept it this day, rolling up 126 yards in 10 carries. The Assumption speedster scored on option keeps of 38 and 57 yards in the first quarter. The Royals sealed the victory with a 19-play drive that consumed most of the fourth quarter. It culminated with a 28-yard field goal by Mike Ritchay, making it 17-10. For the third year in a row, Assumption defeated the Dons. Kroll remarked, "They were just more physical than us, especially in the second half."

The following Saturday night, Chuck Krier's 57-yard TD dash on the third play of the game at Chippewa Falls gave CHS a 6-0 victory. McDonell dominated the line of scrimmage in the second half. Unfortunately for the Macks, their game-tying score with 55 seconds left was nullified by a penalty, allowing Columbus to hang on for the win. Sophomore nose guard Pat Kraus played his best game of the year, as did two other defenders, "Hughie" Hughes and Steve Zygarlicke. In La Crosse the next week the Dons managed just one first down in their 20-0 loss to Aquinas. The Blugolds win was their seventh in a row and ninth in their last 10 starts. Kroll acknowledged, "The Blugolds were too big, too tough, too quick. Their physical dominance just began to wear us down. They simply outclassed us." The first half was played in near perfect weather but it started to pour as the teams went to the locker rooms for halftime.

When lightning joined the rain with about two minutes remaining, the game was terminated. Despite the defeat Kroll praised defenders Dick Stevens, Brian Morgan, and Jeff Weister. In a good, hard-hitting season finale at Beell Stadium against once-defeated Pacelli, the Dons fell 14-3. Rob Wagner burned the Cardinals on sweeps of 11, 21, 11, 12, and 19 yards en route to a 100-yard game. Pacelli coach Bob Raczek said, "It was a typical Columbus-Pacelli game. We always have tough ones." Kroll added, "We had a darn good season. We made week-to-week improvement."

Eleven seniors played their final game against Pacelli: Frank Baltus, Tim Connaughty, Greg Dean, Dave Fait, Paul Hughes, Joe Koenig, Keith Koenig, Chuck Krier, Mike Scherr, Rick Schreiner, and Steve Zygarlicke. Jon Radlinger led in scoring with 54 points, followed by Dick Stevens (31), Rob Wagner (26), Larry Olsen (20), Dave Fait (18), Frank Baltus (18), and Chuck Krier (12). Two Dons were named All-CWCC: Paul Hughes at linebacker and Olsen at defensive end.

1979 CWCC Standings	W	L	TP	OPP
La Crosse Aquinas	6	0	164	29
Stevens Point Pacelli	5	1	144	44
Wis. Rapids Assumption	4	2	95	73
Marshfield Columbus	3	3	73	54
Wausau Newman	2	4	57	78
Chippewa Falls McDonell	1	5	33	108
Eau Claire Regis	0	6	28	208

1980 – 1989

1980: State Champions!

The 1980 team brought Marshfield its first state high school football championship. A packed Beell Stadium breathed a sigh of relief when Kevin Kennedy intercepted a Waukesha Catholic Memorial pass in overtime to secure the thrilling victory. It capped a perfect 12-0 season. These Dons were relentless, scoring 345 points, more than any other Columbus 11. Their 28.75 per game scoring average was eclipsed only by the 1965 team at 30.11 points per game. The stingy defense shutout six of 12 opponents, a record that would stand. The Dons allowed a scant 5.25 points per game, bested only by the 1957 squad's 4.57. The defense's remarkable string of 18 scoreless quarters reminded long-time fans of the 20-quarter streak achieved by the 1970 team. For Columbus it was a fourth undefeated season. The 1980 squad joined those from 1957, 1958, and 1967 in attaining perfection. Those teams, however, played fewer games and did not have a playoff system to lengthen their season.

The Dons drew formidable strength from their overall balance on offense, defense, and kicking game. Junior quarterback Brian Morgan set a conference accuracy mark, connecting on 61.5% of his passes, breaking the 1968 record held by Bill Draxler, also of Columbus. Morgan tossed 11 TD passes while being intercepted only twice. The potent backfield triumvirate consisted of the elusive Robby Wagner, bulldozing Jon Radlinger, and fleet-footed Larry Olsen. The Kennedy twins, Kelly and Kevin, joined Tom Nikolai to give Morgan key passing targets. Morgan doubled up as the punter and seemed to kick better the more dire the situation. Junior Dick Stevens became the most prolific kicker in team history when he converted a late-game extra point against Assumption. It was his 60th career kicking point, shattering Steve Seidl's record of 59. Stevens also broke the single-season record with 44 points. In addition, he connected on five field goals, tying the 1975 Ken Kraus mark. Finally, his 40-yard field goal, into a brisk wind at Carson Park in Eau Claire, was the longest in CHS history until then. Overall, the Dons led the loop in defense but McDonell, with their prolific aerial game, nudged them out for conference offensive honors. The season marked the first time since 1967 that the Dons claimed a CWCC crown outright.

Edgewood appeared to be fed up with losing annually to Columbus in their season opener, having lost five in a row. Playing on a soggy field in Madison, the Crusaders dominated the first half by limiting the Dons to 30 yards and causing two CHS turnovers. Edgewood led 12-7 at halftime. Whatever was said in the locker room motivated Columbus. Like a charm. The defense, led by Rod Retterrath, Kevin Hamann, and Jon Radlinger, limited the Crusaders to five net yards in the final two stanzas, allowing neither a first down nor a pass completion. Brian Morgan looked sharp in his first start at QB. Coach Walt Kroll felt that the turning point was Morgan's 25-yard TD pass to Larry Olsen just before halftime. The resurgent Dons scored 25 second-half points and rode home with a 32-12 win.

Auburndale was no match for the Dons the following Saturday night in the home opener at Beell. Columbus bolted to a 34-0 halftime advantage on a warm, mosquito-filled evening. The Dons reserves played the last quarter and a half. Kroll cited Tom Nikolai's outstanding receiving and the defensive play of sophomores Tom Reigel and Duane Wanta in the 41-0 win. In the first of three straight Saturday afternoon contests, the Dons dismantled the Wolves 31-0 in Winneconne. With only a 12-0 halftime lead, Kevin Hamann's early third quarter blocked punt put the ball on the opponent's 4 yard line. Jon Radlinger scored on the next play. Rob Wagner added two more third quarter TDs. Kroll praised Kevin Kennedy, Derold Martin, Hamann, and Radlinger for their offensive contributions. On defense, Pat Kraus had his best game. Kroll also complimented Wally Schuetz for his play. He was unhappy, though, with the number of penalties his team was incurring. Manitowoc Roncalli came to Beell Stadium undefeated and unscored upon in the young season. They didn't leave that way. Columbus notched a 21-0 win over the Jets on slippery turf. Middle guard Eric Fehrenbach and tackles Pat Kraus and Kevin Hamann played key roles in the team's third consecutive shutout, according to their coach. A 35-0 homecoming win over Newman allowed the Dons to up their defensive string of shutout quarters to 18. Ranked #2 in the

WISAA Class A poll, the Dons put three touchdowns on the board in three and a half minutes before halftime to give the alumni much to cheer for. Dave Drach, a 1970 Columbus grad and former grid star under Kroll, was coach of the Newman team. While the entire defense played well, Kroll mentioned the play of Jon Radlinger, Pat Kraus, Kevin Hamann, and Kelly Kennedy.

Assumption's Shawn Montgomery, the reigning conference 100-yard dash champion, ended CHS's defensive scoreless streak with a 67-yard touchdown run on the third play of the game the following Saturday night in Wisconsin Rapids. Before the first quarter was over burly Craig Gerlach also tallied for the Royals to give AHS a 14-0 lead. Dons QB Brian Morgan shepherded a comeback, tying the game before half. Afterward, the Dons methodically moved down the field in nine plays to score the go-ahead TD on a Rob Wagner 6-yard run. Columbus' ability to control the ball in the last two quarters spelled doom for Assumption, which ran only 15 plays. With a 35-14 win at Witter Field, the Dons enjoyed a 17-10 advantage in the all-time series with their county rivals. "Morgan's leadership and pinpoint accuracy kept us in contention when things were still a little shaky," Kroll noted. McDonell brought their aerial circus to Beell Stadium the next Saturday night and made history by passing 46 times. No other team had ever attempted so many against Columbus. The Dons picked off four of those attempts. Late in the first quarter Brian Morgan found Kevin Kennedy for a 32-yard reception. Kennedy was knocked out of bounds at the 9-yard line but not before stunning the crowd with his spectacular, diving catch. The drive stalled and the Dons settled for a 19-yard field goal by Dick Stevens, who also nabbed three interceptions. The Dons cruised to a 31-6 victory.

Everyone knew the Aquinas game in Marshfield the following Saturday evening was essentially the 1980 CWCC championship game. Aquinas was also undefeated in conference play and only an early season loss to crosstown rival La Crosse Central marred its record. The Blugolds also boasted a seven-game win streak over the Dons. After nearly a week of rain, field conditions were slippery on game night. Hard hits reverberated around the stadium, though both teams failed to score in the first half. Brian Morgan's punting put CHS in good field position all game long. The Dons caught a huge break when an Aquinas punt snap sailed out of the end zone for a two-point team safety in the third quarter. The Dons ended up on the Aquinas 42-yard line after the Blugolds' free kick following the safety. Morgan threw a perfect pass to Kevin Kennedy to cover the 42 yards for a TD on the next play. In 20 seconds the Dons had turned a scoreless draw into an 8-0 advantage. Aquinas Coach Dave Reinders said, "That caught me by surprise. It was a beautiful throw, the best of the night." Dick Stevens added an insurance field goal to make the final tally 11-0. The Dons defense shut down the league's top offense. "That was absolutely super team defense," Kroll said. "Rod Retterath played as great a game at linebacker as anybody ever has, at least while I've been here, and Jon Radlinger was right beside him on every play." No past victory had made him happier than this one, he claimed. Columbus routed an 0-8 Regis team the following week in Eau Claire, 43-6. Dons reserves saw plenty of action and the final CHS tally came from the second offensive unit. Just before halftime Stevens booted a school record 40-yard field goal—into a stiff 15 mph wind. The Dons closed out their 1980 regular season with a convincing 29-0 shutout of Pacelli in Stevens Point. Jon Radlinger and Rob Wagner rushed for 133 and 129 yards, respectively. Even though it was Parents Night for Pacelli, there were twice as many Dons fans on hand at Goerke Field.

Sporting a perfect 10-0 record, Columbus was an easy choice for one of the four coveted WISAA Class A playoff berths. The Dons traveled to Manitowoc to face Roncalli the following Saturday night. The Jets were 7-2 and Fox Valley Christian Conference champs. (One of their two losses had come against the Dons earlier in the season.) The wind was whipping at Municipal Field, with gusts up to 40 mph, and all game points were scored with the team that had the wind advantage. Roncalli had the choice of getting the ball or going with the wind to start the third quarter. They chose to go with the wind. The dependable Dons defense rose to the occasion, holding the hosts to 30 yards in the third frame. The only Roncalli pass caught in six third-quarter attempts was a Columbus interception. Trailing 13-10 late in the fourth, 155-pound senior fullback Jon Radlinger found daylight after clearing the line of scrimmage and out ran three defenders for a 38-yard go-ahead touchdown with two minutes left in the game. Dick Stevens' extra-point kick made it 17-13. Because Radlinger had blocked an earlier Roncalli extra-point try, the Jets now needed a TD to win. The Dons held on for the victory.

A Marshfield team winning a Wisconsin state championship in Marshfield will probably never happen again. But it did happen on Saturday, November 15, 1980. In what Kroll described as "the greatest game a Columbus team has ever played," his Dons hung on in overtime to defeat Waukesha Catholic Memorial 19-12 for the WISAA Class A state football title at Beell Stadium. Both teams wanted to go on defense first in the overtime but Memorial won the toss. Columbus chose the north goal toward the flag pole and the concession stand, away from the scoreboard at the end of the jam-packed stadium. Both teams got one set of downs from the 10-yard line. Jon Radlinger picked up four yards in two rushing attempts for CHS. Facing third down from the 6-yard line, halfback Robby Wagner knifed through the tough Memorial line for a 6-yard TD. Dick Stevens' point-after was perfect, giving the Dons a 19-12 advantage. The Crusaders knew what they must do to retain their state championship crown—score a touchdown and then decide whether to kick for one point to send the game into another overtime or gamble on a two-point conversion for sudden victory or sudden defeat. Surprisingly, Memorial did not go with their 212-pound senior workhorse Mike Reuteman in the overtime period. Facing second-and-10, the Dons blitzed two linebackers forcing Memorial QB Joe Houk to hurry his pass into the end zone. Kevin Kennedy made the interception for the Dons to seal Marshfield's first-ever state football championship. Catholic Memorial coach Bill Young explained, "We went away from Mike because we knew they would be looking for him."

Early in the game, the burly fullback wasted no time making people wonder why he had been chosen Most Valuable Player in the previous year's championship game. He raced 68 yards for a touchdown on the first play. His extra-point kick attempt, however, sailed wide left leaving the Crusaders with a 6-0 lead 28 seconds into the championship game. The Dons caught a break when a bad punt snap allowed a bevy of Dons to swarm Memorial's punter and take over on the 31-yard line. Seconds later, facing third-and-goal from the 12, Kevin Kennedy made a sensational end zone catch while surrounded by three defenders to even the score. The *News-Herald* account said, "The angular senior honor student made a diving catch of the deflected ball for a touchdown." Later in the second quarter Dons senior linebacker Rod Retterath shredded the Memorial line to block a Crusaders punt. The Dons recovered at the Memorial 18-yard line. With everyone thinking deep pass, Columbus executed a perfect screen pass from Brian Morgan to Rob Wagner for 16 yards. Jon Radlinger lunged over from the 2-yard line for the go-ahead score with 40 seconds left in the half. The Crusaders blocked Dick Stevens' kick, leaving the Dons ahead 12-6 at halftime.

Near the end of the third quarter Catholic Memorial drove 56 yards in seven plays, mainly using Mike Reuteman, to even the score at 12. The Crusaders surprised a lot of people by going for two points. However, their pass fell incomplete. A Columbus face-mask penalty allowed Memorial another attempt. This time Reuteman's kick sailed left. Larry Olsen couldn't find the handle for the Dons on the ensuing kickoff and Memorial recovered the elusive pigskin on the Dons' 24-yard line. The Crusaders eventually plowed to the 2-yard line. They faced fourth-and-1 for a first down. Everyone in the stadium knew who was getting the ball. Fullback Mike Reuteman was stopped six inches short on an epic goal-line stand. While saved for the moment, the Dons were still in the shadow of their own goal posts. Reuteman blitzed and had Radlinger in his grasp in the end zone. Only a Herculean effort from the tough-as-nails fullback allowed him to escape being tackled for a safety. Neither team was able to score again and the regulation game ended in a 12-12 deadlock. "It all went down to the kicking game," a glum Memorial coach Bill Young said after the game. "We haven't muffed a kick or had a punt blocked all season... But everything went wrong tonight and in the end that was the ball game." Despite the loss, Memorial's Mike Reuteman was named Most Valuable Player. Besides picking up 199 yards in 31 carries and scoring all of the Crusaders points, he was a terrifying menace for the Dons on defense and blocked a crucial extra point attempt. In the lead up to the game, coach Kroll had declared this group of Columbus athletes as "without a question, the best team in my 17 years at Columbus."

Seventeen seniors crowned their careers with a state championship on home turf: John Braem, Ray Burrill, Eric Fehrenbach, Kevin Hamann, Kelly Kennedy, Kevin Kennedy, Derold Martin, Kevin Merkel, Joe Michalski, Tom Nikolai, Larry Olsen, Aric Prickett, Jon Radlinger, Rod Retterath, Wally Schuetz, Pat Stangl, and Jeff Weister. Eleven Dons scored in the 345-point season, led by Rob Wagner with 96 points. He was followed by Radlinger (66), Dick Stevens (44), Olsen (42), Kevin Kennedy (32), Kelly Kennedy (22), Brian Morgan (16), Nikolai (12), Tom Kraus (6), Rick Ploen (6), and Jim Bloczynski (1). More Dons were named All-CWCC in 1980 than ever before. On offense, end Kelly Kennedy, tackle Derold Martin, QB Brian Morgan, halfback Rob Wagner, and guard Lyle Lang were chosen. Larry Olsen was selected at defensive end for the second year in a row. Defensive tackle Kevin Hamann, linebacker Jon Radlinger, and defensive back Dick Stevens rounded out the all-conference picks.

1980 CWCC Standings	W	L	TP	OPP
Marshfield Columbus	6	0	184	26
La Crosse Aquinas	5	1	152	41
Chippewa Falls McDonell	4	2	152	84
Stevens Point Pacelli	3	3	118	69
Wis. Rapids Assumption	2	4	82	138
Wausau Newman	1	5	43	224
Eau Claire Regis	0	6	33	182

1981: Less of More

The 1981 Dons had pressure thrust upon them like no other team. Coming off an undefeated state championship season, expectations were high. The early schedule was brutal. A strong Edgewood team, a perennial WISAA power from the Milwaukee area, and a WIAA state champion were on the docket. Coach Walt Kroll was relieved to come out of that stretch with two wins. But the Dons faltered once in conference play, to McDonell's national record-breaking aerial attack. Their third loss in a fine 9-3 campaign came in the State Class A WISAA championship game, a narrow 14-7 defeat by Milwaukee Thomas More. They shared the conference title with Chippewa Falls McDonell and Stevens Point Pacelli.

Coach Joel Maturi brought his 64-player Edgewood squad to Beell to open the campaign. With 15 lettermen, the Crusaders had their strongest teams in years. One of them was 5'9", 205-pound senior center Chris Farley, who would go on to comedic fame with Saturday Night Live. The Dons eked out a 6-0 win on the strength of a 45-yard John Olsen punt return that set up the game's lone score. "Olsen tackled great the whole game and his blocking impressed me as much as anything else," said Kroll. The coach also singled out the defensive play of Steve Meyers, Al Gripentrog, and Shawn Morgan. All told, seven Dons players had never started a game before this home opener.

Jim Haluska, a former star QB at Wisconsin, ushered his Milwaukee Metro Conference champion Thomas More Cavaliers to Beell Stadium for the second game. The Cavaliers were 9-1 in 1980 and had lost a total of five games over the previous five years. With 700 boys to choose from at an all-boys school, More didn't have to rebuild year to year. They just re-loaded with a senior-laden squad every new season. Thomas More had an impressive passing attack. Tom Bishop, the Cavalier QB, delivered on-the-money balls to sure-handed receivers. More defeated Columbus 17-10 after they stopped a fourth-down CHS QB sneak late in the game at their own 25-yard line. "It was a fine high school football game by two good teams. It just turned out on that night Thomas More was a little bit better," said Kroll. "Maybe that loss will take that win-streak pressure off. The players were under some pressure to try and play up to the excellence of last year's team right off the bat." The Cavaliers ended the Columbus streak at 13.

Two Rivers brought their 1980 WIAA Division 3 state championship laurels with them to Beell the following Saturday afternoon.

Earlier in the week, Kroll told a reporter, "Each season is a new season and each team is a new team... I'm satisfied with the progress the young players have made in the first two games." His defense, starting four sophomores, yielded only 23 points to clever and well-run attacks. Fullback Joe Baierl emerged in the Two Rivers game, getting CHS's only TD in the second quarter. A third-quarter 28-yard Dick Stevens field goal gave the Dons a 10-6 win. The victory snapped a 13-game Two Rivers win streak. The year's first road game was another afternoon game, in Wausau for Newman's homecoming. The Dons did not cooperate with the celebration, dumping the Cardinals 55-0. Kroll was now 17-0 against Newman. The Dons had two runners who topped 100 yards in the Thom Field trouncing: Rob Wagner (145) and Dick Stevens (114). Columbus played a third straight afternoon game when they hosted Assumption for homecoming the following Saturday. After falling behind on an 80-yard TD dash by Shawn Montgomery, the Dons settled down and prevailed 12-7. Kroll praised the defensive efforts of junior Pat Mancl, sophomore Al Gripentrog, and senior Mark Zimmerman. He also applauded Tom Kraus and Steve Jones for exceptional catches. Star running back Rob Wagner suffered a bruised shoulder and sat out the second half.

The Dons ran smack into the Dave Geissler-led McDonell aerial attack the next weekend at Dorais Field in Chippewa Falls. Every week the senior Macks quarterback flirted with the national high school record of 35 completions in a game. His first-half performance was otherworldly, connecting on 16 of 20 passes for 223 yards. "His passing was remarkable but the receptions were even better," Kroll said. Trailing 21-14 late in the game, the Dons tried an onside kick but it didn't quite go 10 yards, giving McDonell possession and the win. Kroll spotlighted the play of Dick Stevens, who ran for 124 yards and "was in on almost every tackle. ... We were outplayed up front," Kroll lamented. In La Crosse the following Saturday night, both Aquinas and Columbus scored on their opening drives. The Dons, though, imposed their will on the Blugolds at the outset of the second half. A Stevens interception put the ball on the Aquinas 16-yard line, setting up Rob Wagner's TD three plays later. On the first Aquinas play from scrimmage after the kickoff, Steve Meyers recovered a Blugold fumble that led directly to Stevens' 26-yard field goal. Wagner, back at full strength, played his finest game of the year in the 20-14 Columbus win.

The Dons beat Regis 26-6 on a muddy field in Marshfield the following Saturday night. For the second week in a row, their defensive pass rush created havoc. John Olsen returned to the lineup after missing four games due to shoulder injury. The Regis TD came with eight seconds left in the game. The following Friday night St. Mary's narrowed the score to 24-15 early in the fourth quarter of a non-conference game at Calder Stadium in Menasha. Columbus exploded for the final 16 points, riding a 40-15 win back to Marshfield. Rob Wagner rushed for a remarkable 209 yards on 24 carries. No Columbus player had gone over the 200-yard mark since Wayne Zygarlicke in 1975 against Onalaksa Luther. Jim Bloczynski returned an interception for a 98-yard TD before halftime only to have it nullified by a penalty flag for clipping. The final regular season game pitted conference-rival and undefeated Pacelli against the Dons in Marshfield. A CHS victory would create a three-way tie for the CWCC crown. The Dons ran 16 plays covering 81 yards in their opening scoring drive to try and establish momentum. Pacelli had the league's toughest rush defense coming into this game, yielding 248 yards total in their previous five league games. Columbus ran for 350 yards in this game alone. So successful was the Dons' running attack that they only attempted one pass. Both Wagner and Stevens rushed for over 100 yards in the 28-14 win, with Wagner gaining 143 and Stevens notching 120. "There's no doubt in my mind that this was the best game we've played all season," said Kroll.

Columbus hosted one of the two WISAA Class A football championship semi-final games on a Friday night in Marshfield. Fond du Lac St. Mary's Springs brought their 10-0 record and newly minted Fox Valley Christian Conference championship crown with them. Kroll said the offensive line "really opened up some nice holes against a line that had registered six shutouts in ten games." The Dons ended the Ledgers' 15-game win streak with a bruising ground game—and a 21-10 victory. Again, Wagner and Stevens topped 100 yards rushing (150 and 110, respectively). Kroll commented, "We got a tremendous game from Wagner. Pat Kraus was outstanding, as was Rich Nikolai, but basically our whole defense was that way." The Beell win propelled the Dons into the state championship game for the second year in a row, this time against Thomas More, whom they had lost to early in the season. At Titan Stadium in Oshkosh, the Dons dominated a scoreless first half with More failing to reach midfield. But they were unable to score when things were going their way, which proved to be their undoing. Falling behind 14-0 early in the fourth quarter, the Dons rallied with a 14-yard Wagner run and a point-after kick by Stevens to close the gap to 14-7 with nine minutes left. Columbus was unable to score on their last three possessions and simply ran out of time. Dons defenders played the Thomas More ends much tighter in this game than in the earlier encounter. But the Thomas More defensive alignment that took away CHS's coveted inside run game, thwarting Stevens, proved to be more effective in the Cavaliers 14-7 win. For the southside Milwaukee team it was a fourth overall WISAA football title.

Fifteen seniors ended their Dons careers playing in back-to-back state championship games: Joe Baierl, Bill Hakl, Pat Kraus, Tom Kraus, Jim Krier, Lyle Lang, Brian Morgan, Tim Nikolai, John Olsen, Tony Pichler, Rick Ploen, Greg Sebastian, Dick Stevens, Rob Wagner, and Mark Zimmerman. Stevens scored just over 40% of the team's points. He booted a school-record six field goals. With his 19 point-after kicks and 11 rushing TDs, he racked up 103 points, winning the conference scoring crown. Other leading scorers were Wagner (36), Olsen (24), Morgan (24), Steve Jones (18), Chris Zukowski (12), and Jim Bloczynski (10). Seven Dons were named to eight All-CWCC positions. On offense, center Greg Sebastian, guard Lyle Lang, tackle Pat Kraus, and running backs Rob Wagner and Dick Stevens were selected. All were seniors. Lang, Wagner, and Stevens were repeaters on the all-conference team. Two Dons defensive linemen were accorded seats on the elite squad: Pat Kraus (the only player to make both teams) and junior

Rich Nikolai. Walt Kroll was named CWCC Coach of the Year for the second consecutive year.

1981 CWCC Standings	W	L	TP	OPP
Chippewa Falls McDonell	5	1	136	80
Marshfield Columbus	5	1	166	62
Stevens Point Pacelli	5	1	131	69
La Crosse Aquinas	3	3	76	74
Wis. Rapids Assumption	2	4	118	72
Wausau Newman	1	5	23	191
Eau Claire Regis	0	6	28	119

1982: Road Warriors

This Columbus squad proved an unexpected delight. Delivering steady, opportunistic play with few miscues, they found themselves in the WISAA Class A state championship football game for a third year in a row. These over-achievers played nine of their 12 games away from Marshfield in compiling a stellar 10-2 mark and claiming the CWCC title outright with a thrilling overtime win over Pacelli in Stevens Point. Going into the game both teams were undefeated in league play. In their first three tilts, the Dons played a revamped Edgewood team, Thomas More (defending WISAA champs), and Two Rivers (defending WIAA Division 3 champs)—all in their home stadiums. And they won them all. Columbus' team-oriented style of play put seven straight wins on the board before a loss to perennial Upper Peninsula power Menominee on their home turf. Two weeks later they handed Pacelli their first loss in overtime. Columbus kickers paved the way for a 6-3 win over DePere Pennings before coming up short in a well-played championship game in Oshkosh. Milwaukee Marquette prevailed in that one, 7-0.

In the season opener Columbus scored its eighth win in a row over Edgewood, 14-7. The Crusaders, under the new tutelage of 1974 EHS grad Tim Martinelli, gave the Dons all they could handle in Madison. The Dons capitalized on two Edgewood mistakes. Shawn

Morgan recovered a Crusader fumble on the opening kickoff to lead to the first tally. When Edgewood tried a third-down quick kick in the second quarter, Morgan broke through the line and blocked the punt. Craig Duellman found paydirt for the Dons from five yards out. Edgewood responded with an impressive 12-play, 75-yard march down the field before halftime to narrow the gap to 14-7. While no scoring occurred in the last two quarters, both punters were exceptional. Mark Rae had boots of 45 and 48 yards for the Dons. In addition, Steve Jones had two noteworthy punt returns of 30 and 41 yards for the navy-and-white. Thomas More, which won the 1981 state championship game over CHS in Oshkosh, faced the Dons at St. Francis High School in the south Milwaukee suburb this time. In the second quarter, senior QB Jim Bloczynski engineered a 75-yard scoring drive to give the Dons the only score they would need, a 13-yard strike to Steve Jones. Bloczynski injured his knee returning a punt a bit later and was lost for the season. Mark Rae, his junior backup, took over signal-calling duties. Timely defensive plays helped Columbus shut out the Cavaliers 14-0.

Jerry Bonino's Two Rivers football team came into the 1982 season with back-to-back WIAA Division 3 state championships and an impressive 32-3 record over a three-year span. This Saturday afternoon affair was a tense back-and-forth game with plenty of thrills. The Purple Raiders got their fans out of their seats with a 52-yard opening kickoff return. The drive was later halted by Steve Jones' one-handed, juggling interception at the CHS 15-yard line. Wind played havoc for both teams. Columbus was buoyed when it held Two Rivers scoreless when they were with the wind in the third quarter. Playing like the champions they were, the Purple Raiders mounted an impressive 80-yard drive against the wind to take a 19-15 lead with just over four minutes left in the game. Columbus fought back. Running a down-and-out pass pattern, Steve Jones leapt high for a Mark Rae pass. "Jones seemed to spear the ball by the nose and then hauled it in as he crashed to the ground," the Marshfield newspaper reported. All were amazed. A short while later, Rae fooled everyone when he ran wide and untouched on a 2-yard QB bootleg. After John Rasmussen's extra point, the Dons led 22-19 with 1:14 to play. Mike Saviage picked off a Purple

Raiders pass and sped 60 yards with the interception for a cherry-on-top touchdown with 27 seconds left. The 29-19 score was not indicative of the nail-biting nature of the seesaw contest.

The Dons' fourth straight away game to open the season was just down the road in Wisconsin Rapids. The conference opener pitted the quickness of Columbus against the power of Assumption. On this day, quickness prevailed. Mike Saviage intercepted a Royals pass on the third play, giving the Dons the ball on the AHS 28-yard line and setting up the first touchdown. CHS later capped an 80-yard drive with Mark Rae's perfectly thrown over-the-shoulder ball to Steve Jones in full stride for a 29-yard score. After Assumption responded with a long run, Doug Nikolai returned a punt 52 yards for six points before halftime. "The punt return was the turning point in the contest," Assumption coach Rod Tafelski said. The Dons departed the Wood County seat with a 27-15 triumph. Coach Walt Kroll credited George Olsen and pulling guards Duane Wanta, Jim Hanson, Paul Rasmussen, and Tom Reigel for the success of the buck trap play. "I'll tell you one thing, there's no team in the state that's played four quality opponents, all on the road, and won them all," Kroll stated.

McDonell's aerial barrage came to Beell Stadium for the home opener (and homecoming game) the following Saturday afternoon. All scoring was done in the first half with the Dons subduing the Macks 9-6. The Dons set the tone early with a Doug Nikolai theft of a Macks pass on the third play of the game. The second CHS swipe came near the end of the first half with McDonell knocking on the door from the Columbus 8-yard line. Rob Nikolai picked it off to preserve the 9-6 halftime lead. The Columbus running attack controlled the ball in the second half. When the Macks did get their hands on it, especially in the fourth quarter, the Dons were there to thwart any positive movement. Five of the seven CHS interceptions came in the last stanza. The only CHS sad note in the narrow win was that running back Tom Borowski injured his knee.

Both Aquinas and Columbus had identical 5-0 records when they met at Beell the next Friday night. The Dons bolted from the gates with a nine-play, 71-yard scoring drive. Aquinas fumbled on its first possession and an alert Shawn Morgan recovered on the

Aquinas 38-yard line. Eight plays later the Dons were on the board again, another TD pass from Mark Rae to Steve Jones. "They sure jumped on us quick," said Aquinas coach Dave Reinders. "We had only run three plays from scrimmage and they were already ahead 14-0." Aquinas never got closer than the Columbus 25-yard line in the 21-0 shutout. The following Saturday night saw quagmire-like conditions in Eau Claire's Carson Park, which prevented Columbus from running wide against Regis. Rain during UW-Eau Claire's homecoming game earlier that afternoon left field conditions less than desirable. Nevertheless, the Dons sloshed to a 17-0 victory with Mark Rae running 51 yards for one of the scores. Kroll commended linebackers Al Gripentrog and Pat Mancl for their inspired play.

Menominee is a Michigan school with as rich a football tradition as Columbus. Maroons head coach Ken Hofer was on a three-year hiatus when the Dons defeated Menominee twice in the early 1970s. The Maroons were now in the middle of facing three undefeated teams in a row: Escanaba (they beat them), Columbus, and Antigo. Kroll said before the game, "We know they have a fine team and we want to win, but we're not afraid to lose. It's the competition we like. We like to play good teams." Menominee was big and physical. Their single-wing, shotgun-like offense depended heavily on a good fullback. At 230 pounds Paul Pedersen fit that bill nicely for the Yooper squad. He scored both of their TDs in the 14-7 Dons loss. Menominee was averaging over 200 yards passing per game. The Dons held them to just 22 with their staunch pass defense. The third and final home game had the Dons facing Newman, who had beat Columbus in 1954, 1955, and 1956. It was the last time the Dons fell to Newman. The schools did play to a tie in 1959. Otherwise, the Dons dominated this series like no other. And 1982 was no exception. CHS led 49-0 with 6:53 left. Sophomore Hap Wolfgram ran for three scores and John Rasmussen scored on six extra points (five by kick and one by run). Newman probably knew what kind of day they were in for when Rasmussen's initial extra-point kick two minutes into the game was blocked. The ball came right back to Rasmussen and he ran it in for a two-point conversion. The final tally stood at 49-14. The regular season finale in Stevens Point saw two 5-0 CWCC teams play head-to-head for the conference title.

"It's a game of champions, played by champions, for the championship, and you can't ask for more than that," said Kroll. The Pacelli front line averaged 193 pounds, with their backfield players even bigger. The teams battled to a 7-7 tie in regulation. Columbus won the coin toss and chose to go on defense in overtime. Kevin McNamara booted a 31-yard field goal to put the Cards up 10-7. On their possession, the Dons ran Craig Duellman three straight times, with the last burst over left tackle good for three yards and the game-winning, conference-clinching touchdown. The name of the game, according to Kroll, was the punting of Mark Rae.

The Dons next faced DePere Pennings in a WISAA semi-final playoff game at the Squires' home venue, Minahan Stadium. Over the years in five tries, the Dons had yet to defeat DePere. Heading into their playoff contest, both teams had matching 9-1 records and spotless conference records. Wind played a major role on the 32-degree game night. Both teams came in with powerful kicking games. Todd Gregoire of Pennings was 26 of 27 kicking extra points and 11 of 15 kicking field goals with his longest registering 47 yards. John Rasmussen was no slouch for the Dons either, connecting on 21 of 24 extra points and booting two field goals. Gregoire also punted for Pennings. Mark Rae was averaging 39 yards per boot for Columbus. Pennings, backed by the wind in the second quarter, scored first on a 50-yard Gregoire field goal. Holding tightly to their 3-0 halftime lead, the Squires decided to go with the wind in the third stanza. Columbus negated that choice as much as possible by controlling the ball for 15 of the quarter's 23 plays. John Rasmussen knotted the game 3-3 with a 37-yard field goal with 5:30 to play. With 42 seconds left, Pennings punted 16 yards into the wind, allowing Steve Jones to fair-catch the boot on the Squires' 33-yard line. Thirty-five seconds showed on the scoreboard. An option available to any receiving team that chooses to fair catch after a punt is a free kick. Under the rules, Rasmussen was allowed to have the ball teed up, with the opposing team forced to fall back and give a clear shot at the goal post. "He took full advantage, splitting the uprights with a much stronger kick than the 37-yarder that had tied the game," the *News-Herald* reported. The 43-yard free-kick field goal was the longest in Columbus history. With only

27 seconds left after the historic boot, the Dons held on for a 6-3 win. Gregoire would go on to score 278 points for the Wisconsin Badgers from 1984 to 1987. His 65 career field goals stood as a UW record for 31 years.

With the win, Columbus was playing in an unprecedented third consecutive state championship game. It was on the road, too. The Dons had met Marquette High once before in 1974 in Milwaukee and had come away with a 28-13 victory at the end of the regular season. This match-up was another David vs. Goliath scenario, given that the Milwaukee school had nearly three times as many students. David got the better of it at the start. Columbus tallied four first-quarter first downs and 60 yards rushing compared to just 17 yards and no first downs for the Hilltoppers. The momentum shifted in the second quarter. One minute before halftime, Marquette's Pat Christie scored on a 2-yard run, climaxing a 91-yard drive. Chris Kasun's point-after made it 7-0. With the Dons driving in the fourth quarter, QB Mark Rae threw a third-down interception from the Marquette 6-yard line. Tom Klar of the Hilltoppers made a spectacular diving catch in the end zone. "Klar was one heck of a linebacker who knew what was going on out there," said Kroll. Marquette was marching toward a second score at the end of the game. Dick Basham's Hilltoppers, with the state title clearly in sight, graciously allowed the clock to run out with the ball resting on the Columbus 1-yard line, content with their hard-fought 7-0 state championship victory. "We played 12 good games this season. We played as hard as we could Saturday night, but Marquette played just a little bit better," Kroll said. Five hundred people were on hand to welcome the team back to Marshfield.

Seventeen Dons seniors ended their careers playing in three straight state championship games: Dave Adler, John Bersalona, Jim Bloczynski, Tom Borowski, Jim Hansen, Steve Jones, Pat Mancl, Pete Moore, Shawn Morgan, Rich Nikolai, Steve Norfleet, Paul Rasmussen, Tom Reigel, Mike Saviage, Randy Spencer, Duane Wanta, and Chris Zukowski. The season's 206 points were well distributed. Jones led everyone with eight touchdowns for 48 points, followed by kicker and end John Rasmussen with 42. Barrel-chested fullback John Bersalona scored 30 and sophomore wingback Hap Wolfgram had 24. Craig Duellman managed to put 18 points on the board, Mark Rae 14, and Chris Zukowski 12. Seven Dons were selected for All-CWCC honors. On offense, end Steve Jones, tackle Randy Spencer, guard Paul Rasmussen, and place-kicker John Rasmussen were named. The defensive choices were end Rich Nikolai, linebacker Pat Mancl, and punter Mark Rae. All were seniors except the two kicking specialists. It was Nikolai's second year recognized at defensive end. Walt Kroll was named Coach of the Year for the third straight time.

1982 CWCC Standings	W	L	TP	OPP
Marshfield Columbus	6	0	136	45
Stevens Point Pacelli	5	1	175	33
La Crosse Aquinas	4	2	134	77
Chippewa Falls McDonell	3	3	119	62
Wis. Rapids Assumption	2	4	78	137
Wausau Newman	1	5	74	225
Eau Claire Regis	0	6	41	178

1983: Three to Start, Three to Finish

Coach Walt Kroll continued his quest to schedule tough non-conference foes, no matter the location. But doing so in 1983 left the Dons with three quick defeats at the hands of Edgewood and first-time opponents Cudahy and Janesville Parker. Narrow league wins over conference competitors Assumption and McDonell enabled Columbus to face Aquinas in an early showdown of undefeated CWCC teams. It wasn't much of a contest, though. Sporting one of the best teams ever in the 44-year history of the league, Aquinas dismantled the Dons 34-0 at La Crosse's Memorial Field. Aquinas would finish 6-0 in the conference, scoring 163 points and yielding a miserly six. Yes, six points in six games! A loss to a re-tooled Regis had the Dons staring at an uncharacteristic 2-5 mark. Three consecutive wins, including one in double overtime over Menominee, enabled the Dons to finish with a 5-5 record. Columbus and Assumption, both 4-2, tied for second place in the conference.

One of the last times Edgewood beat Columbus, second-year EHS coach Tim Martinelli was on the field as a player. He shredded the Dons with a nine-reception, 101-yard performance in a 14-0 Crusaders win. That 1973 game was followed with a 15-8 Edgewood triumph the next year. Then the navy-and-white exerted eight years of dominance in the series. In 1983 the game ended 0-0 in regulation. Just before halftime, the Dons were on the Edgewood 4-yard line when time expired. CHS had two timeouts to use and used neither. In overtime John Rasmussen's field goal was eclipsed by Mark Geske's 1-yard TD plunge for the Crusaders' streak-ending 6-3 win. The outstanding play of halfback Jim Michalski and guard Al Gripentrog drew plaudits from Kroll. Also coming in for praise were the running and punting of Mark Rae and the tackling of lineman George Olsen.

Cudahy's last game prior to meeting Columbus was a setback to Antigo in the 1982 WIAA large-school championship. In the previous six years of play, the Packers had fallen only seven times. Cudahy coach Jerry Bowe had many Marshfield connections via relatives and friends. With a comfortable 27-0 fourth-quarter cushion, Bowe inserted his reserves. The Dons quickly scored two touchdowns and the Packers mentor hastily put his first unit back on the field to quell the uprising. Cudahy won 27-14. "I think the big difference was our physical advantage in the line," Bowe said. "We had great pass protection and they just couldn't get to our passer. I know one thing. That (Mark) Rae kid is the best high school punter I've seen in 25 years of coaching." At Janesville the following Saturday night, the Dons dominated first-quarter play against Parker. The Vikings turned the tables by shoving the Dons around in the second half. Protecting a slim 6-3 lead, Parker chewed time off the clock with strategic first downs that denied Columbus the ball. The navy-and-white finally got their chance with one minute left and with 85 yards to travel. Advancing the ball to the 28, QB Mark Rae threw a perfect pass to Doug Nikolai but it went through his hands. The Dons headed home sitting at 0-3.

At the homecoming game, John Rasmussen's 42-yard field goal attempt with 16 seconds left fell short sending CHS into overtime with Assumption. Having battled to 7-7 in regulation, the Dons caught a break by winning the overtime coin toss and playing defense first. The Royals booted a field goal in their overtime possession. As the Dons lined up for their four chances to score from the 10, thunder crackled and the skies opened. With rain coming down in torrents, Al Gripentrog cleared a path for Craig Duellman on a 1-yard TD burst, giving CHS a 13-10 win. The following Saturday night pass-happy McDonell struck first in Chippewa Falls. Throwing on almost every down, the Dons showed the Macks that when you live by the pass, you can also die by it. Columbus stopped all three of their opposition's fourth-quarter drives with interceptions. They returned from Dorais Field with a 17-6 triumph. Next up, Aquinas. The 1983 juggernaut boasted 22 seniors on a 5-0 team coming into the Columbus game. Four of the Blugold victories had been shutouts. They added a fifth in a 34-0 whitewash of the Dons. It was the worst CHS defeat since 1972. Columbus didn't get their initial first down until the final minute of the first half. "We were manhandled," Kroll acknowledged. The following Saturday night, former Marshfield High assistant football coach Pete Gust, in his second year at the helm of Regis, brought his 4-2 Ramblers to Beell. The two defeats had pushed Regis' record-setting conference losing streak to 30. But this time, except for a brief span in the third quarter, Regis dominated the game and rode back to Eau Claire with an emotional 18-13 victory. Regis was officially back.

The Dons rebounded the following Saturday afternoon in Marshfield with a double overtime win over highly touted Menominee, a Michigan team. The Maroons were sitting on a 5-1 record with only a 14-8 loss to Wisconsin's top-ranked private school, Fond du Lac St. Mary's Springs. The scoreless first half turned into a punting duel between Mark Rae and Menominee triple-threat Phil Kloida. The Dons culminated a 12-play, 71-yard scoring drive with 3:23 to play on a 41-yard TD pass from Rae to John Rasmussen. Trailing 8-6, Rae ran for the crucial two-point conversion. Rasmussen settled matters in the second overtime with a 22-yard field goal for an 11-8 victory.

Kroll started star QB Mark Rae at safety for the first time all year for Newman's homecoming game the next Saturday afternoon in Wausau. It worked as Rae intercepted the Cardinals twice and threw for two TDs himself en route to a 34-17 victory. Jim Michalski ran for a career-high 116 yards, the first 100-yard rushing game for Columbus all year. In the season finale against Pacelli at Beell, "our backs ran with a lot of authority," Kroll said. "Our line came off the ball real good and opened some daylight for our runners." Craig Duellman capped his Dons career with a stellar 12-carry, 144-yard performance. The 318 rushing yards were the most in a game all year. The Dons prevailed 27-7.

Ten seniors finished their careers with three straight wins: Al Baierl, Bob Bare, Craig Duellman, Al Gripentrog, Steve Meyers, Doug Nikolai, Rob Nikolai, George Olsen, Mark Rae, and John Rasmussen. Besides catching six touchdown passes, Rasmussen also connected on four field goals and 11 extra points. His 59 points led the team. He was followed by Meyers (30), Duellman (20), Rae (14), Hap Wolgram (6), and John Michalski (6). Three Dons were selected for five spots on the All-CWCC team. Rasmussen was named to two positions on the offensive team, end and place-kicker. Guard Al Gripentrog and quarterback Mark Rae were chosen by the league's coaches, too. Rae also was recognized as best punter. Rasmussen and Rae's kicking talents were cited at the conference's highest level for the second consecutive year.

1983 CWCC Standings	W	L	TP	OPP
La Crosse Aquinas	6	0	163	6
Marshfield Columbus	4	2	104	92
Wis. Rapids Assumption	4	2	101	46
Eau Claire Regis	3	3	55	78
Chippewa Falls McDonell	2	4	79	93
Stevens Point Pacelli	2	4	73	113
Wausau Newman	0	6	31	167

1984: Four to Close

All five interior offensive starters returned for the 1984 team: center Mike Olsen, guard David Stevens, guard Paul Crowder, tackle Mark Earll, and tackle Paul Gordee. They averaged 189 pounds. "This could be one of the best offensive lines we've had at Columbus," coach Walt Kroll said. Indeed, John Michalski had a banner year running behind the veteran line. He rushed twice for 200 or more yards and five times for 100 or more en route to 1,326 yards on the ground. Kroll made a major adjustment with his players this season. Instead of platooning an offensive team with a separate defensive unit, Kroll rotated 20 players on offense and 18 on defense. Perhaps he picked up the idea while coaching the North team in the Wisconsin Shrine All-Star game in the summer of 1984. Another change came from higher up: the number of WISAA playoff participants increased from four to eight. But that didn't help these Dons. Though they closed out the year with four consecutive wins, including three shutouts, they finished 6-4 overall and 4-2 in the conference.

Kroll's new rotation system worked against Edgewood in Madison. Twenty-seven players saw action in the 21-13 road win. The *News-Herald* said the Dons were "operating behind an offensive line that opened up holes with the precision of a skilled surgeon." Columbus had drives of 51, 72, 42, 77, and 71 yards. John Michalski picked up his first 200-yard rushing game with 22 carries at Mansfield Stadium. Like Columbus, the Cudahy Packers had a strong football tradition. The Milwaukee Suburban Conference team had finished with a 6-3 mark in 1983. End Tom Lisota was a 6'6" high jumper and the rest of the team was big and physical, too. "Overall, they have one of the best football programs in the state," Kroll said. The Packers won at Beell, 20-6. One bright point was Michalski, who had 166 yards on 15 carries.

A new nine-year series of games against Marquette University High School began the following Saturday night. "The Marquette game was a whale of a contest, reminiscent of the 1980 WISAA championship game with Waukesha Memorial," Kroll said. It was an exciting game with a hard-to-swallow finish. The Dons drew first blood with a perfectly executed draw play midway through the second quarter. Michalski romped 35 yards for the score. A 25-yard Bill Saviage field goal with just over four minutes left had Dons fans feeling good with a slim 10-7 lead. But Marquette QB Bob Herman broke a tackle on the ensuing kickoff and was finally downed on the Columbus 38-yard line. Twelve plays later on fourth down, 215-pound Jim Ganzer rumbled in from two yards out over left guard. The Hilltoppers returned to Milwaukee with a 13-10 victory.

Bill Saviage's 23-yard field goal with five seconds left gave Columbus its own 31-28 come-from-behind victory the next Saturday night at Beell. Before the heroics, McDonell QB Todd Harings connected on 24 of 47 passes. Both were records against a CHS team. Trailing 28-14 with eight minutes left in the third quarter, the Dons rallied on long, ball-control drives. John Michalski continued his stellar play, ripping off 275 yards on 41 carries. It was the most yards gained in a game by a Dons ball carrier since Bobby Koch's 304-yard effort against Pacelli in 1965. "He's been tremendous," Kroll said of Michalski. "He's a great high school two-way player." A noteworthy Aquinas team steam-rolled Columbus 28-0 the next Friday night in Marshfield. The 1983 Aquinas club ran the ball 90% of the time; this Blugold squad had rifle-armed 6'4" John Hoch at the helm of a well-balanced offensive attack. This quicker, smaller Aquinas team had no one listed over 200 pounds. The Blugolds scored in every quarter on lengthy drives of 76, 80, 80, and 55 yards in a one-sided affair.

Regis held on to a 10-7 halftime lead for the win the next Saturday afternoon in Eau Claire. The Ramblers' only touchdown was helped along by a Jim Michalski punt-snap miscue on the CHS 21-yard line. Even though Regis was keying on him, John Michalski ground out 102 yards in the loss. After two tough conference losses the Dons travelled to Baraboo the following Friday night for a non-conference match. The Dons dominated, and walked away with a 6-0 win. Thunderbird coach Doug Freiermuth admitted, "We were lucky the score wasn't a lot worse." John Michalski erupted for 156 yards in 27 trips. Newman took the Dons into overtime on homecoming the following Saturday afternoon before falling

17-14. Bill Saviage's 19-yard three-point boot was the difference. The Cardinals outplayed Columbus and ran 66 plays compared to 44 for the Dons. It was the 25th consecutive win over the Wausau school. Eight days later, a 34-yard Saviage field goal as time expired in the first half stood up in a 3-0 win over Assumption. The Dons used a sustained 12-play, 61-yard drive to set up the game's only score. They dampened the Royals homecoming festivities with the win. In the season finale, Columbus blanked Pacelli 25-0 in Stevens Point. John Michalski, helped by the cohesive CHS line, concluded the season with a 143-yard rushing performance.

Fourteen seniors capped their careers with four straight wins: Shawn Carlson, Jim Christy, Paul Crowder, Jeff DeSmet, Mark Earll, Paul Gordee, Tom Krier, Jim Michalski, John Michalski, John Odegard, Mike Olsen, Bill Saviage, Dave Stevens, and Todd Zygarlicke. John Michalski ran for ten touchdowns (60 points), accounting for nearly half of the team's points. Bill Saviage was the only other player to score more than one touchdown. His 36 points came from two TD runs and an additional two dozen as kicker. Those logging one touchdown were Dan Zygarlicke, John Werner, Lee Pritzl, Scott Herkert, and Shawn Carlson. Bruising senior running back John Michalski was selected for the All-CWCC team. He finished second in CWCC rushing yards. For the third year running a CHS place-kicker was selected as the circuit's top booter. The honor went to Saviage, who kicked 12 extra points and four field goals. Three were game winners.

1984 CWCC Standings	W	L	TP	OPP
La Crosse Aquinas	6	0	190	9
Eau Claire Regis	5	1	105	67
Marshfield Columbus	4	2	83	80
Stevens Point Pacelli	3	3	54	77
Chippewa Falls McDonell	2	4	162	178
Wausau Newman	1	5	57	154
Wis. Rapids Assumption	0	6	38	117

1985: Play-Off Berth for Young Team

The first play of the 1985 season was a 72-yard TD pass from Eric Helms to Scott Herkert. It was emblematic for, within that moment, three things were apparent. First, the team was young. Helms, an untested sophomore, was among a dozen sophomores and juniors forming a healthy core of coach Walt Kroll's 22nd team at Columbus. Second, this team was still led by seniors, even though fewer in number than most years. Herkert, a senior, snared five touchdown passes to lead the Dons in scoring. The only All-CWCC pick was another senior, linebacker Dan Zygarlicke. Third, this team could score, at least compared to their CWCC peers. While the Dons finished second in a five-way logjam with a 3-3 mark, no other conference squad scored more points.

The Dons' road opponents were scattered to various corners of America's Dairyland. After a home win against Madison Edgewood in Marshfield (near the center of the state), Kroll took his charges to Door County (Southern Door), The Driftless Area (Aquinas), metro Milwaukee (Marquette), and the Chippewa Valley (McDonell) on successive weekends. Late season games Up North (Medford, Wausau) completed the travel itinerary. Kroll's heady scheduling of highly regarded opponents allowed the 6-4 Dons to displace 7-3 Pacelli as one of the teams selected in the expanded WISAA Class A playoffs. The Dons' 14-0 whitewash of Pacelli in the finale didn't hurt, either. All WISAA schools knew strength of schedule was an important factor. QB duties were shared by Helms and junior Jim Pankratz. Both performed far above average, throwing a combined ten touchdowns. More impressive, they were accurate, connecting on 54% of their passes. Pankratz's 64% completion rate was among the best-ever for a Dons signal-caller. A trio of talented receivers (Scott Herkert, Lee Pritzl, and David Scheuer) helped keep the accuracy percentage high.

The Dons scored on the first play of the season at Beell Stadium. They controlled the ball throughout to gain a 21-7 win over Edgewood. It was Dan Zygarlicke up the middle and Earl Miranda around the end to the tune of 125 and 109 yards, respectively. "They don't fumble and they don't make mistakes," Edgewood coach Tim

Martinelli said, "and that is their game. They always seem to play well against us." Key Columbus defensive stops were made by Pat Hughes and Lee Pritzl. Next game, Columbus players endured bad traffic on their long bus ride to Door County. Southern Door coach Jesse Harness was literally one of Kroll's past students (summer wing-T coaching workshop), and he adopted the finesse offense for his Eagles. They had gone 7-1 in 1984. Extreme humidity on this early September eve caused wet field conditions. Using seven sophomores as regulars, the Dons eked out a 10-7 win. Extra time was taken between quarters, and many players cramped in the second half. In Wauwatosa the following Saturday night the Dons ran into a championship-caliber team in Marquette. The Hilltoppers' stonewall defense and high-powered offense were evident. Marquette coach Dick Basham used 30 players a game, led by split end Chris Wagner. The veteran coach said, "Chris is probably one of the best players in the state of Wisconsin." He had three catches and a 37-yard run in a 28-0 Dons loss. "They were just too big and physical and skilled to allow us to do anything offensively or defensively," said Kroll.

At Dorais Field in Chippewa Falls the next Saturday afternoon, Columbus fell to McDonell, 21-19. Jeff Rothbauer nabbed TD passes of 51, 31, and 30 yards for all three McDonell scores. As was becoming customary in the yearly McDonnell air-fest, the 30 completions and 48 passing attempts against CHS were both records. Kroll said, "We don't have a solid group of seniors and it can be difficult to throw young players in there and expect them to do real well right away." Even in defeat Kroll cited the play of safety Scott Herkert, linebackers Dan Zygarlicke and Lee Pritzl, defensive ends Mike Nikolai and Randy Schueller, and defensive back Eric Helms. At game time the following Saturday night in La Crosse, a light rain was falling. As the game progressed, the rain turned into a downpour. The Memorial Field turf was a sloppy mess. Aquinas held a 7-0 lead with two minutes left in the contest. A 1-yard TD plunge by Dan Zygarlicke with 1:45 to go made it 7-6. David Herkert's extra-point kick failed, leaving the Dons with no option other than an onside kick. David Scheuer and Dan Zygarlicke executed a successful kick-and-recovery that gave the

Dons the ball. With 35 seconds to play, Jim Pankratz found Mike Brown for a game-winning 21-yard TD. The David Herkert extra-point kick made the final score 13-7. Pankratz had a superb night connecting on seven of nine attempts and passing for 142 yards in less than ideal conditions. Even though the Dons had to come from behind for the win, they dominated the game both offensively and defensively throughout.

Heavy rain and a muddy field didn't seem to bother Regis the next Friday night in Marshfield. It did hamper the Dons, though. The navy-and-white coughed up the ball 11 times, losing six fumbles to the Ramblers. Columbus did not record a first down until the fourth quarter. The relentless Regis running attack kept the Dons defense on the field most of the game. Regis won 24-0. The following Friday night in Medford brought another muddy field, limiting the runners' ability to make hard cuts without slipping. Trailing 13-7 with five minutes to go, the Dons launched a 74-yard scoring drive that ended with Dan Zygarlicke's touchdown plunge. David Herkert added the extra-point to give the Dons a narrow 14-13 win. The game featured a lot of punting as both coaches played for field position. Medford coach Carl Alberti had been an assistant to Kroll during the 1984 Shrine All-Star game when both coached the North team.

All streaks must end. Newman's Kurt Kraimer made sure there would be no 29th straight loss to Columbus at Thom Field. The Wausau 180-pounder combined power and quickness to amass 221 yards on 42 carries. His three touchdowns, including an 87-yard punt return, were all the points Newman needed in a 20-14 victory. The senior fullback broke three Newman rushing records in the process. His coach, Russ Grundy, noted, "We've been frustrated for a very long time. The kids have played hard all year, but this is something special." Fielding a team mostly of sophomores and juniors, the Dons headed home from Wausau with an emotional loss, their first to Newman since 1956, when a 6-0 Newman win allowed the Cards to claim the first-ever CWCC title. It was Newman's only title claim in the 44-year history of the league.

Homecoming turned into a jubilant 33-0 victory celebration over Assumption the following Saturday afternoon at Beell. Ball control and a stiff defense spelled doom for the visiting Royals. A week later, pre-game chatter centered on Pacelli being one of eight teams likely to be chosen in the newly expanded WISAA playoffs. Their 7-2 mark and second place hold in the conference were facts. But the Dons scored an impressive 14-0 All-Saints night win over the Cardinals to create a five-way tie for second place. Two short TD bursts by Earl Miranda were enough for the rain-soaked win. A Randy Schueller fumble recovery set up the first one. The second was aided by a fake field goal from the 35-yard line. Holder Eric Helms connected on a screen pass to Miranda. On the next play Miranda ran it in from the 4-yard line. Columbus got another shot at an 8-1 Regis team in the first-round of the WISAA Class A playoffs the next Thursday night in Eau Claire. The Ramblers still proved to be the better team and won 19-13. Sophomore QB Eric Helms went six for seven in passing, throwing for 95 yards and one touchdown.

Six seniors ended their careers in the rugged playoff game at Carson Park: John Bell, Glenn Draxler, Scott Herkert, Pat Hughes, Lee Pritzl, and Dan Zygarlicke. Ten Dons scored points in 1985. Leading the way was Scott Herkert with 32. David Herkert's 11 point-after kicks and a field goal added to his two unusual touchdowns (a lateral and an interception return) for 26 total points. They were followed by Dan Zygarlicke (18), Earl Miranda (18), Eric Helms (14), David Scheuer (13), and Mike Brown (12). Linebacker Dan Zygarlicke was the only Dons player selected for All-CWCC honors.

1985 CWCC Standings	W	L	TP	OPP
Eau Claire Regis	6	0	87	23
Chippewa Falls McDonell	3	3	84	75
La Crosse Aquinas	3	3	59	45
Marshfield Columbus	3	3	93	72
Stevens Point Pacelli	3	3	73	90
Wausau Newman	3	3	85	71
Wis. Rapids Assumption	0	6	15	120

1986: Next Man Up

With Columbus returning 20 lettermen, coach Walt Kroll planned to deploy a two-quarterback attack, using the considerable talents of senior Jim Pankratz and junior Eric Helms. "This is a very coachable group," said Kroll. "They're very bright and they catch on to material quickly. Also, within this group there are some outstanding competitors." The non-conference schedule was ruthless with road games in Madison and Austin (Minnesota). No one could have foreseen that the first five Columbus opponents would all be undefeated when the Dons clashed with them. Nonetheless, CHS came out of the first half of the schedule with a 4-1 record and won their next four games, setting up a final-game showdown against Pacelli for the CWCC title. Injuries to key personnel created a lot of disappointment and opportunity. The Dons lost Pankratz to injury early in the Austin game. Helms stepped up to take over the field-general role full-time—until he got hurt. Helms missed the last four games and Kroll turned to wide receiver David Scheuer to take the QB reins to finish the season. Sweep-runner extraordinaire Earl Miranda also missed the last three contests. But the "next man up" attitude that Kroll instilled took the Dons far.

Columbus used only three running plays and one pass play in amassing nearly 300 yards in the Edgewood opener. Miranda ran around the end for one TD and Pankratz galloped in on a QB bootleg for the other in a 16-0 victory. The defense was tenacious and recorded seven sacks. Defensive end Mike Nikolai had five of them. The Crusaders never crossed the midfield stripe and finished with a negative 18 yards on the night. Kroll praised the play of Jim Herkert, Jason Reigel, Rob Cooper, and Kent Altmann in this defensive gem. A Friday trip to Austin to face one of the top large school teams in Minnesota proved more than worthwhile for those making the journey. Austin already had a 41-13 win over Rosemont, a large Twin Cities area school. "These kids are used to playing up," Kroll said of his Dons. "Austin has a beautiful stadium and it will be fun for the boys to play there." With the hard-fought game knotted 6-6, Dons place-kicker David Herkert got his chance to win the game with a 30-yard field goal. It sailed wide left. Austin went first in overtime and scored on a fourth-down pass that was tipped by a CHS defender. Dons QB Eric Helms bobbled a fourth-down snap, ensuring the 12-6 overtime victory for Minnesota's #6 ranked Class AA team. Senior QB Jim Pankratz left the Austin game in the first half with a season-ending knee injury. Pankratz ended his abbreviated Dons career completing 61.7% of his passes, one of the finest marks ever. Kroll said, "When you lose a senior QB, it's a real blow to the team."

Defending WISAA state champion Marquette entered sun-drenched Beell Stadium the next Saturday afternoon. The game lived up to its billing with precision passing by both quarterbacks and hard-hitting defense. All of Marquette's TDs were set up by long pass plays, including a 21-yard throw from punt formation. The Dons went to their bag of tricks in the double overtime affair. On a double-reverse option, end David Scheuer tossed a 31-yard pass to Earl Miranda for one quirky score. David Herkert ran 28 yards on a lateral from a hook-and-ladder pass for another. But it was a nine-minute, 17-play fourth quarter drive that allowed the Dons to tie the game at 21 in regulation play. Marquette kicked a 20-yard field goal to take a 24-21 lead in the second overtime. David Herkert, however, scored on a short run for the Dons in their second overtime turn to earn the exciting 27-24 victory. Eric Helms passed for 132 yards for the Dons but Hilltoppers QB Todd McLees topped him with 212. Linebacker Chris Hendler earned plaudits from Kroll for his outstanding effort. CWCC teams went 17-1 against non-conference opponents (the only loss being the CHS defeat by Austin).

McDonell came into Beell Stadium looking for a win via their aerial barrage. The Dons did their best to keep the ball out of dangerous hands by possessing it 70% of the game. With its unique pass-first offense, McDonell was capable of scoring on every play. The Macks connected on a 16-yard TD pass with 1:26 left in the game. But they were still trailing 21-20. McDonell coach Jerry Uchytil opted to go for the win. When the extra-point pass failed, Columbus escaped with a narrow victory. Uchytil was clear on the matter, saying, "We're not here to make things look good. We're here to win." Aquinas was the fifth straight undefeated Dons foe.

On Saturday afternoon CHS took the opening homecoming kickoff and put together a 13-play, 69-yard drive. David Herkert's 1-yard run and Pat Earll's extra-point kick stood up for the remainder of the game in a tight 7-6 win on a sloppy field. Herkert, at safety, came up with two key QB sacks to help preserve the win. "He is one of the guys we count on in big situations," Kroll said.

The Dons travelled to Eau Claire the following Saturday night and came home with a win against Regis that fans still talk about. Trailing 8-6 after taking over on downs on their own 23-yard line, Columbus had 91 seconds to cover 77 yards. The navy-and-white wasted no time. Eric Helms immediately found Todd Maurer on a 22-yard pass. Maurer was hit quickly but teammate David Herkert took a lateral from Maurer and sprinted 55 yards for the go-ahead score with 1:01 left. The Ramblers did not fold. It wasn't until Mike Brown intercepted a Hail Mary pass on the Dons' 2-yard line with seconds remaining that the improbable 13-8 win was added to CHS football annals. Up next was Milwaukee the following Saturday afternoon. The Dons manhandled a young John Marshall team, 28-0. The Dons ran 90 plays to just 22 for the Eagles, resulting in 405 yards to 40. Fourteen players had at least one rushing attempt for Columbus, the highest on record. Marshall never crossed the 50-yard line. But the easy win proved costly. Columbus lost QB Eric Helms to a broken thumb. The injury jinx continued the next week at home versus Newman. Earl Miranda, the team's top rusher, dislocated his right elbow. Miranda was having his best game of the year with 100 yards rushing on 10 carries. The Dons held top conference ground-gainer Brian Rheinschmidt to 48 yards in a 21-13 Columbus victory. Miranda was replaced at running back by defensive end Mike Nikolai and sophomore Joe McCormick. David Scheuer was moved from end to QB. "The whole way we responded to a new quarterback was very good," Kroll said. "The whole team made a good account of themselves."

For the third time in the season, the Dons used a hook-and-ladder pass to perfection, scoring the first touchdown in their Wood County battle with Assumption at Witter Field. David Scheuer hit Todd Maurer for an 8-yard completion. Maurer once again lateraled to a streaking David Herkert, who ran the last 14 yards for the second-quarter score. Running backs Mike Nikolai and Scott Reigel combined for 89 yards to go with Herkert's 83 yards on the ground as the Dons blanked the Royals 21-0.

A Halloween night game in Stevens Point matched Pacelli with Columbus, the two CWCC schools with 5-0 conference ledgers. "This is pretty much what we had in mind when we rearranged the conference schedule (beginning in 1977) so that Columbus and Pacelli could always play the last weekend of the year," Kroll said. "It's really a good, healthy rivalry because of the fact that both teams' players have a great deal of respect for each other. In many instances, warm friendships have been created." A light but steady rain created a soggy setting for the championship game at Goerke Field. Pacelli was 8-0 and ranked second in the WISAA poll. Columbus was 7-1 and ranked third in the statewide poll of private schools. Pacelli's break in the scoreless duel came with 1:30 to go. After David Herkert picked up 12 yards near midfield, the ball squirted out of his hands. Greg Flees recovered for the Cardinals. With 13 seconds left, sophomore Scott Van Order drilled home a 28-yard field goal for a 3-0 Pacelli win and the conference crown.

The Dons travelled to Chippewa Falls the next Thursday night for a first-round WISAA playoff game. Columbus and McDonell had identical 8-2 records. The Dons would once again face the wide open style of the Macks. As for the Dons, Kroll said, "It's not easy taking your top receiver (David Scheuer) and making him your quarterback and having a good passing game right away." But it was McDonell's defense that proved resilient. CHS could not sustain any second-half drives. The Dons roused the faithful with a 34-yard TD pass from David Scheuer to Chris Hendler with 1:15 left, tightening the game to 21-14. The ensuing onside kick failed and the Dons ended their season at 8-3. McDonell coach Jerry Uchytil was complimentary afterward: "I knew they were playing with a number of starters banged up and injured and I think it's a tremendous credit to Walt Kroll to see how well they played in that situation."

Seven seniors ended their careers at Dorais Field: Jeff Boh, Mike Brown, Rob Cooper, Brian Louis, Mike Nikolai, Jim Pankratz, and Dave Saviage. In a tight scoring race, David Herkert (50 points) nudged out Earl Miranda (44) by a touchdown. Other top scorers were Todd Maurer (24), Pat Earll (20), Scott Reigel (12), and David Scheuer (12). Four Dons were named to the All-CWCC team. Both offensive picks were linemen, center Brian Louis and tackle Rob Cooper. End Mike Nikolai and back David Herkert were selected on defense.

1986 CWCC Standings	W	L	TP	OPP
Stevens Point Pacelli	6	0	121	32
Marshfield Columbus	5	1	83	50
Chippewa Falls McDonell	4	2	128	117
La Crosse Aquinas	3	3	108	92
Eau Claire Regis	2	4	99	84
Wausau Newman	1	5	64	109
Wis. Rapids Assumption	0	6	25	144

1987: A Game of Inches

The 1987 Dons proved to be an offensive juggernaut that could score points. Only the 1965, 1974, and 1980 teams scored more points. Coupled with a defense that limited opponents to 11 points a game, coach Walt Kroll had the recipe for another stellar squad. He made no secret of his game plan. "We are going to try and establish our basic running game, utilizing the halfback in the sweeps and running the fullback on our traps through the middle," he said. "We will also be throwing some play-action passes which are a complementary part of our running game." It helped that he had experienced leaders at key positions. One area of concern, though, was the offensive line where only one player had varsity experience. As it turned out the interior quintet of Chris Hendler, Rob Heller, Derek Dieringer, Dale Newman, and Geoff Weinfurtner jelled early in road games against formidable opponents. Long-time opening opponent Edgewood was dropped from the schedule and replaced with La Crosse Central and Rochester (Minnesota) John Marshall to open the campaign, followed by perennial state powerhouse Marquette High in Wauwatosa. The tough competition readied Columbus for the CWCC slate. The team's leaders always seemed to step up when needed and came into the final conference game at Pacelli undefeated in loop play at 5-0. Pacelli was 4-1 and looking to claim a share of the crown. The annual season finale with the Cardinals, more often than not, showcased the best of Wisconsin high school football.

The opener at Memorial Stadium in La Crosse pitted the Dons against the defending Big Rivers Conference champion Central Red Raiders. "I thought the line controlled Central's line from the start," said Kroll, calling out tackles Geoff Weinfurtner and Rob Heller for special mention. The last CHS touchdown featured a spectacular catch by David Scheuer. He leapt up between two defenders and snared a 27-yard pass in the end zone to increase the score to 32-0. The Columbus defense recorded six QB sacks. The Red Raiders finally managed to score against deep reserves to make it 32-6.

The last time a Columbus team had travelled to Rochester, Minnesota, for a game was in 1950, the inaugural year of Dons football. They faced Lourdes that day. This time they played a much larger public school, John Marshall, the defending champions of the Big 9. "They have one of the best programs in the state," Kroll said. "They lost to Apple Valley in the (Minnesota) state playoffs last year and Apple Valley went on to win the big school championship." The navy-and-white eked out a 13-0 win in a game that Kroll always fondly remembered as the quintessential high school football contest. The first CHS score was set up by a pass off a reverse to David Scheuer, an end. Scheuer had to come in to play quarterback at the end of the 1986 campaign so #85 was no stranger to throwing the ball. His pass to David Herkert covered 26 yards. QB Eric Helms hit Scheuer for a 13-yard TD on the following play. The Dons went back to the option pass off the reverse to Scheuer in the second quarter. It worked for a 25-yard touchdown to Todd Maurer. The Dons hung on for a 13-0 victory on a perfect fall football evening.

Eric Helms injured his finger during mid-week preparation for the upcoming Marquette game. Andy Pankratz took over at QB but Helms retained his defensive safety and punting duties for the Hilltoppers contest in the lush Milwaukee suburb of Wauwatosa. "Our players are used to these competitions with top-quality teams," Kroll explained. "They know what we're shooting for. We want to improve each time and play four good quarters of football when we take the field." The Hilltoppers scored on two long pass plays to earn an 18-7 victory. "We got the two 'home runs' and that was the difference in the game," Marquette coach Dick Basham said. "They blitzed like mad, taking a chance that we wouldn't complete the passes. Give Columbus credit, they threw our timing off." Kroll said the Dons defense came to play. "Andy Pankratz did a remarkable job in directing the team," Kroll added. "Overall, had we not dropped several passes that Andy put on the money, the outcome could have been different." The following Saturday night the Dons travelled down Highway 13 for their CWCC opener at Assumption. The Royals were bedeviled with dealing with a new coach almost every year. They hoped to stop the revolving door with the young, energetic Bob Freund. But the inexperienced Assumption 11 was no match for the senior-laden Dons, who won 44-0. Guard Chris Hendler had some bone-crushing blocks on David Herkert's four-TD performance. Dons defenders again recorded six quarterback sacks. After playing away from Marshfield in their first four tilts, it truly felt like homecoming the following Saturday afternoon at Beell Stadium. The Dons exploded for 56 points, the fourth highest in program history. Columbus came into the festivities ranked #5 in the statewide WISAA Class A poll. The Dons worked on their air attack during the Newman game, knowing they would need it later in the year if they wanted to make any end-of-season headway. The final score was 56-22.

Columbus made life difficult for sophomore QB Ben Gardow of McDonell the following Saturday afternoon in Chippewa Falls. The pass rush and blitzes against the inexperienced field general produced five sacks and 10 plays where Gardow had to scramble because of intense pressure. Gardow had numerous hurried throws but also attempted more passes (55) than anyone ever had against the Dons. While the offense scored four times in the 28-7 victory, this win was really a nod to the strong Dons defense. Craig

Lewin, a sophomore, was starting to make people notice his running ability. Kroll cited the play, both ways, of linebacker and offensive guard Chris Hendler. David Scheuer threw his third option pass of the year for a touchdown in the win. Next up: Fond du Lac St. Mary's Springs. The Ledgers came to Beell Stadium ranked #2 in the WISAA statewide poll; Columbus was #5. Any Bob Hyland-coached team was always a challenge for the Dons. Still, they recorded their third shutout of the season with a 12-0 win. Columbus used a strong first-half defense and a second-half offensive surge to earn the win. On the 78-yard third-quarter drive that secured CHS's second touchdown, QB Eric Helms threw to Andy Pankratz in the backfield. Pankratz passed back to Helms and he fired it 41 yards downfield to David Scheuer who reached over a Ledgers defender to pull in the pass. Three plays later Earl Miranda scored to give Columbus a 12-point margin of victory.

With 3:22 left in the Aquinas game the following Saturday night in Marshfield, Pat Earll tried tacking on three points to a 14-7 CHS lead. The 20-yard attempt from the left hash mark hooked wide to the left. Aquinas got possession but had 80 yards to go. Aquinas QB James Gilbert took to the air and moved the Blugolds down field quickly. Gilbert lofted a pass into the corner of the end zone and Craig Weisbrod made a sliding catch for a 14-yard TD. With 29 seconds left in the game, Aquinas coach Dave Reinders made the decision to go for two points for the win. He explained, "We don't play for ties. We were going to go for two all the way." Columbus stopped the extra-point run and escaped with a 14-13 win. Earlier, Earl Miranda had improvised during the quest for CHS's second and final touchdown. With the ball on the 3, Miranda appeared stopped for no gain but managed to pitch the ball back to an alert Eric Helms, who raced in for the unconventional score. The following Saturday night in Eau Claire, Regis took it right to the Dons by scoring on their opening drive. The Dons responded quickly with three unanswered TDs. The Ramblers managed only 14 more yards in the entire first half after their initial burst. Regis coach Ken Zagzebski, a former standout running back at D.C. Everest High School, said, "Miranda and Herkert are two guys that are going to break tackles because they just keep twisting and turning when they get hit." The Dons prevailed in this one, 31-21.

The table was set for another Columbus-Pacelli showdown for the CWCC title. Because McDonell had beaten Pacelli 37-25 earlier in the year, the Cards needed a win to claim a share of the title with the Dons, who were undefeated in conference action. Pacelli made late-season tweaks to their offense. To give some relief to Pacelli standout halfback Steve Mannebach, the Cards shifted QB Kurt Soderberg to the other running back position. Doing so allowed sophomore Scott Soderberg to come in to guide PHS. The Dons assistant coach was Jeff Soderberg. Pacelli offensive coordinator Don Soderberg was the father of all of them. No wonder some referred to this as "The Soderberg Game." The Dons' failure to score on a first-and-goal from the 5 at the start of the fourth quarter hurt. With the Dons trailing 21-6, the Pointers administered the same sustained, time-killing drive that the Dons often inflicted on opponents. The Dons did score late but the onside kick did not work. Pacelli beat Columbus 21-13 for a share of the crown. Kurt Soderberg scored all three Pacelli touchdowns and tallied 154 yards on the ground. On the losing side, Kroll said Eric Helms had "a brilliant game. Definitely his best game of the year." The Dons were co-CWCC champs.

Beell Stadium was the site for a first-round playoff game with Regis. Only a fortnight before, the Dons shredded the Ramblers defense with 347 yards rushing. Ironically, the tables were turned this evening, as Regis ran with authority against the Dons. Columbus was lucky that two field goals were enough to earn a 6-6 regulation tie. Just before half, standout Eric Helms dislocated a bone in his right wrist on a tackle on a kickoff return. Backup Andy Pankratz did a respectable job as his substitute. In overtime, Regis struck first with a touchdown and extra point to go up 13-6. Regis was whistled for pass interference on CHS's first attempt to score from the 10-yard line. The penalty advanced the ball to the 5. From the new starting position, Pankratz bootlegged to the 2. Craig Lewin got it to the 1, and David Herkert was stopped for no gain on third down. Kroll and the Dons called a timeout to discuss matters. They decided to go with Craig Lewin off tackle on fourth down but came up short. The goal-line stand ended the Dons' 1987 campaign at 8-3. Regis coach Zagzebski was ecstatic. "That was a fantastic goal-line stand," he said. "Columbus is a super team, the best we've faced all year, and to stop them on the goal line makes the win even sweeter." After Helms got hurt the Dons moved Herkert from linebacker to safety. Zagzebski said, "It was to our benefit when they moved him away from the line of scrimmage. It allowed us to do more things on offense. He's the best defensive player we've faced all year."

Twelve seniors saw their careers end inches short of the goal line at Beell Stadium: Kent Altmann, Joe Bersalona, Mike Earll, Pat Earll, Eric Helms, Chris Hendler, David Herkert, Todd Maurer, Scott Michalski, Earl Miranda, Pat Perner, and David Scheuer. Four Dons scored 30 or more points: Herkert led with 79 tallies, followed by Miranda (42), Scheuer (36), and Pat Earll (31). Helms notched 18 and Craig Lewin, Joe McCormick, and Todd Maurer each scored 12. Five Columbus players, all seniors, were selected for seven spots on the All-CWCC team. Scheuer and Helms were named to both the offensive and defensive teams, Scheuer at end and linebacker and Helms at quarterback and defensive back. Other honorees were Herkert at running back, Hendler at guard, and Maurer at defensive end. Hendler was further recognized as CWCC Lineman of the Year.

1987 CWCC Standings	W	L	TP	OPP
Marshfield Columbus	5	1	186	84
Stevens Point Pacelli	5	1	150	65
Chippewa Falls McDonell	4	2	157	114
Eau Claire Regis	4	2	143	78
La Crosse Aquinas	2	4	126	82
Wausau Newman	1	5	49	205
Wis. Rapids Assumption	0	6	21	204

1988: Toughest Kroll Year

Sometimes coaches take on opponents that are superior to their charges. Coach Walt Kroll had a good feel for the minor art of scheduling non-conference opponents but even he admitted he miscalculated in 1988. After a pair of early season humiliations, Kroll said, "I've concluded that this year we overscheduled. That is my fault, not the players' fault." The Beell Stadium opener had the Dons scoring on their first play from scrimmage, a 79-yard jaunt down the west sideline by senior running back Joe McCormick. It was a seesaw affair, with the Dons offense trying to make up for troubles on defense against the strong La Crosse Central power game. Just before half Dons QB Andy Pankratz passed 9 yards over the middle to Steve Scheuer. He lateralled to Joe McCormick, who raced 41 yards to the end zone to give the Dons a 20-12 halftime advantage. McCormick also ground out 166 yards in the 27-24 win. The opener gave valuable game experience to nine new offensive players.

All-boys powerhouses from Minnesota and Wisconsin were next. The first of three consecutive Saturday afternoon games took place in St. Paul the next weekend. St. Thomas Academy (STA) elected to play in Minnesota's largest division though not required. Like Columbus, it had 12 post-season playoff appearances in the 1980s. STA's offense and defense mirrored those of the Dons. The comparisons ended there. The Tommies routed Columbus 41-14. "By halftime they had broken our morale and we were disorganized and down at that point," said Kroll. "Overall, it wasn't a good day for us." The 41 points Columbus yielded were the most any Kroll team had given up since 1966. Marquette High was again coming off a WISAA state championship when they entered Beell Stadium for the season's third game. The Hilltoppers dominated. Backup QB Kendrick "Save Us" Davis wowed the fans with his flashy moves. The former flanker also returned a punt 73 yards to bury the Dons 28-0 on a warm afternoon. Dons end Tom McCormick showcased his receiving skills by going over the middle to snare seven Pankratz passes for 118 yards in the losing effort. Lessons were learned by the young Dons in those defeats and they came right back with two conference wins, racking up 83 points.

The Dons grabbed a 26-0 halftime lead on homecoming against Assumption and coasted to a 33-14 win to even their record at 2-2. Second-year AHS coach Bob Freund said, "You know what Columbus is going to do. They only run three plays, but they just executed." It was the first time the Royals had scored on Columbus since 1983. Meanwhile the Dons scored the first four times they had the ball. The navy-and-white also had two ball carriers top 100 yards, Joe McCormick with 155 and Andy Pankratz with 109. In Wausau the Dons scored a program-record 31 points during the second quarter of play the following Saturday night on their way to a 50-26 triumph over Newman. Right halfback Joe McCormick had one of CHS's all-time great individual performances against the Cardinals. In the second quarter alone, he scored four touchdowns on runs of 85, 62, 49, and 4 yards. "Our guards made the wide stuff and the trap plays go," Kroll said. "Our backs ran with authority, especially Joe McCormick and Craig Lewin." The win left Columbus at 3-2 and 2-0 in CWCC play.

McDonell came to Beell Stadium the following Friday night with a new coach and a slightly different approach to their pass-happy ways. Kurt Geissler wanted his Macks to mix the run with a robust passing game. A careless whistle robbed the Dons of a touchdown on an interception return before intermission. A referee inadvertently blew his whistle as Joe McCormick neared the 15-yard line, meaning the TD did not count. Instead of trying for an extra point to tie the game, the Dons were first-and-10 from the 15-yard line. Andy Pankratz threw an interception on the next play. The teams headed to the locker room with the Macks holding a 7-0 lead. McCormick narrowed the gap to 7-6 early in the fourth frame but McDonell responded with a time-consuming 76-yard drive to go up 14-6. McCormick rambled in from 23 yards out to close the lead again. It was 14-12 with 5:33 left. The score held. "We had our chances but we weren't sharp. Over the years we've lost very few games that we should have won. We felt we should have won," Kroll said. The Dons were no match for the top-ranked WISAA team the following Saturday afternoon in Fond du Lac.

It was a homecoming contest for St. Mary's Springs. Their coach Bob Hyland was a bit surprised his team was sitting at 6-0 considering they lost 29 players from the previous year. "They have a big veteran line and a group of fine running backs," Kroll said after the 34-0 spanking. The Ledgers held Joe McCormick to 30 yards on 10 carries.

Aquinas came from behind to overcome the Dons 26-22 the following Saturday night in La Crosse. Their coach Dave Reinders had revamped his offense during the off-season. He felt the Blugolds' style of play had become too conservative. He leaned on his young assistants to come up with a more exciting style. Aquinas was 4-0 in league action coming into the game and had a near 50-50 balance between the run and the pass. All seven touchdowns in this game were scored on TD passes, an oddity in high school football. Aquinas mounted a 15-play, 89-yard winning drive after falling behind 22-19. The next week Regis was sitting on an early 15-0 third-quarter lead when Dons QB Andy Pankratz twisted his ankle. Sophomore backup Pat Schueppert came in and ignited the Dons offense with a 49-yard strike to Joe McCormick to narrow the gap to 15-7. But the Ramblers duo of QB Mike Blang and Greg Prince proved unstoppable. Prince, a tight end, made several key catches after the Dons scored, including a 4-yard TD catch to give the Ramblers some breathing room at 21-7. Schueppert responded by connecting again with Joe McCormick with five minutes left. With Steve Scheuer's point-after boot, the Dons tightened matters to 21-14. But the Ramblers literally ran out the clock and scored an icing-on-top TD with 24 seconds left to depart Carson Park with a 29-14 win. McCormick ran for 56 and caught five passes for 100 yards in the loss. The Dons added one new look, sometimes moving 190-pound offensive tackle Dale Newman to fullback. He picked up 73 yards in 13 carries but fumbled twice, helping Regis gain the upper hand.

Pacelli needed a win over Columbus in the season finale to gain entry into the WISAA playoffs. The Dons, sitting at 3-6 and 2-3 in the loop, could only play the role of spoiler. The game did not live up to the #1 offense (CHS) vs. the #1 defense (PHS) hype. The Cardinals cast aside the Dons 22-2. "They outplayed us in every facet of the game," Kroll said. Both teams' reserve quarterbacks started because of injuries. Pacelli's Jeff Flees ran the QB option to perfection and torched the Dons for 113 yards on 26 carries. Sophomore QB Pat Schueppert tossed five interceptions to a lightning-quick Pacelli defense. "Schuep is only a sophomore and he is going to be an outstanding player for us," Kroll predicted. The five-game losing streak to end the season left Kroll with his third, and last, losing campaign. In 31 years of guiding Columbus gridders, the 3-7 mark of the 1988 team was his worst.

Ten seniors concluded their careers: Eric Gordee, John Kohlbeck, Joe McCormick, Mark Meyers, Dale Newman, Jason Reigel, Pat Scheuer, Mike Schiferl, Tom Weister, and Sam Zwaschka. McCormick scored well over half the team points with 15 touchdowns and an extra-point run for 92. Place-kicker and end Steve Scheuer tallied 16. Other scorers were Craig Lewin (12), Tom McCormick (12), Andy Pankratz (8), and Tom Weister (6), who ran in a fumble recovery from 30 yards for the year's oddest score. Two Dons were honored with selection to the All-CWCC team. Both were on offense and both were seniors, guard Eric Gordee and halfback Joe McCormick. "Eric and Joe really worked together well and made our sweep play as effective as it was this season," Kroll said. For Gordee it was also his first earned letter. "Eric proved to be one of the best pulling guards that has ever played for us," Kroll noted. McCormick tied two CWCC records—most TDs in a season (12) and most points scored in a CWCC season (74). Kroll said, "Joe's play has been outstanding all season long, despite the fact that defenses have been geared to stop him." The senior running back set a conference mark for yards per carry with an average of 8.4 yards.

1988 CWCC Standings	W	L	TP	OPP
La Crosse Aquinas	6	0	159	35
Eau Claire Regis	5	1	133	75
Stevens Point Pacelli	4	2	119	57
Chippewa Falls McDonell	3	3	112	109
Marshfield Columbus	2	4	133	131
Wis. Rapids Assumption	1	5	67	170
Wausau Newman	0	6	80	226

1989: New Foes, Stinging Defeat

The 1989 team opened at home against some new foes, the Reedsburg Beavers and the Nekoosa Papermakers. The Dons took care of business in both contests. Milwaukee Marquette again proved to be robust, and a revamped Newman squad fought a good match—for a while. The Dons edged McDonell but then dropped two in a row. Rhinelander was in its fourth year under coach Fred Kuhl and he had the Hodags humming. The green-clad gridders ran over the Dons 34-18 up north. Aquinas came to Beell Stadium for homecoming the next week and was downright inhospitable. But Aquinas only counted for one game and after the next two CWCC conquests (Regis and Assumption), the Dons trekked to Stevens Point to claim their share of the CWCC crown. Pacelli was sitting with two losses but the Dons and Aquinas only had one each. In a big turning point in Columbus football history, Pacelli drilled the Dons, 43-0. Aquinas stood alone atop the league standings. With 20 teams now gaining entry into the WISAA playoffs, in three separate divisions, the 6-4 Dons were given a first-round home playoff game against DePere Abbott Pennings High School. The Squires had listened to a stunning announcement earlier on that November 2 day: the three Green Bay-area Catholic high schools—Premontre, St. Joseph's Academy, and Pennings—would be merging to become Notre Dame High School the next year. The Marshfield game that night could be the last one in the 90-year history of the fabled school.

Reedsburg saw the Dons in what seemed like mid-season form in the opener at Beell. The Beavers were flummoxed by the Dons' offensive deception and spectacular execution, and fell behind 41-0 after two quarters. The Dons opened with a five-play scoring drive and never let up in the first half. Coach Walt Kroll tested all 63 Dons players in the 48-20 win. The offensive ring-leader was senior QB Andy Pankratz. "Andy is the steadying influence on this football team. He's very bright and cool—the perfect Columbus quarterback," Kroll said. Cited for their defensive prowess against the Beavers were nose guard Steve Scheuer, tackle Craig Lewin, and tackle Robbie Pankratz. "They're the foundation we've built our defense around," the coach said. Fourth-year Nekoosa coach Paul Nistler fashioned much of his Papermakers offense around the Columbus Wing-T attack. Nekoosa started four sophomores and only four seniors. As might be expected, the over-matched squad fell to Columbus, 24-8. But Kroll offered kind words. "He's a good young coach," he said. Though Columbus lost 14-0 to Marquette at a rainy Hart Park in Wauwatosa the next Saturday afternoon, it amounted to a great high school football game, according to Kroll. "Our defense was just tremendous. We played them toe-to-toe," he said. Marquette coach Dick Basham, an 18-year veteran, said it was a tough game. "We needed someone to really smack us, and that's what Columbus did. We were happy to win. They have a very fine team." Marquette stood at 3-0 on the year and no one had yet to score on them. Coming off two straight titles, they wore with honor the right to be called WISAA state champs. Numbers were never a problem with the Jesuit school of 1,000 boys. The Hilltoppers suited up 67 players, all juniors and seniors. Basham mused on the relationship between the schools, saying, "It's a pleasant rivalry. We enjoy going to Marshfield and they enjoy coming here. After every game between the two schools, the teams get together for a cookout."

Newman and Columbus were deadlocked 14-14 in the third quarter the next Saturday afternoon in Marshfield when Andy Pankratz picked off an errant Cardinals pass and raced 35 yards for the go-ahead score. The Dons added three rushing touchdowns in the fourth frame for a 41-14 victory. Second-year Newman coach Dan Sullivan said of the Dons, "They get more out of their kids every year than any other team in the conference." Three Grundy-family coaches were present for this affair. Russ Jr. and Kevin, former Newman players, were now assisting Walt Kroll on the Dons sideline. Their dad, Russ Sr., had gotten the itch to come back after retiring. He directed the Newman defense. The 3-0 Cardinals were ranked fifth in the statewide WISAA poll before the game. The Dons were eighth. Newman had not had a winning season in 17 years. Hope abounded in Wausau that the streak would disappear by year's end. Kroll lauded the play of senior offensive right tackle Rob Pankratz. "Robbie played an outstanding game, both ways for us." The match was marked by a spectacular Scott Kundinger catch near the Newman bench. Unfortunately, sophomore backup QB Mike Magistrelli dislocated a thumb and left the game.

For the third week in a row the Dons faced an undefeated opponent. McDonell was sitting at 4-0 for their homecoming game against Columbus. Aggressive play by the secondary accounted for three critical interceptions in the 27-13 CHS win. But the story of the night was Steve Scheuer's outstanding 294-yard performance carrying the ball on 42 attempts. He averaged 7 yards per tote. Kroll called his achievement "just tremendous. He's the biggest and hardest runner we've had in a long, long time." Only Bobby Koch's 304-yard game in 1965 bettered Scheuer's feat. Scott Kundinger of the Dons broke his leg during the game. McDonell would go on to win WISAA Division 3 later in the season. The week before encountering Columbus, Fred Kuhl had his Rhinelander Hodags riding high with a 31-0 trouncing of arch-rival Antigo. The Dons went north to meet the 4-1 Hodags and were turned back 34-18. Even in defeat to the well-oiled Rhinelander machine, Kroll managed to find a few bright spots. He commended the play of offensive tackle Jason Wrensch and the running of Steve Nugent. Additionally, 5'6" 150-pound senior Garret Seebandt drew praise for filling in admirably for Scott Kundinger. Rhinelander coach Kuhl said afterwards, "I have so much respect for Walt (Kroll). He's a tremendous human being. He instills class in the kids, and they always let that come out, win or lose."

The Columbus homecoming game was the following Saturday—a cool, sunny afternoon at Beell. Aquinas brought 28 seniors. Nine started on the 1988 conference championship team. They departed with a crisp 25-0 victory. The *News-Herald* called the Dons' performance lackluster. QB/DB Andy Pankratz was sick and did not play. His play at defensive back was sorely missed. Rocket-armed Mike Magistrelli filled in behind center and completed 11 of 29 pass attempts. "Mike did a good job. We dropped a number of passes we could have hung onto," Kroll said. Seven passes from Troy Venner to P.J. Esten for 129 yards dismantled the Dons. Columbus racked up 52 points the next Saturday in Marshfield against Regis. The game was all but over at halftime with Columbus ahead 40-0. The final tally on a perfect autumn afternoon was 52-29. The Ramblers were rebuilding and had only six seniors on their squad. End Tom McCormick made an impressive leaping catch in the back of the end zone for a touchdown in the second quarter. Two sophomores played well in their first start: center Paul Heiting and defensive back Steve Nugent. Kroll also lauded junior Keith Nikolai in his first start at tackle. In comfortable fall weather, the Dons headed 31 miles to Wisconsin Rapids to take on Assumption the following Friday night. Executing their ball-control offense to near perfection, the Dons rode back home with a 35-7 victory. "Our inside trap play and belly play were going really well," Kroll said, citing the lead blocking of left tackle Derek Dieringer. "A lot of our offense was directed behind him." Both Steve Scheuer (163) and Ross Gliniecki (106) picked up over 100 yards on the ground. Kroll named linebacker Jeff Burrill as the driving force on defense.

The final CWCC showdown between Columbus and Pacelli once again had championship implications. Aquinas had already completed loop play with a 5-1 record. The Dons were 4-1 and Pacelli stood at 3-2. A Dons triumph would allow them to share the crown with the Blugolds. Pacelli controlled the line of scrimmage and was led by QB Scott Soderberg, the fourth Soderberg to play quarterback at Pacelli. Their father, Don, had defeated the Dons in 1956 when he led his Thorp Cardinals to victory at Beell. Most contemporary Dons fans did not remember that the elder Soderberg had also coached football at Columbus from 1966 to 1971 under Walt Kroll. Pacelli prevailed this time. "To make a long story short, it was a championship game and we didn't come to play," Kroll lamented after the 43-0 rout. The *Stevens Point Journal* reported that Kroll replaced all of his starters at the start of the second half. The second offensive unit, especially QB Mike Magistrelli, looked sharp. On a positive note, halfback Steve Scheuer claimed the CWCC rushing title.

With the expanded WISAA playoffs the 6-4 Dons found themselves hosting a first-round game against Abbott Pennings the following Thursday night. Pennings was coached by seven-year veteran Al Groves, the defensive coordinator for the Squires in 1982 when the Dons achieved their only program win over the DePere school in six starts (a quirky 6-3 win on a free kick). Pennings walked away with another victory, 24-14. It proved to be the next-to-last game in the storied history of the all-boys high school. Pennings started out as St. Norbert High School in 1898 and retained that name until 1959 when it moved to its Third Street location. Going forward, DePere youth wishing to receive a Catholic secondary education would attend newly formed Notre Dame High School.

Thirteen seniors saw their Dons careers end: Jeff Burrill, Derek Dieringer, Ross Gliniecki, Brad Heiting, Craig Lewin, Jason Maurer, Tom McCormick, Andy Pankratz, Rob Pankratz, Bryan Revolinski, Steve Scheuer, Garret Seebandt, and Peter Taddy. Scheuer led the scoring with 78 points. Twelve other Dons scored, among them Gliniecki (38), Pankratz (30), McCormick (30), place-kicker and backup QB Mike Magistrelli (23), Lewin (12), and Steve Nugent (12). Three Dons were selected for five positions on the All-CWCC team. Burrill and Scheuer were named to both the offensive and defensive units. Burrill, a guard, was picked as co-CWCC Lineman of the Year. Scheuer led the conference in rushing and was honored at running back. On defense, Scheuer was top nose guard and Burrill was tabbed at a linebacker. Tom McCormick received a spot at safety.

1989 CWCC Standings	W	L	TP	OPP
La Crosse Aquinas	5	1	211	84
Chippewa Falls McDonell	4	2	171	118
Marshfield Columbus	4	2	155	131
Stevens Point Pacelli	4	2	209	107
Wausau Newman	3	3	102	148
Wis. Rapids Assumption	1	5	73	166
Eau Claire Regis	0	6	87	254

Dons preparing for the 1956 season opener. 35 players reported for action.

56.08.23.001a NWCHS *Marshfield News Herald* Collection

Ralph Jensen gains six yards on a QB keeper for the Dons in the 1959 season opener against Colby. The 25-6 triumph was their 17th consecutive win—a feat never again matched in program history.

59.09.12.001c NWCHS *Marshfield News Herald* Collection

Mike Wallschlaeger hangs on for a six-yard pass completion in the opener at Colby.

59.09.12.002c NWCHS *Marshfield News Herald* Collection

1961 Dons cheerleading squad. Left to right: Sharon Mech, Paula Whittington, Katie Felker, Karen Connaughty, Kris Ley, and Kerry Coleman.

61.R13.11 NWCHS *Marshfield News Herald* Collection

Warren Rhyner (33) turning the corner in 1961 against Colby. Corky Wilczewski (66) and Larry Meress (blocking #20) lead the way.

61.10.R1.38 NWCHS *Marshfield News Herald* Collection

Bobby Koch (48) on his way to one of his six touchdowns vs. St. Paul Cretin to open the 1965 season season at Beell Stadium. The Raiders only gave up 15 points the rest of the year and finished 7-1.

65.Sept.7 NWCHS *Marshfield News Herald* Collection

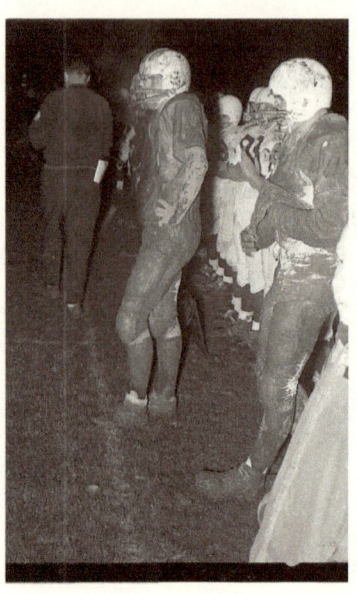

Mark Smith and Giggs Mancl await game re-entry in 1967. Kroll walks the sideline.

67.Oct.9 NWCHS *Marshfield News Herald* Collection

Jim Haselberger (60) blocks for QB Bill Draxler (14) in 1968 against Wausau Newman.

68. Sept.16.R1.41 NWCHS *Marshfield News Herald* Collection

Coach Walt Kroll with budding stars Jim Haselberger (26), Paul Mancl (42), and Willy Wilcott (23) in 1968. #32 Chuck Koch graduated the year before Kroll arrived from Milwaukee Lincoln. The elder of the athletic Koch brothers starred at South Dakota.

68.47.R2.17 NWCHS *Marshfield News Herald* Collection

Paul Mancl (13), Ed Smrecek (75), and a closing in Paul Blum (46) tackle an opponent in 1968. Aggressive gang tackling was a defensive staple of most Dons teams.

68.Oct.7.R1.2 NWCHS *Marshfield News Herald* Collection

Lyle Lang (61) and Kevin Merkel (65) lead block for Larry Olsen (20) in 1980. Olsen shares the school 100-meter dash mark with Bobby Koch. Only eight Dons linemen achieved All-CWCC status in two seasons. Lang was one of them.

Eric Gordee (67) and Jeff Burrill (66) lead block for Joe McCormick (21) in 1988 against Milwaukee Marquette at Beell. Kroll loved pulling guards.

Kroll mulls over matters in 1989. The Pacelli loss to end the season that year would be the Dons last CWCC defeat for five years.

Adam Michalek (31) driving the point home against Newman at Beell 1989.

Eric Heiting (42) goes wide against the Rhinelander Hodags in 1992. That team was the top offensive unit in school history.

92.Sept.26 NWCHS *Marshfield News Herald* Collection

Coach Walt Kroll going over strategy at intermission in the 1994 WISAA state championship game at Camp Randall Stadium in Madison. The Dons managed a fourth quarter score to earn a 6-0 win over Winnebago Lutheran. Kroll joked that the weather was mild compared to the year before. It proved to be his last halftime chat with the boys.

1990 – 2000

1990: First Camp Randall Appearance

The longest season in Columbus football history was also one of its most successful, ending in a state championship game at Camp Randall Stadium on the campus of the University of Wisconsin in Madison. Playing in their 13th game of the year, the Dons succumbed to a large Whitefish Bay Dominican team that Sunday afternoon. These talented Dons finished the year 10-3 overall and 6-0 in conference. A 13-game season would never occur again for Columbus.

Talent abounded. Junior QB Mike Magistrelli came into his own this year, tossing 15 TD passes and almost breaking Bill Draxler's mark of 16 set in 1968. The gifted signal-caller set a CWCC record that can only be equalled. Magistrelli became the only starting QB in CWCC history to never throw an interception during conference play. He connected on 51% of his passes. His back-to-back 200-yard-plus passing games against Pacelli within a six-day span is a feat never surpassed. Both games were at Beell Stadium, one to end the regular season, the other in the first round of playoffs. Senior superstar Pat Schueppert ran for almost 1,200 yards on the year. He also led the conference in scoring with 78 points on 13 touchdowns in six conference games. "Schuep" also became the first Dons player in eight years to return a punt for a TD. Four times the Dons had two rushers top 100 yards in the same game. It would have been five but Schueppert, with his brilliant off-tackle running, fell 1 yard shy in the Aquinas game. Columbus dominated league play, fielding the circuit's best offensive and defensive squads and taking coach Walt Kroll, in his 27th year helming Columbus football, to Camp Randall Stadium for the first time. His previous WISAA championship game appearances were at Titan Stadium in Oshkosh (three times) and Beell Stadium (one time), the memorable 1980 championship game.

Rain interrupted the season opener at Reedsburg. Both teams waited an extra 30 minutes at halftime to let the heavy rains pass. Pat Schueppert and Steve Nugent rushed for 143 and 120 yards, respectively, leading to a 22-8 win. Nekoosa was next. Like Columbus, Nekoosa ran a wing-T offense. Their inexperienced 1989 squad turned into a polished 1990 team. The overpowered Dons fell to the Papermakers 20-7 at Holland Field in the southern reaches of Wood County. Nekoosa's long sustained drives mimicked the trademark style of the Dons. Coach Paul Nistler had his Nekoosa machine running smoothly. But the Dons struck first, in stunning fashion. Columbus stopped Nekoosa's initial thrust just short of the goal line. Dons QB Mike Magistrelli rolled to his right and threw a perfect strike to a streaking Steve Nugent down the right sideline. The swift junior raced 94 yards for the longest TD pass play in CHS history.

Marquette High arrived in Marshfield from Milwaukee with wins over Madison West and Waukesha North already on their resume. The Hilltoppers had 400 yards of total offense and left central Wisconsin 3-0 after a 25-14 win. It was obvious that their 41-game Metro Conference win streak was no fluke. The rigors of a tough non-conference slate produced immediate results when the Dons opened conference action on a rainy night in Wausau. Pat Schueppert ran up the middle for 136 yards in a 28-0 shutout of Newman before a slim crowd at Thom Field. The Cardinals got their initial first down with nine minutes remaining. The stubborn CHS defense allowed only 39 total yards. The Dons feasted on homecoming by carving up McDonell 43-8 the following Saturday afternoon. The offensive line opened holes for Schueppert (167 yards) and Nugent (108 yards). "Homecoming is a real big week for Columbus," Kroll said. "I'm really happy for our players, our fans, and our alumni." Getting ready for the unique Macks passing attack is everyone's favorite week of practice, he said. "McDonell is not only a fun team to watch but also a fun team to play and coach against," he noted. Kroll was all smiles as the Dons' game plan worked brilliantly with five QB sacks and four interceptions.

The Hodags of Rhinelander were 34-14 victims of a balanced Dons attack that featured 170 yards of passing to go along with the reliable ground attack. Justin Casperson "really gave us a lift," said Kroll. "We can always count on Pat Schueppert." The pair accounted for 95 and 86 yards in a game with a lot of tempo. Aquinas was again undefeated in CWCC play when CHS visited Memorial Stadium the following Saturday afternoon for the Blugolds homecoming game. Aquinas reigned as conference champs two years running but this day belonged to the Dons. "Our defensive ends, Tom Bores and Michael McCormick, played outstanding. Our sophomore inside linebackers, Al Talens and Justin Casperson, are improving and getting better every game," Kroll said after the 25-0 win. He was also ecstatic with fan support 105 miles from home: "Our fans outnumbered them on their homecoming."

The Dons rolled over Regis 60-14 the following Saturday night in Eau Claire. It was the third highest point total for a Columbus team up to then, surpassed only by the 68 against Campion in 1974 and the 61 against St. Agnes in St. Paul in 1951. Every Dons player who suited up played. Kroll remarked on the temperament of the 1990 team: "Our team this year has played the same in every game—even keel—right from the start." He sang Adam Michalek's praises at defensive tackle, describing him as "one of the best linemen in the conference." And of his QB, he said, "Mike Magistrelli is a very good QB. His ball handling and faking is a big part of our offense." An improved Assumption team came to Beell the next Friday night and left with a 47-14 loss. The Dons defense continued to get better. But, Kroll said, "We still feel there's room for improvement." Steve Nugent's 61-yard TD scamper on the first play from scrimmage in the second half broke Assumption's back. Damian Mancl, an Assumption freshman, had two long TDs—a 68-yard pass reception and an 87-yard run in the loss.

CHS was 7-2 overall and 5-0 in the CWCC going into the season finale against Pacelli (5-4, 3-2). Aquinas was sitting with only one loss so the Dons had to win to claim the CWCC title outright. The game featured five second-quarter touchdowns, four by Pacelli. The Cards led 27-13 midway through the third quarter. After PHS's Sean Cashin moved the ball down to the Dons' 9-yard line, the navy-and-white defense stiffened with a stellar defensive stand and killed the scoring threat. Trailing 27-21 with six minutes remaining, Magistrelli connected with Michael McCormick on a 45-yard score. After a long discussion among officials, it was ruled that an inadvertent whistle wiped out the play. "I don't know what happened," Kroll said. "The officials were very vague on their explanation." Instead of scoring the Dons had to punt. But with 51 seconds left in the game, Magistrelli and McCormick teamed up for a TD pass, this time from 13 yards out. Magistrelli's extra point boot tipped the scales to 28-27 in favor of the Dons. Columbus held on for the come-from-behind win and their first solo league championship since 1982. Pacelli coach Bob Raczek said, "Our defensive secondary let us down tonight. We're not real quick back there and Magistrelli took advantage of that."

Pacelli found themselves right back at Beell Stadium six nights later for a first-round WISAA playoff game on an unseasonably warm night. With the score tied at 7-7 seconds before halftime, Pacelli faced fourth down on the Columbus 2-yard line. Instead of kicking a field goal, the Cardinals went for it. Michael McCormick and Tom Morrell sacked the Pacelli QB to end the threat. Like the week before, the Dons were facing a deficit, this time 14-13 with only two minutes left. Magistrelli fooled defenders and scored on a 12-yard QB bootleg. The Dons' second come-from-behind victory over Pacelli in less than a week advanced them. "It's hard to describe, but this team seems to have the energy to rally themselves to victory," Kroll said. It was their first playoff win in eight years. "I felt the line play by both teams tonight was just excellent. There was a lot of hard-hitting going on," Kroll observed. The Dons made quick work of Manitowoc Lutheran, 48-6, the following Tuesday night in Marshfield. The Dons' Steve Nugent scored on a 71-yard jaunt on CHS's second play from scrimmage to set the tone for the evening. Schueppert and Nugent had 110 and 104 yards rushing. But Kroll's focus was elsewhere. "Our defense really played exceptionally hard. We're very pleased with the chance to go to Madison," he said.

For the first time the Dons appeared at Camp Randall Stadium for the WISAA Division 2 state championship. The Whitefish Bay Dominican Knights, their opponents, were 7-4. The Dons were 10-2. But the Knights were big. Senior tackle James Key was listed at 6'7", 330 pounds. He was the younger brother of Marquette University basketball standout Damon Key. Several other regulars ranged from 235 to 290 pounds and up to six-foot-five. The Dominican offensive line averaged nearly 270 pounds per player. The Dons missed a second-quarter field goal and trailed 7-6 after Tom Bores scored on a 36-yard run early in the fourth quarter. But Dominican sophomore fullback Stoney Craig answered with a 63-yard breakaway to give the Knights a 14-6 lead and the state championship. "Dominican was able to overpower some of our smaller linemen and put a lot of pressure on our quarterback," Kroll said. "Mike is very accurate when given the time to throw the ball but it's very difficult when people the size of the Dominican linemen are in his face." Kroll added, "We had a great season. We're very proud of the way our players performed."

Six seniors made their last appearance in a Dons uniform: Tom Bores, Scott Kundinger, Michael McCormick, Keith Nikolay, Pat Schueppert, and Scott Treglowne. The team amassed 381 points in 13 games, the most so far by any Columbus team. Schueppert led with an impressive 120 points on 20 touchdowns. Junior Steve Nugent tallied 78. Place-kicker and QB Mike Magistrelli notched 51 followed by Kundinger's 48 on eight TD receptions. McCormick had 38, Justin Casperson 20, and Bores 18. Six Dons were selected for eight positions on the All-CWCC team. Pat Schueppert and Adam Michalek were named to both the offensive and defensive units. Schueppert was selected at running back and defensive back. League coaches named him Back of the Year. Michalek was honored at tackle, both offensively and defensively. The hardworking Michalek, a junior, was named Lineman of the Year. Three other Dons were chosen for the offensive unit: center Keith Nikolay, QB Mike Magistrelli, and running back Steve Nugent. The talented backfield duo would return next year. Senior defensive end Michael McCormick completed the tally of Dons on the prestigious squad.

1990 CWCC Standings	W	L	TP	OPP
Marshfield Columbus	6	0	231	63
La Crosse Aquinas	5	1	163	67
Stevens Point Pacelli	3	3	103	98
Wausau Newman	3	3	70	79
Wis. Rapids Assumption	3	3	68	145
Chippewa Falls McDonell	1	5	86	131
Eau Claire Regis	0	6	52	190

1991: Perfect Until Cashin

The 14-year tradition of playing Pacelli in the finale came to a close. The traditionally tough Cardinals-Dons game became the first conference encounter of the year. But before that game in Stevens Point, Columbus faced two battle-tested teams, Nekoosa and Milwaukee Marquette. Senior quarterback Mike Magistrelli drew attention as one of the state's premier signal-callers. Coach Walt Kroll moved CWCC Lineman of the Year Adam Michalek to tight end to help catch Magistrelli's bullets. It worked. Michalek caught six of Magistrelli's 13 TD passes. Those, plus 15 in 1990 and two in 1989, gave Magistrelli 30 career TD passes, shattering the previous school high of 23 set by Bill Draxler in the late 1960s. The Dons began their year on a roll. "The fact that we were able to win those first three games really set a tone for the balance of the season," Kroll said. Columbus ran through the rest of the regular season with relative ease. The high-powered offense and stingy defense meant no opponent got closer than 22 points. Until the playoffs. Then the 9-0 Dons team squared off once more against Pacelli.

The Dons opened the season at home against Nekoosa, the South Central Conference champs. The Papermakers had also been selected for WIAA playoff action the year before. "We've been able to establish a good rivalry with Nekoosa in recent years," Kroll said. "I have a lot of respect for Paul Nistler (head coach) and Dick Hyland (assistant), and I enjoy the relationship we have coaching against each other." The Dons came away with a thrilling 14-7 victory when Magistrelli rolled to his left and outran several defenders for the 5-yard go-ahead touchdown with 58 seconds left. Kroll cited both Magistrelli and Eric Heiting for their fine play. The following Saturday night found the Dons at a warm Hart Park in Wauwatosa, the home turf of Marquette High. The Hilltoppers dominated the tough Milwaukee Metro Conference. Their 48 straight conference wins and six consecutive league titles proved it. "Marquette epitomizes everything that is good about athletics as well as academics and we are always up for them as they are us," Kroll said. The Dons used a swarming defense and Magistrelli's remarkable punting to good effect. Leading 7-6 with one minute to play, Magistrelli placed his final punt at the Marquette 3-yard line. Nose guard Adam Michalek, all 6'2" and 225 pounds of him, sacked Marquette QB Dan Kaminsky for a safety in the end zone with 40 seconds left to ensure a 9-6 Columbus victory. It was one of Michalek's 10 tackles. "I thought Jeremy Maurer had one of his best games for us," said Kroll. "Also, Craig Eckes played well at D-back. To defeat a team like that is a choice victory for us. The heat took a toll on us. We were fortunate to hang on."

The Pacelli game was in Point on Friday the 13th, and the Dons played scarily good, dominating from start to finish and never allowing Pacelli to get into scoring position during the 28-0 win. Adam Michalek anchored the defense. Steve Nugent carried for 171 yards as the offensive line came into their own at Goerke Field. "Adam played a great game," said Kroll. "Al Talens and Eric Heiting at the inside linebacker spots were playing well also. When you get a shutout, you have to be very, very happy." The Dons amassed 322 total yards while yielding a mere 49 total yards. In Chippewa Falls the next Saturday night, the Dons managed to corral McDonell's wide-open pass offense en route to a 36-12 victory. Kroll explained his approach: "Each season when we face McDonell, we tell our rush people we can't expect to sack the quarterback on every play. But we want constant pressure on him every play to make him throw early. In our secondary, we want to play an aggressive break on the ball and look for the interception rather than conceding receptions." Nugent picked up 138 yards on the ground and Michalek gathered five catches for 126 yards. "Mike Magistrelli had a great game," Kroll said.

"He was poised in picking out his receivers and good at establishing a rhythm." The quick-paced game was unusual. Neither team converted any extra points.

The Dons' fourth straight road game was a non-conference affair in Rhinelander. The Hodags got all the way to the 1-yard line on their opening drive before CHS stopped them. Magistrelli responded by orchestrating a 99-yard scoring drive with passes of 35 and 51 yards to Michalek to set up Jeremy Maurer's 4-yard TD plunge. The Dons cruised to a 36-14 win. Kroll enthused about Magistrelli's play: "That's five great games he's played for us this year and he's getting better every game." The Dons returned to Marshfield the following Friday night to face Aquinas on a rain-soaked field. The relentless CHS defense allowed no Blugold penetration beyond the 47-yard line. Alfred Talens and Eric Heiting picked up 124 and 112 yards. "But our little mentioned offensive line has been outstanding," said Kroll. "Our two offensive guards, Brian Hoerneman and Jeremy Sternweis, have been a real force in terms of our sweep play. Our junior tackles Tom Backaus and Tom Morrell have continued to improve as each game goes by, and Victor Michalek shows improvement as he gets more and more experience." The Dons left muddy and victorious, 28-0.

Columbus catapulted to a 34-0 halftime lead in their Saturday afternoon homecoming tilt. Regis was 5-1 overall and 3-0 in the conference. But their success was derailed. The final score was 50-16. Nugent scored four touchdowns and Magistrelli tossed for three. "Winning for homecoming is always nice. To win in the style we did against a team in first place is very satisfying," Kroll said. The Ramblers managed only one first down. The Dons took their stellar 7-0 mark to Wisconsin Rapids the following Saturday night and annihilated Assumption 43-7. The Royals were decimated by injuries and only had 18 bodies for their practice sessions that week. The game's first touchdown belonged to AHS. The Dons used a balanced team effort—five interceptions, 374 total yards, and five QB sacks—to gain the victory. "Eric Heiting had a tremendous offensive game as did his alternate 'Dumptruck' Maurer. These guys are real hard to get down once they get going," Kroll said. "Justin (Casperson) also had a great game. He played well both ways." The season finale was a 41-6 rout of Newman at Beell Stadium. The Cardinals finished 0-9, the mirror opposite of Columbus. Magistrelli found Adam Michalek on three of his four TD passes. "It was a great season for us," Kroll said. "Week to week we improved with every game of the season." The Dons held a 34-0 lead 13 minutes into the game.

Pacelli and Columbus faced each other in the playoffs, and expectations were high. The previous year the navy-and-white had come from behind twice to defeat PHS in both the regular season and the playoffs. This year's early season 28-0 whitewash by the

Dons also had left a bitter taste for the Cards. So it was a pent-up Pacelli 11 that came to Beell, eventually. The scheduled Friday night matchup was cancelled due to a day-long rain. The rescheduled Saturday night game also was moved due to an early November snowstorm. So it was on Monday night that the teams finally met in a frigid Beell Stadium with temperatures in the teens. The frozen and snow-covered turf yielded four touchdowns, three in the all-important fourth quarter. Pacelli's Sean Cashin tormented Columbus. The swift Cardinals running back gained 269 yards on 38 attempts and scored 20 of Pacelli's 21 points. The Dons were outdistanced in total yards, 328-115. Not surprisingly, that difference resulted in a 21-7 Pacelli win. "We have to take our hats off to them tonight because truthfully they were the better team," Kroll said. "Now we know how they felt last year." The Pacelli playoff loss would be the final one that really stung Kroll. "It's disappointing for the players. We were being outplayed up front and couldn't get our normal attack going." Still, the coach lauded Pacelli. "They're always a well-coached team and their players are always very competitive. It's fun playing a team of that type when you know you have to play a solid game for four quarters."

The Dons finished the year 9-1. Mike Magistrelli capped his brilliant career by leading Columbus to two undefeated CWCC titles, cementing his standing as the most prolific Columbus quarterback to that point. Two-way senior superstars Adam Michalek and Steve Nugent also played key roles. Nine seniors made their last appearance in the frigid November air at Beell: Magistrelli, Michalek, Nugent, Ryan Beaver, Brian Hoerneman, Cody Casperson, Jason Hertel, Todd Weber, and P.J. Wilcott. Nugent led the scoring with 68 points, followed by Eric Heiting (52), Magistrelli (51, including 21 extra-point kicks), Michalek (38), Jeremy Maurer (26), Jason Hertel (12), and Rick Merkel (12). Many others scored in single digits. Seven Dons were named to 11 spots on the All-CWCC team. For the second year running, Adam Michalek was named Lineman of the Year and was rewarded with spots at tight end on offense and interior line on defense. Steve Nugent was picked as Back of the Year and was also selected at running back and defensive back. Mike Magistrelli copped honors for punting, place kicking, and quarterback. Four juniors were honored: tackle Tom Backaus and guard Jeremy Sternweis on offense and end Jeremy Maurer and linebacker Eric Heiting on defense. Walt Kroll was named Coach of the Year.

1991 CWCC Standings	W	L	TP	OPP
Marshfield Columbus	6	0	226	41
La Crosse Aquinas	5	1	183	97
Stevens Point Pacelli	4	2	139	90
Eau Claire Regis	3	3	136	160
Chippewa Falls McDonell	2	4	150	188
Wis. Rapids Assumption	1	5	134	158
Wausau Newman	0	6	12	245

1992: Perfection and Points

The most prolific scoring team in Columbus football history ran the table to a 12-0 mark and secured Columbus' second state football championship. It would be the fifth, and last, undefeated team in Dons lore. Size, speed, and talent—the 1992 squad had it all. They were the first Dons to score more than 400 points in a season, their 434 tallies amounting to a 36.2 scoring clip per game. In the playoffs alone, the navy-and-white outscored opponents 128-22. It was a unique team with a long list of accomplishments: two rushers with more than 1,000 yards, a first-team All-State place-kicker, the best offensive and defensive teams in the conference, and a member who scored in all four seasons.

Their opener pitted two defending conference champions against each other at George Holland Field in Nekoosa. The Dons came away 27-0 victors after scoring on their first drive. "I thought our offensive line made a statement on our very first series of the night," said coach Walt Kroll. "We dominated the line of scrimmage and with our two big backs Eric Heiting and Jeremy Maurer pounding it up the middle and with Ricky Merkel, Justin Casperson, and Al

Talens all running well behind them, it made it pretty tough to defend." The nine-year early season Marquette High non-conference series came to a close in 1992 at Beell. Long-time Marquette coach Dick Basham experienced his first losing season (4-5) in 1991. Cuts in the Marquette athletic budget were cited as the reason for dropping the encounter between football powers from different parts of the state. In their last battle, Ricky Merkel intercepted the Hilltoppers with 46 seconds left for a 13-7 triumph on Saturday afternoon. "To beat Marquette two years in a row is a very satisfying situation for us," said Kroll, who praised the play of sophomore signal caller Mike Scheuer. "Mike played very well against a Metro team with a great reputation."

On a picture perfect night in front of a noisy throng at Beell, the Dons and Pacelli Cardinals battled evenly to the end. With 13 seconds left and trailing 24-23, Pacelli coach Bob Raczek decided to go for the win rather than a tie. Kevin McCormick thwarted the two-point conversion try by Shorty Flees, allowing the Dons to escape with a one-point victory. The game-saving tackle gave the Dons their 13th straight conference win, breaking the previous mark of 12 set by Aquinas. With almost their entire team back, including stars Sean Cashin and Flees, Pacelli was formidable. Despite the victory, this thriller exposed a weakness against a scrambling QB; Flees ran for 91 yards. The next Saturday afternoon the Columbus offense routed McDonell, 44-12. The Dons hounded pass-happy Macks QB Jake Goettl (seven sacks, two interceptions) en route to the win. "Craig Eckes continues to improve each game and was very alert in his play all day long," Kroll said. "Nate Sanders at defensive end also put forth a very strong effort." Eric Heiting ran for 178 yards on 16 carries.

The non-conference Friday night home game against Rhinelander featured four nifty TD runs by sophomore QB Mike Scheuer. The rushing attack and stifling defense prevailed, 36-14. "The quarterback keeper has always been a big part of our attack," said Kroll. "Mike made some real good decisions and advanced the ball very well. All of our quarterbacks have been very adept at using that play during the course of our games." Next, the Dons returned two interceptions for touchdowns in a 42-14 win against Aquinas. "I thought our defense was very alert and played very physical. Justin Casperson, our safety, is the one who sets the tone with his physical play," Kroll said. "This was a big victory for us, coming down to La Crosse and getting the win on the road." The Columbus defense stymied Regis the next Saturday afternoon in Eau Claire and came away with a 17-0 shutout. "Kevin Ahmann's field goal and two extra points proved to be important points," Kroll said. "His kickoffs gave us a lift as far as field position."

The Dons dismissed Assumption 42-14 on a homecoming Saturday afternoon the next week. It didn't help the Royals that their transfer QB from Nekoosa, Blake Knutson, hurt his ankle shortly before halftime. The Columbus run game was so effective the team didn't go to the air once in the 470-yard performance. Justin Casperson and Al Talens accounted for 174 and 142 yards, respectively. "Our counters were very effective today. Our misdirection got us a lot of yards," Kroll said. The Dons welcomed back Ryan Kolbeck after an early-season injury. Kroll praised his play. The 61 points the Dons tallied against Newman the following Saturday night tied for the second most ever posted by a navy-and-white squad. The 61-14 Beell Stadium win featured Kevin Ahmann breaking the CWCC record for most kicked extra points in a season. Ahmann shattered the old mark of 24. He raised his total to 29 in the conference finale. Casperson ran for 177 yards in 12 carries and found the end zone four times. "He's a great high school back and certainly ran with a lot of determination tonight," Kroll said. Mike Scheuer also ran for three scores.

Marshfield hosted Onalaska Luther for a first-round WISAA Division II game the next Friday night and sent them away with a 56-6 loss. Casperson accounted for 238 yards on the ground in just 14 carries, and Kevin Ahmann connected on all eight of his point-after boots. The offense collected 539 total yards. The following Saturday night, Manitowoc Roncalli invaded Beell. The Jets were 8-2 and had been in the 1991 state championship game. But they had difficulty stopping running backs Al Talens (179 yards) and Casperson (124 yards) in a 44-6 CHS win. The score had been 14-6 at the half.

The Division II state championship game at Camp Randall pitted the Dons against Pacelli in a high noon showdown. The Cardinals' only blemish on their 10-1 mark was their loss to Columbus early in the season. The Dons left no doubt as to who was the better team on this mid-November day and posted a relatively easy 28-10 win to claim the school's second state football championship. Like the 1980 state champs, the 1992 contingent also finished with a perfect 12-0 record. Kevin McCormick set the defensive tone early in the contest when he batted away a Shorty Flees pass on fourth down at the 2-yard line on the opening PHS drive. Al Talens ran for 139 yards on six carries and his three touchdowns earned him game Most Valuable Player honors. Casperson notched 100 yards. Pacelli's Sean Cashin (running) and Jake Mihm (receiving) topped 100 yards apiece, as well. "I'm real happy for our team, our school, and for Marshfield," said Kroll. "Our defense played exceptionally well. I thought it was one of our better defensive games of the year." It was Kroll's 200th win at Columbus.

Seventeen seniors bid farewell to their high school grid careers at Camp Randall Stadium: Kevin Ahmann, Tom Backaus, Jim Bob Beining, Justin Casperson, Eric Heiting, Rob Klumb, Tom Kohl, Ira Martin, Jeremey Maurer, Kevin McCormick, Rick Merkel, Tom Morrell, Scott Osbourne, Nate Sanders, Chris Spencer, Jeremy Sternweis, and Alfred Talens. For the only time in their history, the Dons had four players score 60 points or more in a season: Casperson (108), Ahmann (80), Heiting (66), and Mike Scheuer (60). Talens notched 48 tallies, followed by Nate Bennington (24), McCormick (18), and Maurer (18). Maurer joined a select group of players who tallied points in all four years of high school. Only Chuck Koch, Steve Seidl, Tom Stangl, Dick Stevens, and Steve Nugent had managed the feat before. As conference champs once again, the Dons placed six players in eight slots on the All-CWCC team. On offense, Eric Heiting at running back, Tom Backaus at tackle, and Jeremy Sternweis at guard/center were unanimous picks. Kevin Ahmann was chosen as the league's best place-kicker. On defense, Heiting and Backaus were unanimous selections for line-backer and defensive lineman. Justin Casperson also was selected unanimously at defensive back. Jeremy Maurer was named to the select team for the second year in a row at defensive end. For the third year running, CWCC Lineman of the Year was a Dons player, Tom Backaus. Heiting shared Back of the Year honors with Shorty Flees of Pacelli. Ahmann was further honored as Wisconsin's first-team All-State place-kicker.

1992 CWCC Standings	W	L	TP	OPP
Marshfield Columbus	6	0	230	77
Stevens Point Pacelli	5	1	173	73
La Crosse Aquinas	3	3	112	136
Wis. Rapids Assumption	3	3	115	113
Chippewa Falls McDonell	2	4	112	161
Eau Claire Regis	2	4	66	103
Wausau Newman	0	6	59	204

1993: Conference Streak Continues

Any thoughts of a long winning streak after the undefeated 1992 season were put to rest in the season opener at Beell by Nekoosa of the South Central Conference. The Papermakers blanked the Dons 20-0 but the experience gained in that loss paid off. The Columbus squad proved to be a model for coach Walt Kroll's expectations, a young team that continually improved. The Dons, however, did keep alive their record-breaking streak of conference wins, which they extended to 23 by year's end. The Dons had yet to lose a conference game in the 1990s. The first time Columbus won the state championship in 1980, a three-year span of state championship appearances followed. Would history repeat itself with more championship games after the second state crown in 1992? Kroll seemed to take the Nekoosa loss in stride. "Nekoosa is one of the teams we play where I really admire their coach (Paul Nistler) and coaching staff and how they handle their players," he said. It didn't hurt that Nistler had 14 seniors and a solid core of juniors from a conference champion team. All points came in the second stanza when the Papermakers stung the Dons with long-range touch-downs—a 72-yard punt return and a 75-yard interception return. In between, they bolted in from four yards.

The last of the great non-conference school series that Kroll scheduled started at East High School, early home of the Green Bay Packers. The opponent, though, was the high school on Green Bay's northeast side, Preble. The Hornets struck first in the Friday night contest on Labor Day weekend. The Dons responded with 14 points in the second quarter. The lead stood up for a 14-6 win. Mike Scheuer and Aaron Rasmussen each scored on 1-yard bursts. It proved to be a good defensive win for a young team on the road. Preble's defensive end, Dana Bongle, at 6'5" and 240 pounds, would later be named first team All-State. Andy Dean was key on defense for the Dons, with two fumble recoveries and an interception that led to the winning TD.

The entire Columbus squad got to play in the McDonell game in Chippewa Falls the following Saturday night, a 56-13 victory. Eleven ball carriers toted the pigskin 408 yards in the one-sided affair. CHS led 49-7 at the half. The Macks operated from the shotgun pass formation on every play. The clock ran continuously the entire second half because of the "35-point rule." Scot Cook connected on eight point-after kicks. The Dons found themselves 20 minutes south of Madison the following Friday night, at Oregon High School. They used a great defensive effort to shut down the Panthers 27-0. The pass combo of Mike Scheuer and Nate Bennington clicked for 79 yards on five catches. Ryan Beck ran for 100-plus yards for the second week in a row, and Aaron Rasmussen chipped in with 88 yards rushing. The Dons physically dominated the game.

The CHS defense came up big for the third straight week when they beat Aquinas 7-6 in overtime at Beell in the conference opener. Kroll knew going in that getting their 19th consecutive conference win would be a challenge. "They're a big team physically, proba-bly the biggest team we will play this year," he said. An overtime touchdown yielded by the Dons was the only TD they allowed in over eight quarters of play. Aquinas penetrated CHS territory only twice during the regulation game. Steve Stenslien's run for the two-point conversion fell short as he was gang-tackled. The Dons went second in overtime. Mike Scheuer was chased from the pocket and ran in from 10 yards out to tie the game. Scot Cook's kick ended what Kroll called "a great high school football game between two good teams." Scheuer's play caught Kroll's eye. "Scheuer's last two games have been the best he's ever played for us. His leadership and presence have been very evident," he noted. Kroll also applauded lineman Ryan Kolbeck, saying he has played "very well in every contest. He's been a real standout for us."

For the second time in CHS history, the Dons took back-to-back games into overtime. Unlike in 1986, they won both this time, escaping Beell on homecoming with a 13-10 win over Regis. It was the last overtime game in program history. Regis was 5-0 coming into the game and led 7-0 with 5:20 left. That's when the Dons took over 69 yards from their end zone. They struck fast. Mark Mineau grabbed a 15-yard Scheuer TD pass with three minutes left and Scot Cook tied the score. In overtime, Regis booted a go-ahead 27-yard field goal. The Dons answered with a winning 15-yard TD pass to Andy Dean. "Hats off to the Regis front wall," said Kroll. "They stymied us up front." The Dons were held to 10 yards rushing as a team. Nate Bennington caught seven more balls for 80 yards. The following Saturday night the Dons humbled Assumption 38-7 in Wisconsin Rapids. Ryan Kolbeck recovered an Assumption fumble on the opening kickoff and the Dons never looked back. Junior QB Mike Scheuer passed for 163 yards, including six receptions to Bennington. "He's our key receiver and he showed it tonight," Kroll said. Brian McCormick "had his best game he's ever played for us," the coach added. Craig Eckes gained 116 yards, more than collected by Damian Mancl, the league's top rusher at game time.

The Dons hosted La Crosse Logan the following Friday night. The Rangers were 6-1 when they hit the Beell turf. The Dons came away with a narrow 21-19 win. The winning points came on a 60-yard pass from Bennington to Mineau. Earlier in the third quarter, Mineau had saved a touchdown by tackling Logan's Denver Harris at the CHS 11-yard line. Kroll was pleased with his team's performance, saying, "We've beat three big public schools this year … That's very satisfying. We were able to maintain our composure." Columbus extended their 22-game conference streak in the season finale in Stevens Point. They drove the 35 miles back to Marshfield celebrating a 22-16 win and a fourth consecutive conference title. Helping Kroll were assistants Russ Grundy (defense) and Kevin Orr (freshmen). "It's to coach Grundy's credit that our defense has played so well this year," he said. "His expertise has played a big role in the development of our three down linemen and our defensive ends." Kroll praised the defensive play of Craig Eckes, whom he called "the leader of our secondary." Junior Mike Scheuer had now led the Dons to victory 19 times in his 20 starts at quarterback. The previous winter, Scheuer had been in a serious auto accident but he had recovered amazingly well. Scheuer and Bennington switched roles on a second-quarter trick pass that found Scheuer on the receiving end of a 43-yard Bennington aerial.

The Dons scored 60 points six times over their 51 years. One of them was two weeks later on a Saturday night at Beell. Columbus thrashed Lake Geneva Northwestern Prep 60-6 in a first-round WISAA Division III playoff game. The Dons had moved down to Division III in 1993. Division I and II still had eight teams vying for state titles. Division III had been reduced to four teams, hence the bye week before entertaining the Falcons. The Dons scored on nine of their 12 possessions and took a 40-6 lead into the halftime. All suited Dons got to play. "It's nice when you can do that," said Kroll. "All our reserves worked hard all season long and it's moments like this they will always treasure."

The WISAA Division III state championship was set: Regis vs. Columbus at Camp Randall Stadium. "Having the opportunity to play in the state championship at Camp Randall is a moment every high school player in the state yearns for," Kroll said. The Sunday night affair was played in a cocktail of pouring rain with cold, ice, and sleet as the ingredients. After a scoreless first half, Regis controlled the ball and the clock in the second half on their way to a 14-0 win. The Dons appeared to take an early lead when Mike Scheuer ran 59 yards on the second play of the game. But off-setting penalties wiped out the score. All-State Regis defensive back Brian Walter, 6'4" and 185 pounds, was named the game's Most Valuable Player. "He's a good athlete and he produced when he had to," Kroll said. A quarterback on offense, Walter was the

CWCC's leading rusher, the only time a QB copped the running title. Understandably, Walter was named the Back of the Year as well. In two contests with Regis in 1993 the Dons managed a paltry 37 yards rushing. Kroll saw the game clearly. "We missed some opportunities and we had some turnovers that spelled our doom," he said. "We have to give credit to Regis. They played hard and they played well. I thought we played well for all four quarters, but it wasn't in the cards." Kroll reflected on the season with pride in his players: "The loss can't diminish the 9-2 season we experienced. Overall, it was a nice season."

Seven seniors made their last appearance for the navy-and-white: Nate Bennington, Craig Eckes, Victor Michalek, Ryan Kolbeck, David Treglowne, Charles "Rocky" Schueppert, and Tim Wilcott. These seven are forever unique in Columbus football history. In their four years of high school, they never experienced a loss in the Central Wisconsin Catholic Conference. The team's 258 points were evenly spread. Junior QB Mike Scheuer led with 62 points, followed by Aaron Rasmussen (36), Mark Mineau (30), Ryan Beck (30), Craig Eckes (26), Scot Cook (24), Nate Bennington (16), freshman Mike Weister (14), and Daryl Konrardy (12). Seven Dons were selected for eight All-Conference slots. On offense, Ryan Kolbeck was a unanimous pick at tackle. Nate Bennington and Rocky Schueppert were named at end and guard. Scot Cook was chosen as top place-kicker. Defensively, Kolbeck on the line and Craig Eckes at back were unanimous selections. Brian McCormick made the select group at end and Andy Dean was chosen as the league's best punter. Kolbeck was further honored as Lineman of the Year, the fourth year in a row CHS had captured the honor. Finally, Walt Kroll was named Coach of the Year.

1993 CWCC Standings	W	L	TP	OPP
Marshfield Columbus	5	0	136	52
La Crosse Aquinas	4	1	135	71
Eau Claire Regis	3	2	111	60
Chippewa Falls McDonell	2	3	111	178
Stevens Point Pacelli	1	4	53	79
Wis. Rapids Assumption	0	5	58	162

1994: An Era Comes to a Winning End

Columbus was successful in 1994—as successful as a high school team could be. The Dons started the season with two shutout wins and finished with three blank slates on their way to their third state football championship, all under coach Walt Kroll. The six defensive shutouts equaled the six posted by the 12-0 1980 state championship squad. What no one could foresee was that, sadly, this would be Walt Kroll's final season. The Wisconsin football legend would die during the off season, in March 1995, closing a long chapter in Columbus High School history.

The 1994 campaign, Kroll's 31st at Columbus, opened with a trip to Nekoosa. The Dons held the Papermakers in check the whole game. But it took the offense until the second half to get moving in the 28-0 CHS win. Kroll praised the play of defensive ends Daryl Konrardy and Brian McCormick for containing and limiting the Nekoosa attack. The following Friday night, with the sounds of the Central Wisconsin State Fair blaring six blocks west of Beell Stadium, the Dons dug in and blistered Green Bay Preble in a 37-0 whitewash. The Dons marched straight down the field in 13 plays covering 76 yards in the first series after the opening kickoff. The navy-and-white drive ended with a 5-yard TD toss from Mike Scheuer to Brian McCormick. It proved to be a big night for Scheuer, who scored on a 12-yard pass, a 16-yard run, and a 72-yard punt return. The next Saturday afternoon, the Dons manhandled the McDonell Macks in Marshfield 56-22. McDonell was 2-0 coming into the game but Kroll had the Dons ready for their passing onslaught. Kroll thought the team improved markedly during the week's preparation due to spirited, enthusiastic practice sessions. Reserve QB Peter Schueppert played the entire second half. Sophomore Mike Weister scored late on runs of 42 and 57 yards in tallying 147 yards rushing on 12 trips.

In Portage the following Friday night, the Dons faced the Warriors in a non-conference confrontation. It was the first game between the schools, each sporting a 3-0 mark. "They pretty much outplayed us in every facet of the game," Kroll said. "Their offensive and defensive lines took control of the game early and they exploited our inexperience in the secondary with their passing attack. When you're outplayed, you have to give credit where credit is due. You can't dwell on feeling bad when the opposition deserves credit." Ryan Beck had 114 yards on the ground in the 29-20 loss. The Portage road defeat toughened the young Dons for their next game, a Saturday night encounter at Memorial Stadium in La Crosse. Aquinas was 4-0 and ranked third in the state's WISAA poll. The Dons were ranked sixth. Aquinas coach Dan Coughlin was wary, especially of Mike Scheuer. "They have a very talented QB. He's ranked as one of the top 25 athletes in the state and can control a game by himself," he said. And he did. In the fourth quarter with Columbus trailing 14-10, the senior quarterback connected with Scot Cook for a 22-yard TD for the lead. Scheuer returned a punt 53 yards two minutes later to pad the CHS lead. After the Blugolds narrowed the gap to 24-20 and again had possession of the ball, defensive back Scheuer ended any Aquinas thoughts of victory by intercepting a Sean Stephens pass. The Dons prevailed 24-20 for their 25th consecutive conference win. The game was mostly a defensive struggle. The Aquinas linemen were much larger than the CHS linemen, yet the Dons were able to neutralize the Blugolds ground game. "A lot of the credit goes to our three defensive linemen Mike Seelen, Richie Seubert, and nose guard Daryl Konrardy, who played great games against this huge offensive line," Kroll said.

For the fourth week in a row, the Dons faced an unbeaten foe when they journeyed to Eau Claire for the annual Regis battle. It was the second straight week they were facing a defending WISAA state champion. After stopping the Ramblers on downs, QB Mike Scheuer went 57 yards on CHS's first offensive drive for a quick 6-0 lead. They kept adding to it. The Dons had four runners with at least 50 yards. Ryan Beck's 109 led the way. Beck also ran 86 yards for a touchdown on a recovered fumble late in the game. It was the longest such TD in CHS history. Kroll remarked about the 38-12 win at Carson Park: "I think what stood out to me was the aggressiveness shown by our defense, which was coming off a good game against Aquinas as well." The Dons had their largest-ever homecoming win the following Saturday afternoon when they disposed of Assumption, 61-7. The 54-point margin easily bested the

44-point homecoming wins of 1951, 1958, and 1965. Columbus played almost exclusively with underclassmen in the second half and still had good results. For decades one of Kroll's foundational strategies was to play as many underclassmen as he could to build his future teams with game-experienced players. "Homecoming is a lot of fun for both myself and the players, the student body, and the faculty," he said. "I think it's a good, healthy experience for these teenagers." Scot Cook sped for 144 yards on wingback counter plays, and sophomore Mike Weister finished two yards shy of 100 on the ground. The Dons trekked back to La Crosse, this time to Swanson Field, to play Logan High School the following Friday night. The Dons were leading 7-0 when Ryan Beck picked off a Rangers pass late in the first quarter and took it 45 yards for another Dons score. They led 28-0 at half and drove home with a 35-0 win over a Big Rivers Conference opponent. "I think the interception took a lot out of us," said Logan coach Bob Christopherson. "We weren't able to get anything going."

The Columbus-Pacelli conference finale at Beell Stadium the following Friday night pitted 4-0 Columbus against the 3-1 Cardinals. A PHS win would give them a share of the CWCC crown. It was a great high school football game, with the Cards eking out a 13-7 road win to end Columbus' 27-game conference win streak. Pacelli came out on a mission, scoring on an opening 82-yard drive. They took a 13-0 lead when their all-run, eight-play, 66-yard drive ended with junior Kevin Sullivan bursting in from four yards out. Those would be the last points ever scored on a Walt Kroll-coached team. The Dons only managed 89 total yards in the first half. Pacelli put tremendous pressure on Mike Scheuer throughout to thwart the attack until the very end. Critical penalties also hurt the Dons. However, the Dons did not go easy into that October 21 night. The Dons converted two critical fourth-down plays on a 10-play drive before Scheuer rolled left and found the end zone with 19 seconds left. Scot Cook's onside kick attempt bounded erratically high and on a perfect angle for CHS's Daryl Konrardy to field it and streak down the sideline. Kevin Sullivan forced Konrardy out of bounds at the 13-yard line. Scheuer threw over the middle in the back of the end zone for a chance at an improbable win. Again, Sullivan was there for the Cardinals and he intercepted Scheuer's pass to end matters. Pacelli held Scheuer to 186 total yards, 99 rushing and 87 passing. "Scheuer is a heck of an athlete. But the kids really hit him," said longtime Pacelli coach Bob Raczek. "He knew he was in a game tonight."

The Dons blanked first-round WISAA Division III opponent Watertown Northwestern Prep 35-0 at Beell the following Friday night. The Hornets were 5-4 but were no match for the Dons. On one exciting play, Columbus scored after Mike Scheuer pitched the ball to Daryl Konrardy, who flipped it back to Scheuer, who found Scot Cook for six points on a 19-yard TD grab. The Dons' second-round game found them at home again, this time against defending state champion Regis. The Ramblers sported a 7-3 mark and came to play. It was a defensive battle but the Dons earned a hard-fought 17-0 win. "I thought our last two games have been our best defensive efforts in terms of consistency," Kroll said after his penultimate win.

A steady rain fell on Camp Randall for the 1994 WISAA Division III state championship game. It was the first-ever meeting between Fond du Lac Winnebago Lutheran Academy (9-2) and Columbus (9-2). "Actually the weather wasn't that much of a factor for either team," Kroll said. "If we compare it to last year's (championship) game where it was cold, icy, and sleeting, tonight was mild." Aaron Rasmussen's 21-yard TD jaunt with five minutes left in the fourth quarter was the game's only score in a narrow 6-0 Columbus win. He helped CHS run out the clock—literally— with his hard running. Altogether, he had 104 yards on 16 totes. Additionally, Rasmussen had nine tackles. He was named Most Valuable Player. "I give a lot of credit to my fellow coaches, Randy Stokke and Justin Casperson, who directed the defense in fine style," Kroll said. "It was a very rewarding season for me because of the team's spirit and cooperation." The Dons had not set a goal of winning a state championship. Kroll reiterated his long-standing coaching philosophy: "Our goal basically was to improve each week, improve each practice, and improve each game. If we do that, we'll be real happy." With Kroll's untimely March 1995 passing, the last game he ever coached was his third state championship. His defense yielded zero playoff points in three playoff contests.

Eight seniors made their last appearance in the cold November rain at Camp Randall: Steve Burger, Scot Cook, Andy Dean, Daryl Konrardy, Brian McCormick, Matt Mineau, Mike Scheuer, and Peter Spencer. The team scored 364 points, the third highest tally by a Dons team to that point. Scheuer led with 78 points, followed by Cook (69), Aaron Rasmussen (68), Mike Weister (48), Ryan Beck (30), McCormick (30), and Chris Fredrick (12). Scheuer became only the seventh Columbus player to score in each year of high school. He concluded his remarkable career with 28 TD passes, two shy of all-time leader Mike Magistrelli. But he was the only Dons field general who led his team to two state crowns. The Dons placed seven players at eight positions on the All-Conference team. On offense, backfield mates Mike Scheuer (QB), Ryan Beck (RB), and Mike Weister (RB) were selected, along with center Peter Spencer and guard Steve Burger. On defense, end Brian McCormick, down lineman Daryl Konrardy, and Scheuer at back were honored. Scheuer's stellar play garnered him Back of the Year honors. Further, Scheuer was named first-team All-State at quarterback and second-team All-State at defensive back. "He started 35 games for us and won 31 of them," said Kroll. "He's experienced and has been highly effective for us at that position, the most important position on the team." The Coach of the Year laurel was shared by each tri-champion: Bob Raczek of Pacelli, Dan Coughlin of Aquinas, and, for one final time, Walt Kroll of Columbus High School.

1994 CWCC Standings	W	L	TP	OPP
Marshfield Columbus	4	1	186	74
La Crosse Aquinas	4	1	146	37
Stevens Point Pacelli	4	1	103	34
Eau Claire Regis	2	3	71	87
Chippewa Falls McDonell	1	4	56	151
Wis. Rapids Assumption	0	5	30	209

1995: First Post-Kroll Season

Tom Passe took over the coaching reins after coach Walt Kroll's death in March 1995. The 25-year-old came to Columbus from Minneapolis Washburn High School, where he was an assistant line coach. He played collegiately in the Minnesota Intercollegiate Athletic Conference at both Macalester and Hamline. Passe's assistant in 1995 was Scott Bleck, a UW-River Falls grad. This also was the inaugural year for the soccer program at Columbus. The first year after Kroll was checkered. The team finished 2-3 in the conference and 5-5 overall. Ryan Beck emerged as a real offensive threat, finishing second for the CWCC rushing title. He averaged 7.4 yards a carry. The squad endured its first three-game losing skid since 1988 but rebounded with a win streak of the same length. Dons ballhawks also returned three interceptions for touchdowns during the season.

The Dons unveiled coach Passe's pro-style offense in a 21-7 win over Nekoosa at Beell Stadium in the season opener. Mike Weister scored all three CHS touchdowns—one on an interception return, one on a run, and another on a Peter Schueppert pass. Passe cited Richie Seubert and Chris Michalski for their defensive play. "He (Seubert) had at least three or four tackles behind the line of scrimmage. Michalski knocked down some passes and made three touchdown-saving tackles," the new coach said. At Green Bay's East Stadium Friday night, the Dons defeated Preble 27-19. The Hornets were big in both physical size and the number of players on their roster. The Dons were cruising with a 27-7 lead in the fourth quarter when Passe put in his reserves. After Preble scored two quick touchdowns to make it 27-19 with 4:41 left in the game, the first-year coach re-inserted his starting unit to preserve the win. Weister again scored three TDs, including an 83-yard punt return. It was the second year in a row the Dons returned a Kevin Stemke punt for a touchdown. Stemke would go on to win the 2000 Ray Guy Award for the University of Wisconsin as the nation's best collegiate punter. His 44.5 punt average his senior year was the best ever by a Badger. Ben Knauf scored the other Dons' TD to go along with his two interceptions.

Columbus fell in the conference opener 33-22 to McDonell in Chippewa Falls the next Saturday night. Macks QB Ryan Stelter tossed four TD passes in a 341-yard aerial assault with their wide-open offense. The Dons got caught up in the airshow, too. Junior Peter Schueppert's 33 pass attempts were the most ever by a Dons quarterback. But it proved to be a case of missed opportunities. The Dons were inside the McDonell 10-yard line twice in the first quarter and came away empty-handed. Mike Weister had a nifty kickoff return TD nullified by a clipping penalty. Passe noted the sharp play of Schueppert. "We played hard right up to the end. We never got down on ourselves and we didn't point fingers," he said. "It would have been easy to say, 'You dropped the pass' or 'you missed a block'." The Dons faced 3-0 River Falls the next Friday night at Beell. The Wildcats had been a Division II WIAA qualifier the year before and were ranked fourth in the state. Matt Kleinbrook, a 185-pound senior, ran through a lot of CHS tackles on his way to picking up 103 yards on 22 carries in the 25-15 Wildcat win. "We got outplayed on both sides of the ball," Passe said. Five River Falls seniors from that team went on to play college football.

Aquinas brought their 4-0 mark to Beell the following Saturday night and departed with a 14-6 win. Andy Marinelli scored the game-winning touchdown for the Blugolds with just over three minutes left on a 3-yard run. It was the first Aquinas win over Columbus since 1989. The defense was robust again and kept CHS in the game. Passe called it the best Dons performance of the year. Unfortunately, Joe Seubert was lost for the season with a back injury. The Dons got back on the right track the following Saturday afternoon against Regis in their homecoming game, blanking the Ramblers 14-0. Two first-quarter Ryan Beck scores, one from 76 yards out, held up. Beck finished the afternoon with 133 yards on 20 carries. But the CHS defense was crucial in the win. The following week the Dons coasted to a 55-0 victory over Assumption on a rainy Friday night in Wisconsin Rapids. Wet conditions contributed to the seven fumbles. CHS, however, recovered all three of their lost balls. Beck erupted for 244 first-half yards en route to a 28-0 halftime lead. He finished with a stellar 277-yard performance on 18 carries. Passe was again pleased with the defense. "The front seven did a good job. Weister and Rasmussen (the linebackers) played the best they've played all year," he said. A long bus trip to Burlington to face non-conference Catholic Central did not deter the Dons from playing what Passe called "the best we've played as a team all year." CHS prevailed 34-6 over the Hilltoppers. "The kids picked it up in the locker room at halftime and that was good to see," Passe said. Two Dons rushers topped 100 yards: Beck with 189 and Weister with 137. Jason Linzmeier had a big day with three catches for 81 yards and two touchdowns.

The conference finale at Stevens Point brought the Dons face-to-face with a skilled Pacelli squad headed by two 1,000-yard rushers in Kevin Sullivan and Adam Rutta. The Cardinals were undefeated at 8-0. On this chilly night PHS special teams enabled the Cards to score two first-quarter touchdowns on the way to a 25-0 Pacelli win. Columbus fumbled the opening kickoff and the Cards recovered it at their own 24-yard line and scored shortly afterward. Adam Mrozek sped 75 yards for his third punt return TD of the year later in the first frame. Mrozek's feat broke the old conference mark held by many, including Brian Fehrenbach in 1973 for the Dons. "Our defense played well," Passe said. The navy-and-white held Rutta and Sullivan to 83 and 35 yards, respectively. Nonetheless, Rutta won the conference rushing crown, and Pacelli proceeded to win the Division III WISAA title a few weeks later.

With Division III now at eight teams, the Dons 5-4 mark was good enough to get into the playoffs. They ventured south to Horlick Field in Racine to square off with Racine Lutheran. The Dons struck first on a Mike Weister 55-yard TD run, setting the early pace. But as the game wore on, so did the physicality of the Crusaders. Lutheran scored on a 14-play, 79-yard drive right before the half to tie things 7-7. Another long Lutheran drive took up most of the third quarter before Ricky Collum scored from 9 yards out to give Racine the lead. Collum scored all 14 of his team's points in the 14-7 Crusaders win. "They are a big, physical football team and they just took over in the second half," Passe said. "We thought the pass would be there. As it turned out, our defense was out on the field the entire second half. That didn't help."

Seven seniors suited up for their last game at Horlick Field: Joe Backaus, Ryan Beck, Jerry Bennington, Kevin Hendler, Brian Mancl, Chris Michalski, and Aaron Rasmussen. Mike Weister led the Dons by scoring 80 of the team's 201 points. Ryan Beck (48), Chris Fredrick (23), Jason Linzmeier (18), and Aaron Rasmussen (12) rounded out the scoring list. Three Dons, all seniors, were named to the All-CWCC team: running back Ryan Beck, tackle Jerry Bennington, and linebacker Aaron Rasmussen.

1995 CWCC Standings	W	L	TP	OPP
Stevens Point Pacelli	5	0	192	13
La Crosse Aquinas	4	1	118	355
Chippewa Falls McDonell	3	2	108	104
Marshfield Columbus	2	3	97	72
Eau Claire Regis	1	4	42	105
Wis. Rapids Assumption	0	5	19	217

1996: A Fourth Journey to State Glory

This Columbus team certainly knew what winning looked like as they made their third appearance in four years at Camp Randall for a state championship. It was a team forged with all the elements of success: experience, strength, size, and speed. They did not disappoint on their way to the school's fourth, and last, state championship—a convincing 42-6 win over friendly nemesis Pacelli. Many long-time records were shattered by this group including most individual points, most rushing yards, most TD passes, most TD receptions, most receiving yardage, and most kickoff returns for a TD. It all added up to a final 11-1 mark. For the first, and only, time both Marshfield schools won a playoff football game in the same season.

Second-year coach Tom Passe had his team ready for the season opener at Nekoosa where the Dons dismissed the Papermakers 25-7. The scoring was indicative of the type of year it would be: Jason

Linzmeier field goals, long Mike Weister kickoff and TD runs, and touchdown receptions from Pete Schueppert to Linzmeier. The only sad note was the loss of two-way lineman Joel Hoerneman to injury for the season. Hoerneman was replaced by 5'9", 260-pound freshman Matt Knauf at center and sophomore Travis Bauer at nose guard. Josh Maurer, another freshman, started at strong safety on defense. Scott Bleck and Kevin Hendler assisted Passe in his coaching duties. The following Saturday afternoon Kevin Stemke and his Green Bay Preble teammates came to a warm Beell Stadium. Stemke was a returning All-State kicker for the Hornets and had already verbally committed to attend Wisconsin. On this day Stemke's 46-yard field goal was sandwiched between two Pete Schueppert TD passes. The field goal would have been good from 56 yards as it cleared the goal post by at least 10 yards. The Dons were in command more than the 14-3 score indicated. Mike Weister rambled for 177 yards on 33 carries and Joe Seubert gathered five passes for 57 yards.

The Columbus defense continued its domination the following Saturday night at Beell Stadium with a 17-0 whitewash of McDonell. New McDonell coach Tom Swoboda emphasized the run more than the pass-oriented attacks of yore. Columbus did not yield a first down to the Chippewa Falls visitors until the third quarter. But the McDonell defense came to play as well. Their aggressive eight-man front caused CHS problems all night. Weister was held to 60 yards on 20 carries. McDonell was the only team to hold the Dons star under 100 yards during the 1996 campaign. "Paul Scheuer did a great job. We're not a blitzing team, but we blitzed in the second half because we needed pressure," Passe said. The Macks generated only 57 yards on offense. At River Falls the following Friday night, spectators saw a classic back-and-forth high school football game between two good teams. The Dons fell 34-28 when their last drive for the winning score petered out on the River Falls 17-yard line with one minute left. "We just got worn down," Passe said. "It's great to play these big schools, but it's tough to compete against them when you have to leave nine guys on the field and they bring in a fresh 11," he said. For Dons fans who weren't too far removed from seeing the wing-T run to perfection under Kroll, it was a bit of deja vu as the Wildcats had two running backs gain well over 100 yards each from that familiar offense. Nick Jenkins scored five times to complement his 176-yard night for River Falls. Jason Linzmeier gathered in three Pete Schueppert TD tosses. A 74-yard Mike Weister punt return kept the game close. "We just didn't expect to get pushed around like that," Passe concluded.

Aquinas would join the Mississippi Valley Conference in 1997 so the 1996 game at Veterans Memorial Stadium was the last between the schools. Aquinas came into the game winless and decided to move senior Nick Forer, a 6'4", 235-pound lineman, to running back. "We just decided we need to shake things up," coach Dan Coughlin said. It worked. Forer gained 172 yards on 23 carries for the Blugolds. Columbus jumped out to a 21-7 halftime lead and things looked good. Though the navy-and-white lost two fumbles deep in Aquinas territory, they appeared in control of the game. But the Blugolds rallied to within one point with under three minutes left. Nick Feuerhelm executed a perfect onside kick for Aquinas. Suddenly the Blugolds were threatening. The drive stalled, though, and Columbus ran out the clock for a 28-27 nail-biter. Mike Weister turned in a grand performance in the final meeting between the schools. His 299 yards on 33 carries was just five shy of the school record set by Bobby Koch in 1965. Weister also caught one pass for 11 yards, accounting for 310 of the Dons' 374 yards. The following Saturday afternoon found the Dons in Elk Mound on a sunny, windy day. Regis moved the game to a village high school football field 14 miles from campus because their Carson Park ground was being resurfaced. Weister rushed for 201 yards in a 45-14 romp. "You never know what's going to happen when he carries the ball," Passe said. "He's the heart of our team." Weister's four TDs included a 62-yard punt return. Future NFL Super Bowl champion Rich Seubert, at 250 pounds, scored his only points for the Dons on a two-point conversion.

A third straight Saturday afternoon game saw the Dons annihilate Assumption 51-8 in Marshfield. Jason Linzmeier's 21-yard TD reception to open the scoring tied him with Ed Sheahen and Brian Fehrenbach for nine career six-pointers. The next time the Dons offense took the field they were ahead 27-0. In the interim, Mike

Weister returned two punts for scores and Joe Seubert returned an errant Royals pass 32 yards for a touchdown. Weister also returned the second-half kickoff 86 yards for another CHS touchdown. He became the only player in Dons' history to return both a punt and a kickoff for touchdowns—and he did it in the same game. Only four players in CHS history had ever returned a kickoff back all the way until then: Russ Truhlar (1957), Paul Mancl (1968), Bill "Sudsy" Seidl (1969), and Weister. Passe complimented the contribution of the offensive line, spotlighting one player who typified the efforts. "Mike Seelen is a guy that goes both ways," he said. "He plays good football and I don't think we give enough credit to our offensive and defensive lines. He's one guy who is a key part of our team." The Dons routed Burlington Catholic Central 52-0 at Beell the following Saturday afternoon. Weister scored six touchdowns, catching one Pete Schueppert pass and running in for the other five to tie Bob Koch's long-held 1965 mark. Weister's final 75-yard burst came with the Dons leading 45-0 with 9:40 left in the fourth quarter. He shattered the single-game rushing mark of 304 yards with 351. Jason Linzmeier also set a single season TD reception record when he recorded his 10th touchdown catch before halftime. Passe also cited the outstanding play of Corey Langreck.

The Dons saved their homecoming game for the conference finale against Pacelli. Columbus was 4-0 and Pacelli 3-1 heading into the Friday night encounter. But the Cards suffered from too much Mike Weister as the shifty running back scored five TDs, leading to an unblemished conference championship with a 38-22 win. Weister broke more career records, this time for exceeding 200 yards in four games and 100 yards in eight games, including seven in a row. Every time Pacelli threatened in the second half, Weister countered with another touchdown. "He wouldn't take himself out of the game," his coach said. "He plays offense, defense, kickoff-return team, punt-return team... He's a good athlete and a good player." Passe also praised Jason Linzmeier and Pete Schueppert for their outstanding games. Linzmeier had three receptions for 97 yards, three interceptions, a 40-yard field goal, and went five-for-five on point-after kicks. Schueppert passed for 220 yards on only six completions.

Newman had officially been out of the CWCC for four years when they met the Dons in Marshfield for a first-round WISAA Division III playoff game. The result followed historical precedent with Columbus prevailing 48-0. Under first-year coach John Raflik, Newman entered the contest 7-2. The Wausau guests were unable to stop a three-touchdown first quarter by the Dons. The scores came within four minutes of each other. Schueppert had four TD passes. With 109 pass attempts on the year through the Newman game, he had been intercepted only four times. The Dons played the second half without all-rounder Jason Linzmeier, who was shaken up in the first half. Weister had 113 yards in the lopsided win. The 9-1 Dons hosted 7-3 Manitowoc Lutheran in round two of the playoffs the next Friday night. Weister did most of the damage for the navy-and-white, reeling off four TD runs between 12 and 31 yards in a 35-8 triumph. Weister's numbers were again on the eye-opening side: 267 yards on the ground and 107 via the air on four receptions. All but 28 of CHS's 402 total yards belonged to the sensational senior. The defense, anchored by linebackers Corey Langreck and Paul Scheuer, allowed only a fourth-quarter score. Senior end Joe Seubert hurt his knee in this game and would miss the state championship.

The championship game began at 11 a.m. Saturday morning at Camp Randall Stadium. It was another battle between Columbus and Pacelli. The Cards were defending champs and sported a 7-4 record. But the Dons dominated both sides of the line of scrimmage and had a 42-0 fourth-quarter lead with a running clock before the Stevens Point crew managed a score. The final was a shockingly easy 42-6 win. It was the fourth state football title in school history. Mike Weister, a 191-pound combination of speed and power, erupted for 218 yards on the ground and ran in, untouched, with a third-quarter 35-yard interception return to complete the scoring. "We've been together four years and it's been the best four years of my life," said Weister. Richie Seubert, who would play collegiately at Western Illinois and professionally for ten years with the New York Giants, added, "It's a sweet feeling. Last year was cut short and this year we were determined. It's such a nice team."

Ten seniors made their last appearance at Camp Randall: Nate Burger, Joel Hoerneman, Jason Linzmeier, Paul Scheuer, Peter Schueppert, Mike Seelen, Joe Seubert, Richie Seubert, Mike Weister, and Nick Yost. The team knew how to score. Their 423 total points rated as the second-highest in Columbus history, averaging 35.25 points a game. Leading the way with 37 touchdowns was Weister. The versatile running back scored touchdowns five different ways—by run, by reception, by interception return, by punt return, and by kickoff return. He also ran in three extra-point tries to give him 228 points. Only 15 of the previous 47 Columbus teams scored that many points in an entire season. Jason Linzmeier was a distant second but his 124 points would have garnered him the top slot in all but one other year (1965). His record-breaking 11 TD receptions in a season, coupled with his record-tying seven field goals, an extra-point pass reception, and 35 extra-point boots accounted for his total. Weister and Linzmeier did 83% of the team's scoring. The only other Dons to score in double figures were Joe Seubert (36) and Corey Langreck (18). Weister scored in each of his four years of high school, a rarity. The Dons filled nine slots on the All-CWCC team with five players. On offense, end Jason Linzmeier, halfback Mike Weister, quarterback Pete Schueppert, guard Richie Seubert, and tackle Mike Seelen were honored. Seubert (tackle), Weister (linebacker), and Linzmeier (back) were chosen on defense, making each a two-way pick. Linzmeier made it a personal triad with his selection as top place-kicker. Columbus snared all the annual awards, as well. Richie Seubert was named CWCC Lineman of the Year; Mike Weister, Back of the Year; and Tom Passe, Coach of the Year.

1996 CWCC Standings	W	L	TP	OPP
Marshfield Columbus	5	0	179	76
Chippewa Falls McDonell	3	2	34	36
La Crosse Aquinas	3	2	133	89
Stevens Point Pacelli	3	2	154	121
Eau Claire Regis	1	4	65	133
Wis. Rapids Assumption	0	5	56	171

1997: New Coach, Tough Times

After one of the most successful football seasons in Columbus history, these Dons proved to be a surprising contrast. In a pre-season survey, coaches picked Pacelli, McDonell, and Columbus as favorites to win the title. However, 1997 was about as different from 1996 as any two seasons could be. First, coach Tom Passe departed for graduate education at the University of North Dakota. A *News-Herald* story said Passe was headed to UND as an assistant coach for tight ends and tackles. "It's always been my goal to go up and get as high as I can," the 27-year-old said. The newspaper reported Passe's move to the college ranks had been in the works for about a year. But given the talented senior class he had returning for the 1996 campaign, he had wanted to coach Columbus for another season. But once the season concluded, Passe focused his search. "It's the right time in my life to do this," he said. Passe said the future of football at Columbus looked bright. Passe was replaced by Roger Capannelli, a Bemidji State University defensive backs coach. In addition to coaching with the Beavers for three years, Capannelli had also played at the northern Minnesota school for four years. He was one of the team's co-captains his senior year. At the time of his hire, Capannelli, an Ontario native, held the BSU record for longest field goal in school history. "I've been in college and now I want to begin in the high school ranks and see what I can do," he said. "I want to be in high school for a long time." Assisting Capannelli were second-year coach Ron Jevaltas and Pat Galligan.

Tailback Chris Fredrick and fullback Corey Langreck captained the squad. Sophomore Jacob Hansen got the starting nod at QB and 275-pound Matt Knauf anchored the line at center. Despite higher hopes, the Dons became one of only two Columbus teams to go winless. They finished 0-8. With the exception of the Assumption game, the contests were not close. The offense was ineffective, averaging a paltry 2.5 points per game, while the defense yielded 30.75 points. The 28.25-point gap between what they gave up and what they scored was the largest in school history.

The campaign started at home with traditional rival Nekoosa. The Papermakers pounded the Dons 42-0 with Paul Nistler Jr. scoring on a long-run four plays into the game. Nistler scored 24 points for Nekoosa, four more than the entire CHS team would garner all year. "Four touchdowns were from blown tackles," Capannelli observed. The new coach cited Josh Klumb and Chris Fredrick for their play. "I couldn't be happier with Klumb on both sides of the ball," he said. Nekoosa's Jedd Sorenson and Nistler combined for 215 yards rushing. Stratford humbled the Dons 35-0 at Beell the following Saturday night. Their stingy defense didn't allow any positive yardage in the second half. Columbus receivers didn't help matters by dropping a lot of Hansen's passes. Capannelli had introduced zone blocking to the Dons' arsenal. "Zone blocking is pretty simple," he said. "It's just executing. You have to realize who you are supposed to block." The coach praised the play of Chris Fredrick, Corey Langreck, and Matt Beck in the loss.

At Custer Stadium in Milwaukee the following Saturday, the Dons had an afternoon match with Milwaukee Washington. After grabbing a 16-0 lead, the Purgolders surrendered a 1-yard TD run to Fredrick before halftime. "We fell apart in the second half," Capannelli admitted. "Our guys go both ways. We were tired." The Dons headed back to Marshfield with the stinging 30-6 defeat fresh in their minds. Matt Knauf injured his shoulders and was lost for the season. On defense, Langreck, Fredrick, and Josh Klumb recorded 12 tackles each and Travis Bauer had 11 stops for the Dons. The rushing attack was led by Matt Beck with 71 yards and Chris Fredrick with 42. Assumption's homecoming game was settled with two Joe Hell field goals for the Royals. The 6-0 AHS victory was Assumption's first over Columbus since 1979.

The win also snapped Assumption's 20-game conference losing streak. With his face covered with tears, Hell said, "It's been so long. This is just so great." Though the Dons allowed only 86 yards, four interceptions on offense undermined them. The offense also squandered good field position throughout the first half. Capannelli remarked on the team's rough start: "They have a great attitude. They could have hung their heads, but our seniors have too much class for that."

Newman got the better of the Dons, 27-7, the next Saturday night in Marshfield. It was the first Cardinals win over the Dons since

1985. Justin Skrzpchak ran for 193 yards for Newman. Chris Fredrick ran in from 4 yards, then kicked the extra point, to narrow the gap to 13-7. Mike Ress hauled in a 50-yard pass from Jay Krambs to lengthen the lead to 20-7. The Wausau gridders were down to 21 players. Capannelli highlighted the play of his defensive line. "Marc Prepulah and Joe Schweikl have done a good job," he said. "But we've got to score some points for the kids' sake." The next Saturday afternoon the Dons hosted Regis for homecoming. The Ramblers spoiled the celebration with a 24-0 shutout. "Our kids are way down," Capannelli revealed. "You can see it in their eyes. We're just not executing. We had dropped passes and penalties on our receivers. I just think it's a lack of confidence."

The Dons ventured to Dorais Field in Chippewa Falls the next Saturday afternoon and emerged on the short end of a 40-0 tally with McDonell. Second-year coach Tom Swoboda was in the process of transforming the Macks into a power-running team behind their big offensive line. McDonell found themselves 6-2 overall and 4-0 in the conference after the win. "We started passing, but we dropped a lot of balls," Capannelli said. "They manhandled us up front." Arnie Swoboda scored four touchdowns and Bobby Swoboda kicked four extra points on the bright, breezy day. The elder Swoboda, coach Tom, sympathized with the Dons. "Columbus has a new coach who came in late and it takes time to get things going," he said. The season finale at Stevens Point found the Dons playing their best half of football despite trailing 14-0 at intermission. After two PHS third-quarter scores, Matt Beck bobbled the Pacelli kickoff. He scooped it, though, and raced 87 yards for the longest TD kickoff return in school history. The Dons finished winless for the first time since 1953. That team scored 14 points; this team scored 20 points.

Seniors Chris Fredrick, Robert June, Josh Klumb, Corey Langreck, and Joe Schweikl experienced the full spectrum of emotions in their four-year careers: two state championships, a .500 season, and now one of the roughest campaigns in program history. The scoring parade was more of a cortege. Matt Beck led with 12 points. Chris Fredrick scored 8. Fredrick's 44 career points were spread over each of his four years of play, allowing him to become the eighth member to ever join that notable group. Senior defensive end Josh Klumb was the lone Dons player selected for the All-CWCC team. His counterpart at the other end, Robert June, received honorable mention.

1997 CWCC Standings	W	L	TP	OPP
Chippewa Falls McDonell	5	0	113	21
Stevens Point Pacelli	4	1	133	58
Eau Claire Regis	3	2	108	54
Wausau Newman	2	3	107	100
Wis. Rapids Assumption	1	4	14	117
Marshfield Columbus	0	5	14	139

1998: The Knauf Era Begins

Columbus Athletic Director Joe Orella hired Tom Knauf to direct the 1998 team, saying, "He's been through 27 football seasons and I think that's something we're very fortunate to have at our school." A 1966 CHS graduate, Knauf was a star guard and linebacker with the Dons' 1965 scoring machine that went 8-1. Eighteen of his 27 coaching years saw him as head at Stratford (12 years) and Marshfield Senior High (six). His 1986 Stratford team won the state title. His most recent posting, as the University of Wisconsin-Stevens Point defensive line coach, helped him re-examine his approach. "Practices, once the regular season begins, will not feature hard hitting day in and day out. The other thing I learned is to calm down a little. You don't need to get excited about things. Kids are going to make mistakes."

Knauf only had 27 players to learn his new offense and defense. Wisely he inculcated those two dozen-plus players with the team's goal—to improve over the course of the season. Assisting him were Pat Galligan (receivers, defensive backs), Jim Conterato (offensive and defensive lines), Dave Knauf, Mike Schumitsch, and Rob Nelles. Columbus improved as the season wore on and the nuances of his plan became more ingrained. The Dons finished 1-8 overall and 1-4 in conference play. The 35-7 win over Newman ended the program's longest losing streak at 13. The offensive lineup featured QB Reed Horswill, halfback Matt Beck, and fullbacks Ben Fredrick and Josh Maurer. The receiving corps included Jake Hansen at wide receiver, Ted Nikolai at flanker, and Chris Seubert at tight end. Matt Knauf centered the line and was flanked by guards Matt Lang and Matt Schmitt, and tackles Scott June, Bryan Hanneman, and Andy Balderas.

For Knauf's CHS debut the Dons traveled to Nekoosa to meet Paul Nistler's well-oiled Papermakers squad. A 1997 WIAA playoff team, Nekoosa was loaded at the skilled positions and guard. The Nekoosa defense held the Dons to 65 total yards and two first downs. The Papermakers dominated, cruising to a 38-0 win. "I told the kids to keep it in perspective because Columbus is rebuilding their program," Nistler said. The next Friday night the Dons ventured 11 miles to Stratford. The Tigers jumped to a 28-0 lead. The Dons managed only 51 total yards and three first downs. Nate Lang led them with 15 yards in five trips. Meanwhile, Stratford used 11 rushers in their 35-0 win. Their coach Cal Tackes said middle linebacker Lee Spindler had a lot to do with stopping the Dons: "He really plugged things up and stopped their run."

In the home opener the next Saturday afternoon, Columbus hosted a large Milwaukee Washington team—large in player numbers and physical size. The Purgolders substituted freely on a hot, humid day at Beell Stadium and overpowered the Dons, 41-0. The inauspicious start was the worst three-game span in CHS history. The Dons yielded 114 points without seeing the end zone themselves. The 1953 squad experienced a similar string during games two through four, permitting 113 points without scoring. While the 1953 Dons were shutout five times during the season, this 1998 team found their offensive legs and were not blanked again. In the Milwaukee Washington loss Knauf cited the play of Ted Nikolai, Dan Treichel, Matt Beck, and both offensive and defensive lines. Washington used eight ball carriers in the lopsided win.

The Dons came up one yard short of victory the following Saturday night at Beell against Loyal. The *News-Herald* reported, "Jake

Hansen hauled in Reed Horswill's desperation pass on the game's final play, but he couldn't keep his feet and skidded down at the 1 as the game ended." The Greyhounds edged the Dons 22-20. CHS had trailed 22-6 with eight minutes left before their feverish comeback. Knauf said the biggest missed opportunity came late in the second quarter when the Dons drove to the 34-yard line but failed to convert on a fourth-and-1.

"That's the one we didn't get that was the difference," the coach said. Columbus led 6-0 at half but the Greyhounds stormed to touchdowns on their first three possessions of the second half. Jake Hansen and Josh Maurer led the CHS ground attack with 60 and 55 yards. The following Saturday afternoon, Vince Udo, Assumption's sophomore speedster, racked up 172 yards on 32 carries to propel the Royals to a 14-6 homecoming win over the Dons at Beell. Assumption marched down the field and scored on their first drive to set the tone. Again, the Dons only engineered 90 total yards and three first downs. "We get an effort out of some people, but we don't get it out of everybody all the time and that's the thing," Knauf said. The Dons' 13-game losing streak ended the next Saturday afternoon in Wausau when they bested Newman 35-7. "Productivity-wise, we had a better game from everyone. It was a situation where everyone was running on the same page for once," Knauf said. The defense shut down the Cardinals. Ben Fredrick ran for 102 yards on seven carries. Josh Maurer added 71 yards; Matt Beck, 49. "The kids were just excited about the whole thing," Knauf noted. "They were singing on the bus on the way home. It was something."

The Dons traveled to Eau Claire's Carson Park the next Saturday afternoon and got clipped 22-7. "The defense I thought played pretty fair. We made them work for everything," Knauf said. He credited the down linemen—John Geldernick, Dan Treichel, Matt Schmitt, Ted Nikolai, Matt Knauf, and Chris Seubert—for making it tough on the Ramblers. He also lauded the job of the CHS secondary (Matt Beck, Jake Hansen, and Chris Dike) in holding down star Regis receiver Nick Simon. Columbus was knocking on the door just before halftime when Mark Hawn picked off a Reed Horswill pass in the end zone. "We had to come away with something there," Knauf said. "That was a big turnaround."

The Dons found themselves ahead 10-0 after the first quarter the following Saturday afternoon on the friendly Beell Stadium turf. However, McDonell stormed to two second-quarter scores and another in the fourth frame to escape with an 18-13 win. Trailing 13-12 with time winding down, the Macks superb QB Bobby Swoboda found Bryan Dahl for a 9-yard TD reception with about three minutes left to take the lead for good. The junior signal-caller threw two other touchdowns passes and gained 219 yards in the air for McDonell. "We had a good effort from a lot of people," Knauf said. Ben Fredrick posted 134 yards rushing on 24 carries. Freshman QB Jon Poehnelt was another bright spot for the Dons. He threw for 42 yards on three completions in four tries.

The season finale against a strong Pacelli team (6-1, 4-0) got interesting early when Reed Horswill connected with Ted Nikolai on a 12-yard TD pass to close the gap to 7-6. Pacelli stomped on the gas pedal after that, and sped off with a no-doubt 42-6 victory. It was easy to see why the Cardinals led the conference in both offense and defense. PHS's only hiccup was getting flagged for 112 yards in penalties. Andy Cashin turned in a 174-yard rushing performance for the conference champions. Jake Hansen finished his Columbus career with 75 yards on the ground.

Five gallant seniors had the fortitude to stick with football through the thinnest times in the program's history: Andy Balderas, Matt Beck, Jacob Hansen, Matt Schmitt, and Chris Seubert. "The past two years, win/loss-wise, haven't been a great thing for them," Knauf said. "They've responded well. You couldn't ask for a better group of kids to work with." Six players scored the team's 87 points. For the second year in a row Matt Beck led (24 points), followed by Ted Nikolai (19), Ben Fredrick (18), Josh Maurer (12), Jake Hansen (8), and Reed Horswill (6). Two Dons made the All-CWCC squad. Linebacker Matt Beck was selected on defense and guard Matt Schmitt on offense.

1998 CWCC Standings	W	L	TP	OPP
Stevens Point Pacelli	5	0	188	18
Chippewa Falls McDonell	3	2	102	89
Eau Claire Regis	3	2	122	77
Wis. Rapids Assumption	3	2	77	89
Marshfield Columbus	1	4	67	103
Wausau Newman	0	5	33	213

1999: Farewell to the CWCC

1999 was the last year of both the Wisconsin Independent Schools Athletic Association and the Central Wisconsin Catholic Conference. Private schools would merge into the Wisconsin Interscholastic Athletic Association (WIAA) for the 2000-2001 school year. Columbus would become a member of the Marawood Conference. The Dons' last season in the CWCC was a competitive one. A tough defense allowed the Dons to stay in every game they played. Back-to-back non-conference road wins in Pepin and Loyal prepared the navy-and-white for the rigors of conference play. Not surprisingly, the last Dons CWCC victory would come over Wausau Newman, 49-0. While Columbus owned the Newman football team over the years, the Cardinals (then known as the Pioneers) won the first three match ups in the mid-1950s. With the 1999 game, the ledger stood at 37-5-1—an 87% CHS winning percentage. The squad finished 3-7 overall and 1-4 in conference play.

In the season opener at Beell, Nekoosa drove 92 yards on the opening drive to remind everyone they were 9-3 in 1998 and had almost upset Colby for the state championship. The Dons trailed 9-0 after three quarters. The Papermakers added two fourth-quarter scores within one minute of each other and came away a 23-0 winner. "We did a lot of things right," coach Tom Knauf said. The next Friday night, again at Beell, the Dons let a 9-6 lead on Stratford slip away with one minute left. Ted Nikolai's 19-yard field goal at the 1:19 mark gave Columbus a startling three-point lead—for two plays. "It was just one of those situations where we got ourselves ahead and that surprised us. We just weren't ready for it," Knauf said. Andy Weigel returned the ensuing kickoff to Stratford for 55 yards, down to the CHS 25-yard line. Chad Landwehr ran 25 yards for what proved to be the winning score on the Tigers' first play from scrimmage, allowing them to eke out a 13-9 victory. Stratford coach Cal Tackes admitted, "Tonight we got outplayed and found a way to win. I can't give enough credit to Columbus." Dons sophomore QB Jon Poehnelt, a first-quarter sub, had a solid game. Knauf gave a nod to his 18 years on the Stratford sidelines, saying, "It's fun to coach against a coaching staff I had a chance to work with for a number of years. You like to play good teams year after year because that's the only thing that's going to make you better." Josh Maurer rushed for 191 yards on 28 carries.

For the 32nd and final time the Dons played away against a Mississippi River foe. The Pepin Lakers provided the opposition on Saturday afternoon. The Dons emerged from the lowest point in their football history (1-18 in their past 19 games) with a resounding 33-15 win near the widest part of the muddy waters. Jon Poehnelt was successful in his first signal-calling start. He tossed two TDs, one to Ted Nikolai and the other to Dan Treichel. Matt Dick also ran for two scores in the team's first win of the year. The Dons made it two wins in a row Friday night at Loyal. They hadn't tallied back-to-back wins in three years. Columbus breezed to a 25-2 halftime lead. Poehnelt threw two more touchdown passes and Josh Maurer romped in on scoring runs of 13 and 29 yards. Maurer was also tackled for a safety. Both of coach Knauf's sons, Matt and Luke, sustained shoulder injuries. Matt, a senior, was lost for the year with a dislocated shoulder. The Dons defense continued their hard-nosed play. The final score was 39-8.

The Dons traveled to Wood County 2000 Field the next Saturday afternoon to face Assumption. Vince Udo, a stellar Royals running back, put his Wisconsin Rapids teammates on his back. His 4-yard run with eight minutes left was all Assumption needed in a 7-0 win. Assumption remained undefeated. Knauf said, "We didn't capitalize on some early opportunities and it came back to haunt us." Udo finished with 205 yards on the ground. The Dons evened their season mark at 3-3 with a solid 49-0 win over Newman the following Saturday night. A running clock was employed the entire second half because of the margin. Columbus had five TD runs of 39 yards or more in the Beell Stadium contest. Josh Maurer, Ben Fredrick, and Pat Michalski each ran for two TDs. Additionally, Maurer and Michalski had 137 and 120 rushing yards, respectively. Ted Nikolai was a perfect seven-for-seven on extra-point kicks. It would be the last CWCC win for Columbus. The following Saturday afternoon Nick Simon, Regis' six-two senior sensation, torched Columbus with three TD catches to spoil homecoming 21-14. Dons linemen tired as the game wore on; most played both ways. Simon's last TD catch with just under eight minutes left proved to be the winner. Regis departed Beell with a 5-1 mark. Josh Maurer notched 125 yards rushing for the Dons. Regis coach Chris O'Connell complimented the Dons. "Columbus is a real physical team, and we had a hard time rushing the ball in the middle of the game," he said.

In the battle of 1-2 CWCC teams, McDonell won 13-0 with two second-half touchdowns at Dorais Field in Chippewa Falls. The Saturday night back-and-forth affair came to life with senior Bobby Swoboda's 54-yard punt return to set up the Macks' first score. "Columbus is a good team," said McDonell coach Tom Swoboda. "We thought going in they were one of the best teams in the conference." Josh Maurer earned 121 yards on the ground in 20 attempts. On Friday night, a cold, late October wind whipped around Goerke Field in the CWCC finale for both Pacelli and Columbus. The Dons took a quick 6-0 lead. But the game's turning point was a Pacelli block of Ted Nikolai's third-quarter punt. Pacelli held a 14-6 lead at the time. Four plays later Pacelli freshman Ahern Cashin scored. In a final quest for victory, the Dons scored with 1:42 left and then recovered their onside kick. But Pacelli intercepted Poehnelt to end the threat and the regular season. Sloppy play was everywhere—133 yards in penalties, three turnovers, and two botched punts. "We've had some great games with Columbus and all the other teams in the 35 years that I've been here," said Pacelli coach Bob Raczek. Somehow the Dons' 3-6 mark got them an Eau Claire WISAA playoff appearance the following Friday night. Regis controlled the line of scrimmage and dominated the Dons 41-20. The Ramblers' 70-yard opening TD march set things in motion. "We doubled down on (Nick) Simon tonight," Knauf said. "But, when you cheat, you get burned in other areas." The Dons closed the gap to 27-20 in the third quarter but that was as close as they would get.

Dons seniors experienced a 15-24 football record in their four years of high school. The highs and lows included a state championship and a winless season. The seven seniors were Dave Adler, Chris Dike, Matt Knauf, Matt Lang, Josh Maurer, Ted Nikolai, and Dan Treichel. Seven individuals scored the team's 176 points. Ted Nikolai led with 48 (five TD receptions and 18 with his foot, including a 19-yard field goal). Josh Maurer ran for seven scores (42) and Matt Dick ran for four and caught one TD (30). Dan Treichel caught all his 20 points (three TDs and an extra-point pass). Pat Michalski (12), Ben Fredrick (12), and Jon Poehnelt (12) each ran for two touchdowns to complete the year's tally. Four Dons made the All-CWCC squad. The offensive honorees were senior running back Josh Maurer, senior center Matt Knauf, and junior guard John Geldernick. Senior defensive lineman Matt Lang was also recognized.

1999 CWCC Standings	W	L	TP	OPP
Eau Claire Regis	5	0	153	61
Stevens Point Pacelli	4	1	148	45
Wis. Rapids Assumption	3	2	116	79
Chippewa Falls McDonell	2	3	79	86
Marshfield Columbus	1	4	75	62
Wausau Newman	0	5	6	244

2000: Welcome to the Marawood

Columbus opened its football campaign in a new conference: the Marawood. The Dons were the perfect team, name-wise, for the new loop. They were the only community whose property lines were located in both counties, Marathon and Wood. Due to massive WIAA conference realignments taking place all over Wisconsin, four new teams were added to the league: Auburndale, Assumption, Newman, and Columbus. Unbeknownst to anyone at the time, 2000 would be the final season for Columbus High School football. Now in his third year at the helm, coach Tom Knauf guided the 2000 squad to a 5-4 record in nine conference games. That was good enough to make the WIAA playoffs against Necedah on the road. Unfortunately, the Dons would fall to a gifted Necedah squad in what was the last game ever played by a Columbus football team.

The Dons opened their first and last football seasons against the same team, Abbotsford. In 1950 CHS prevailed 19-0 at Beell; in 2000 the Falcons won 26-20 in Abby. The outcome was in doubt until the very end. The Dons drove from their own 34 to the Falcons' 17-yard line in the game's last two minutes. Pat Michalski's steal back of what looked like a sure Abbotsford interception kept the drive alive with a 20-yard gain. But Abby linebacker Tyler Beran intercepted a Jon Poehnelt pass in the end zone with six seconds left. "We found out we need to get in better shape," Knauf said. Tyler Kattre, Abbotsford's returning All-Marawood QB, left no doubt to onlookers why he had been chosen as the league's top signal-caller. The Edgar Wildcats had a lot going for them when they entertained the Dons the following Friday night. The list included a 29-game home winning streak, an overall 15-game winning streak, the 1999 WIAA Division 5 football championship crown, and a 35-0 opening game shutout of neighboring Marathon. The Dons didn't fare any better, bowing 31-0. CHS's opening drive proved to be their best offensive effort all night long. The drive faded at the Edgar 36 when Jon Poehnelt's fourth-down pass fell incomplete. Jordan Sinz's second-quarter 66-yard punt return TD was the turning point in the game. Edgar's balanced running attack deflated CHS as four different Wildcats crossed the goal line. Mike Wilke led the Dons with 32 rushing yards.

The third straight away game was a familiar venue for Columbus—Thom Field in Wausau. The Cardinals were just the balm the Dons were looking for in central Wisconsin's largest city. Both teams were 0-2 coming into the game. At half they were tied at zero. After another 10 scoreless minutes of play, the Dons exploded. Joey Altmann got things going with a 2-yard TD run. Justin Poehnelt scored two points for CHS when he corralled a Newman runner in the end zone for a safety. Ben Fredrick returned the ensuing Newman free kick 60 yards for another score. The sparkling 34-0 victory snapped CHS's six-game losing skid. Several freshmen and sophomores saw action as a flu bug kept many Columbus regulars from the gridiron. Remnants of the flu impacted the following Friday night game when the Dons played their home opener. After an initial Marathon second-quarter score, the Dons reeled off 27 straight points en route to a 27-14 win. Their first score just before halftime was set up by a 42-yard Ben Fredrick kickoff return. Jon Poehnelt hit Mark Loveland with a 23-yard scoring strike with just 17 seconds left before intermission to shift the game's momentum. Knauf said of running back Ben Fredrick, "It seemed like the more we gave him the ball, the stronger he got. He fought for a lot of the extra yards by twisting and turning. He had a great night and showed a lot of potential we knew he had." The Dons lost three players to injury during the game: John Geldernick, Matt Elderbrook, and Mark Loveland.

Assumption bolted to a 47-0 halftime advantage and graciously sat on that lead during the running-clock second half the following Friday night in Wisconsin Rapids. Cool, rainy conditions did not keep the Royals offense from scoring at will during the first two stanzas. Still missing three injured players and feeling the last effects of a three-week flu contagion, the under-manned Dons fell 47-0. Assumption coach Brian O'Donnell cited his team captain, Justin O'Shasky, for having an all-around big night. Six of seven AHS touchdowns came from 31 yards or more. The following Friday night the Dons played Pittsville, another Wood County opponent. It was the first time that Columbus played back-to-back away games at

Wood County high schools. In fact, it was only the third time the Dons faced fellow county schools on respective weekends. The 1954 and 1955 Columbus teams concluded their seasons with games against Pittsville Maryheart and Assumption. In 2000, there were eight Wood County high schools: Auburndale, Pittsville, Nekoosa, and Port Edwards in addition to the two public and two parochial schools in Marshfield and Wisconsin Rapids. The Dons came away with a spirited 14-12 win to spoil the PHS homecoming game. "The defense really stepped up tonight," Knauf said. "I was just really happy with the effort from our kids tonight." The aggressive defense stopped a pair of two-point conversion attempts. "You have to give credit to the Dons and their coaching staff," Panthers coach Rick Martin said. "They came out ready to play and we didn't."

The Dons upped their season mark to 4-3 the following Saturday afternoon at Beell with a convincing victory over Rib Lake/Prentice. The winless Hawks trailed the Dons 34-0 after two quarters, allowing the navy-and-white to coast to a 34-6 win. It marked the 300th win (in 486 games) in Columbus history. Knauf and his charges were enjoying a winning team mark for the first time since 1996. In addition to two Ben Fredrick and two Matt Dick rushing touchdowns, the Poehnelt-to-Loveland tandem hooked up for a 60-yard pass to finish Columbus scoring.

Friday the 13th of October proved to be the perfect homecoming game night. After Spencer narrowed the gap to 14-6 in the second quarter, the Dons responded with two TDs within 68 seconds to take a 28-6 halftime lead. Both scores were on Jon Poehnelt passes, one a 21-yarder to Matt Dick and the other a 20-yard strike to Bo Blenker. The Dons prevailed 42-14 on the strength of a good pass rush. "The score is no indication of the type of game this was," Knauf said. "This was a physical game. Spencer is a tough team and they played hard right to the end." With the win, the Dons' third in a row, Columbus qualified for the WIAA playoffs in their first year of eligibility. Defensive back Matt Elderbrook took the Marawood Conference lead with five interceptions despite missing half of the season due to a leg injury. At the time no one knew that this would be the last win in program history.

A 2-6 Athens squad came to Beell the following Wednesday night to conclude the regular season. Coach Joe Feldbruegge had his Bluejays raring to go for their last game of the year. Athens scored on their opening drive, an 18-yard Justin Gajewski run. The Dons also scored the first time they had the ball, on a 6-yard Mike Wilke run. Eric Kraus' extra-point kick made it 7-6. It stayed that way until Gajewski tallied again in the third quarter and then nabbed the two-point pass conversion to account for all his team's points in a stunning 14-7 Athens win. Knauf said Columbus lost the battle at the line of scrimmage. Gajewski ran for 147 yards but Mike Wilke countered with 117 yards on the ground for Columbus.

The Dons could have used momentum when they faced #1 seed Necedah. The Cardinals were 9-0 and 18-1 over the past two years. A Stratford playoff loss in 1999 was the lone blot on their ledger. Their #2 ranking in the state for Division 5 was well deserved. Ryan Seebruck ran 75 yards on the second play from scrimmage and Jason Jump intercepted a Poehnelt pass and ran it in for an 18-yard score 90 seconds later to put Necedah up 14-0 just two minutes into the game. The Scenic Bluffs Conference champions rolled to a 42-0 victory on their home field. Columbus had five turnovers but Ben Fredrick ended his Dons playing career with a stellar 111-yard night on the ground. When the players walked off the field on that Tuesday night, October 24, 2000, none of them knew they had just played the last contest in the 489-game history of Columbus High School football.

Seven seniors ended their careers with a 5-5 mark in 2000: Matt Dick, Matt Elderbrook, Ben Fredrick, John Geldernick, Scott June, Pat Michalski, and Justin Poehnelt. The final-season scoring parade was led by Ben Fredrick with 42 of the team's 178 points. Matt Dick added 30. Bo Blenker and Jon Poehnelt each had 20, followed by Eric Kraus (14), Jason Gorman (12), Mark Loveland (12), and Mike Wilke (12). No Dons were selected for the All-Marawood team. It marked only the second time that a Dons football team was blanked in post-season awards.

2000 Marawood Standings	W	L
Edgar	9	0
Auburndale	8	1
Wis. Rapids Assumption	8	1
Abbotsford	6	3
Stratford	6	3
Marshfield Columbus	5	4
Pittsville	4	5
Athens	3	6
Marathon	2	7
Spencer	2	7
Rib Lake/Prentice	1	8
Wausau Newman	0	9

Appendices

1. The CWCC

History

Marshfield was the first central Wisconsin city to erect a Catholic high school. It graduated its first class in 1952.

Catholic high schools in Wausau, Wisconsin Rapids, and Stevens Point soon followed. Initial play in the newly formed Central Wisconsin Catholic Conference (CWCC) occurred in 1956. Charter members were Columbus, Wausau Newman, Wisconsin Rapids Assumption, and Chippewa Falls McDonell.

The following year, 1957, Stevens Point Pacelli was added and McDonell dropped out. The four central Wisconsin schools remained conference anchors until McDonell re-joined in 1961.

The CWCC eventually built up to eight teams with the addition of Prairie du Chien Campion in 1963, Eau Claire Regis in 1964, and La Crosse Aquinas in 1965. The eight-team conference heyday lasted ten years.

While Columbus rightfully deserved to be called central Wisconsin's oldest Catholic secondary school, they couldn't lay claim as elder in the new octagonal alignment. For that, they were in the wrong century.

McDonell and Campion each traced their lineage to late 19th century starts—1883 in Chippewa Falls and 1880 in Prairie du Chien.

The Chippewa Falls school was the first to produce high school grads in 1889. It was then known as Notre Dame. It changed names to McDonell Central in 1907 when local lumberman Alexander McDonell provided building funds for a new school in the family's name. He did so in memory of his wife, the former Emily Regina O'Neil, who was a Notre Dame alum and three of their children.

Campion started as a college in 1880 and began operating as a high school in 1898. The boys boarding school peaked in the 1960's with just under 600 students. Its namesake, Edmund Campion (1541-1580), was a 16th-century Jesuit priest in England.

Eau Claire witnessed its first Catholic high school graduates in 1932 when the school was named St. Patrick's. When doors to a new campus opened in 1953 it was under the Regis aegis.

Aquinas High School in La Crosse was dedicated September 2, 1928. Four girls comprised the 1929 graduate list at the end of that school year.

Campion Academy's glorious 95-year history concluded in May 1975. The CWCC remained a seven-team confederation from 1975-1992. Newman decided to play an independent schedule starting with the 1992-1993 school year. The Cardinals remained outside the loop for four years.

Aquinas, anticipating the WIAA/WISAA merger slated for the 2000-2001 school year, joined the Mississippi Valley Conference for play in the 1997-98 school year. Newman took its place and the storied conference finished as a six-team assemblage until the curtains closed in May 1999 after 44 yards of athletic play.

Only Columbus and Assumption were league members all 44 years.

All-time team CWCC standings

Team	Years	W	L	T	Pct.	Titles	Solo titles
Aquinas	32	136	60	2	.692	9	6
Columbus	44	169	76	2	.688	15	10
Pacelli	43	139	100	5	.580	12	8
Assumption	44	116	130	1	.472	9	5
Regis	36	101	116	2	.466	4	3
Campion	12	36	44	1	.451	2	1
McDonell	40	96	137	2	.413	4	3
Newman	40	46	176	5	.214	1	1

There were 849 CWCC games played. Best-team-ever claims could be made by the inaugural 1963 Campion team and the 1983 and 1984 Aquinas juggernauts.

Best offensive teams (points per game scored):

43.0 ppg Campion (1963)
39.9 ppg Aquinas (1966)
38.5 ppg Columbus (1990)

Best defensive teams (points per game yielded):

1.0 ppg   Aquinas (1983)
1.4 ppg   Campion (1963)
1.5 ppg   Aquinas (1984)

50.5% of CHS's 489 games were CWCC encounters.

2. The Coaches

In sequential order	W	L	T	Pct.	Years
Marty Crowe	8	8	0	.500	2
Wally Wallschlaeger	3	4	1	.437	1
Earl Perkins	2	13	1	.156	2
Joe Milokna	13	9	0	.591	3
Gordy Clay	31	16	1	.656	6
Walt Kroll	219	99	2	.687	31
Tom Passe	16	6	0	.727	2
Roger Capannelli	0	8	0	.000	1
Tom Knauf	9	20	0	.310	3
Totals	301	183	5	.621	51
Kroll-coached teams	219	99	2	.687	31
Non-Kroll teams	82	84	3	.494	20

Year-by-year tally

Year	Record	Coach	CWCC record	conf. champion(s)
1950	3-5	Marty Crowe	n/a	n/a
1951	5-3	Marty Crowe	n/a	n/a
1952	3-4-1	Wally Wallschlaeger	n/a	n/a
1953	0-8	Earl Perkins	n/a	n/a
1954	2-5-1	Earl Perkins	n/a	n/a
1955	2-5	Joe Milokna	n/a	n/a
1956	4-4	Joe Milokna	2-1	Newman
1957	7-0	Joe Milokna	4-0	Columbus
1958	8-0	Gordy Clay	4-0	Columbus
1959	4-3-1	Gordy Clay	1-1-1	Assumption
1960	3-5	Gordy Clay	1-2	Assumption
1961	6-2	Gordy Clay	3-1	Assumption
1962	4-4	Gordy Clay	3-1	Pacelli
1963	6-2	Gordy Clay	4-1	Campion
1964	4-4	Walt Kroll	3-3	Assumption/Campion

1965	8-1	Walt Kroll	6-1	Assumption
1966	5-4	Walt Kroll	5-2	Assumption/Aquinas
1967	9-0	Walt Kroll	7-0	Columbus
1968	7-2	Walt Kroll	6-1	Regis
1969	5-4	Walt Kroll	4-3	McDonell
1970	6-2-1	Walt Kroll	6-1	Aquinas
1971	3-6	Walt Kroll	2-5	Pacelli
1972	4-5	Walt Kroll	4-3	Pacelli
1973	5-3-1	Walt Kroll	4-2-1	Assumption
1974	8-4	Walt Kroll	5-2	Col/Asn/Pac/Cam/Reg
1975	9-2	Walt Kroll	5-1	Columbus/Assumption
1976	7-3	Walt Kroll	4-2	Pacelli
1977	5-5	Walt Kroll	2-4	McDonell
1978	5-5	Walt Kroll	3-3	Pacelli
1979	6-4	Walt Kroll	3-3	Aquinas
1980	12-0	Walt Kroll	6-0	Columbus *
1981	9-3	Walt Kroll	5-1	Columbus/McDonell/Pacelli
1982	10-2	Walt Kroll	6-0	Columbus
1983	5-5	Walt Kroll	4-2	Aquinas
1984	6-4	Walt Kroll	4-2	Aquinas
1985	6-5	Walt Kroll	3-3	Regis
1986	8-3	Walt Kroll	5-1	Pacelli
1987	8-3	Walt Kroll	5-1	Columbus/Pacelli
1988	3-7	Walt Kroll	2-4	Aquinas
1989	6-5	Walt Kroll	4-2	Aquinas
1990	10-3	Walt Kroll	6-0	Columbus
1991	9-1	Walt Kroll	6-0	Columbus
1992	12-0	Walt Kroll	6-0	Columbus *
1993	9-2	Walt Kroll	5-0	Columbus
1994	10-2	Walt Kroll	4-1	Columbus */Pacelli/Aquinas
1995	5-5	Tom Passe	2-3	Pacelli
1996	11-1	Tom Passe	5-0	Columbus *
1997	0-8	Roger Capannelli	0-5	McDonell
1998	1-8	Tom Knauf	1-4	Pacelli
1999	3-7	Tom Knauf	1-4	Regis
2000	5-5	Tom Knauf	5-4	Edgar (Marawood Conf.)

Asterisk (*) = state championship season

3. The Historical Record

Dons record by decade

Decade	W	L	T	Pct.
1960s	57	28	0	.671
1980s	73	37	0	.666
1990s	70	37	0	.654
1970s	58	39	2	.596
1950s	38	37	3	.506
2000	5	5	0	.500
Total	301	183	5	.621

Playoff games

Year	Opponent	Venue	Score
1974	Milwaukee Thomas More	Hart Park, Wauwatosa	win 17-7
1974	Oshkosh Lourdes	Titan Stadium, Oshkosh	lose 15-14 (2nd)
1975	Fond du Lac Springs	Beell Stadium, Marshfield	lose 20-14
1980	Manitowoc Roncalli	Municipal Field, Manitowoc	win 17-13
1980	Waukesha Cath. Memorial	Beell Stadium, Marshfield	win 19-12 (champs)
1981	Fond du Lac Springs	Beell Stadium, Marshfield	win 21-10
1981	Milwaukee Thomas More	Titan Stadium, Oshkosh	lose 14-7 (2nd)
1982	DePere Abbott Pennings	Minahan Stadium, DePere	win 6-3
1982	Milwaukee Marquette	Titan Stadium, Oshkosh	lose 7-0 (2nd)
1985	Eau Claire Regis	Carson Park, Eau Claire	lose 19-13
1986	Chippewa Falls McDonell	Dorais Field, Chip. Falls	lose 21-14
1987	Eau Claire Regis	Beell Stadium, Marshfield	lose13-6
1989	DePere Abbott Pennings	Beell Stadium, Marshfield	lose 24-14
1990	Stevens Point Pacelli	Beell Stadium, Marshfield	win 19-14
1990	Manitowoc Lutheran	Beell Stadium, Marshfield	win 48-6
1990	Whitefish Bay Dominican	Camp Randall, Madison	lose 14-6 (2nd)
1991	Stevens Point Pacelli	Beell Stadium, Marshfield	lose 21-7
1992	Onalaska Luther	Beell Stadium, Marshfield	win 56-6
1992	Manitowoc Roncalli	Beell Stadium, Marshfield	win 44-6

1992	Stevens Point Pacelli	Camp Randall, Madison	win 28-10 (champs)
1993	Lake Geneva NW Prep	Beell Stadium, Marshfield	win 60-6
1993	Eau Claire Regis	Camp Randall, Madison	lose 14-0 (2nd)
1994	Watertown Prep	Beell Stadium, Marshfield	win 35-0
1994	Eau Claire Regis	Beell Stadium, Marshfield	win 17-0
1994	FdL Winnebago Lutheran	Camp Randall, Madison	win 6-0 (champs)
1995	Racine Lutheran	Horlick Stadium, Racine	lose 14-7
1996	Wausau Newman	Beell Stadium, Marshfield	win 48-0
1996	Manitowoc Lutheran	Beell Stadium, Marshfield	win 35-8
1996	Stevens Point Pacelli	Camp Randall, Madison	win 42-6 (champs)
1999	Eau Claire Regis	Carson Park, Eau Claire	lose 41-20
2000	Necedah	Necedah Athletic Field	lose 42-0

17-14 in playoff games; 11-4 at Beell Stadium.

4-5 in nine WISAA state championship games.

Overtime (OT) games

Year	Opponent	Venue	Score
1974	Aquinas	Beell Stadium, Marshfield	lose 22-14
1976	Pacelli	Goerke Field, Stevens Point	lose 17-14
1977	Pacelli	Beell Stadium, Marshfield	win 9-6 (2 OT)
1980	Catholic Memorial	Beell Stadium, Marshfield	win 19-12
1982	Pacelli	Goerke Field, Stevens Point	win 13-10
1983	Edgewood	Beell Stadium, Marshfield	lose 6-3
1983	Menominee (MI)	Beell Stadium, Marshfield	win 11-8 (2 OT)
1984	Newman	Beell Stadium, Marshfield	win 17-14
1986	Austin (MN)	Wescott Field, Austin	lose 12-6
1986	Marquette	Beell Stadium, Marshfield	win 27-24 (2 OT)
1987	Regis	Beell Stadium, Marshfield	lose 13-6
1993	Aquinas	Beell Stadium, Marshfield	win 7-6
1993	Regis	Beell Stadium, Marshfield	win 13-10

8-5 in overtime games, 3-0 in two overtime games.

Streaks

Longest winning streaks
17 games (1957-59)
14 games (1966-68)
13 games (1980-81)

Longest losing streaks
13 games (1997-98)
9 games (1952-53)

31 winning seasons

Year	Record
1951	(5-3)
1957	(7-0)
1958	(8-0)
1959	(4-3-1)
1961	(6-2)
1963	(6-2)
1965	(8-1)
1966	(5-4)
1967	(9-0)
1968	(7-2)
1969	(5-4)
1970	(6-2-1)
1973	(5-3-1)
1974	(8-4)
1975	(9-2)
1976	(7-3)
1979	(6-4)
1980	(12-0) *
1981	(9-3)
1982	(10-2)
1984	(6-4)
1985	(6-5)
1986	(8-3)
1987	(8-3)

5 undefeated seasons

Year	Record
1957	(7-0)
1958	(8-0)
1967	(9-0)
1980	(12-0)
1992	(12-0)

1989	(6-5)
1990	(10-3)
1991	(10-1)
1992	(12-0) *
1993	(9-2)
1994	(10-2) *
1996	(11-1) *

Asterisk (*) = WISAA state champions

Most team points in a game

Opponent	Year	Score
Campion	1974	68-0
St. Paul St. Agnes	1950	61-6
Assumption	1994	61-7
Newman	1992	61-14
Lake Geneva NW Prep	1993	60-6
Regis	1990	60-14
St. Paul Cretin	1965	59-14
Onalaska Luther	1992	56-6
McDonell	1993	56-13
Newman	1987	56-22
McDonell	1994	56-22
Newman	1981	55-0
Assumption	1981	55-0
Burlington Catholic	1996	52-0
Regis	1989	52-9
Assumption	1996	51-8
Milwaukee Francis Jordan	1968	51-22
Regis	1991	50-16
Newman	1988	50-26

Top 10 offensive teams (by points per game)

Year	Points scored	Games played	Average points per game
1992	434	12	36.17
1996	423	12	35.25

1994	364	12	30.33
1965	271	9	30.11
1990	381	13	29.31
1991	292	10	29.20
1980	345	12	28.75
1968	254	9	28.22
1967	234	9	26.00
1957	175	7	25.00

Top 10 defensive teams (by points allowed per game)

Year	Points allowed	Games played	Avg. pts. allowed per game
1957	32	7	4.57
1980	63	12	5.25
1958	46	8	5.75
1967	52	9	5.78
1982	95	12	7.92
1976	83	10	8.30
1994	103	12	8.58
1991	89	10	8.90
1964	72	8	9.00
1975	104	11	9.45

12 losing seasons

1950	(3-5)
1952	(3-4-1)
1953	(0-8)
1954	(2-5-1)
1955	(2-5)
1960	(3-5)
1971	(3-6)
1972	(4-5)
1988	(3-7)
1997	(0-8)
1998	(1-8)
1999	(3-7)

2 winless seasons

1953	(0-8)
1997	(0-8)

Biggest losses

Opponent	Year	Score
La Crosse Central	1953	53-0
Campion	1962	51-0
Assumption	2000	47-0
Pacelli	1989	43-0
Nekoosa	1997	42-0
Necedah	2000	42-0
Kenosha St. Joseph	1966	48-7
Milwaukee Washington	1998	41-0
McDonell	1997	40-0
Campion	1963	39-0

Note:

1953 team started with being shutout in their first five games; the 1952 team was shut out in their last game, i.e., the Dons were shut out in six straight games.

Dons record vs. opponents

Ten or more games	W	L	T	Pct.
Wausau Newman	38	5	1	.875
Wis. Rapids Assumption	33	14	0	.702
Chippewa Falls McDonell	31	15	0	.674
Stevens Point Pacelli	29	17	1	.628
Nekoosa	8	5	0	.615
Madison Edgewood	13	10	0	.565
Eau Claire Regis	23	20	0	.535
La Crosse Aquinas	17	15	0	.531
Prairie du Chien Campion	8	10	0	.444
Milwaukee Marquette	4	7	0	.364

4-10 games	W	L	T	Pct.
Ashland DePadua	6	0	0	1.000
Green Bay Preble	4	0	0	1.000
La Crosse Logan	4	0	0	1.000
Colby	5	1	0	.833

Mauston Madonna	4	1	0	.800
Mosinee	4	1	0	.800
Menominee (MI)	3	1	0	.750
Rhinelander	3	1	0	.750
La Crosse Central	2	2	0	.500
Milwaukee Thomas More	2	2	0	.500
Thorp	2	2	0	.500
Menasha St. Mary's	3	5	1	.389
Fond du Lac Springs	3	5	0	.375
DePere Abbott Pennings	1	6	0	.143

3 or fewer games	W	L	T	Pct.
Manitowoc Roncalli	3	0	0	1.000
Burlington Catholic Central	2	0	0	1.000
Manitowoc Lutheran	2	0	0	1.000
Onalaska Luther	2	0	0	1.000
Reedsburg	2	0	0	1.000
Two Rivers	2	0	0	1.000
Winneconne	2	0	0	1.000
Auburndale	1	0	0	1.000
Baraboo	1	0	0	1.000
Beaver Dam Wayland	1	0	0	1.000
Brussels Southern Door	1	0	0	1.000
Fond du Lac Winnebago Luth.	1	0	0	1.000
Lake Geneva NW Prep	1	0	0	1.000
Marathon	1	0	0	1.000
Medford	1	0	0	1.000
Milwaukee Francis Jordan	1	0	0	1.000
Milwaukee Marshall	1	0	0	1.000
Monroe	1	0	0	1.000
Oconomowoc	1	0	0	1.000
Oregon	1	0	0	1.000
Pepin	1	0	0	1.000
Pittsville	1	0	0	1.000
Plymouth	1	0	0	1.000
Rib Lake/Prentice	1	0	0	1.000
Watertown NW Prep	1	0	0	1.000

Waukesha Cath. Memorial	1	0	0	1.000
Pittsville Maryheart	1	0	1	.750
Abbotsford	2	1	0	.667
Kenosha St. Joseph	1	1	0	.500
Loyal	1	1	0	.500
Spencer	1	1	0	.500
Superior Central	1	1	0	.500
Milwaukee Rufus King	0	0	1	.500
Oshkosh Lourdes	1	2	0	.333
Antigo	0	1	0	.000
Athens	0	1	0	.000
Delafield St. John's Mil.	0	1	0	.000
Edgar	0	1	0	.000
Janesville Parker	0	1	0	.000
Necedah	0	1	0	.000
Portage	0	1	0	.000
Racine Lutheran	0	1	0	.000
Stanley	0	1	0	.000
Whitefish Bay Dominican	0	1	0	.000
Cudahy	0	2	0	,000
Green Bay Premontre	0	2	0	.000
Milwaukee Washington	0	2	0	.000
River Falls	0	2	0	.000
Little Chute St. John's	0	3	0	.000
Stratford	0	3	0	.000

Dons vs. Minnesota teams	W	L	T	Pct.
St. Paul St. Agnes	2	0	0	1.000
Caledonia	1	0	0	1.000
Rochester John Marshall	1	0	0	1.000
St. Paul Cretin	1	0	0	1.000
Rochester Loudes	1	1	0	.500
Wabasha St. Felix	1	1	0	.500
Apple Valley	0	1	0	.000
Austin	0	1	0	.000
St. Paul St. Thomas Academy	0	2	0	.000

Appendices

Dons vs. Michigan teams	W	L	T	Pct.
Menominee	3	1	0	.750

Dons vs. Iowa teams	W	L	T	Pct.
Waterloo East	2	0	0	1.000
Dubuque Wahlert	0	1	0	.000

Homecoming games

Year	Opponent	Result	Score
1950	Wabasha St. Felix	lose	22-13
1951	Rochester Lourdes	win	44-0
1952	Little Chute St. John	lose	19-0
1953	Menasha St. Mary	lose	6-0
1954	DePere St. Norbert	lose	31-0
1955	Wis. Rapids Assumption	win	13-6
1956	Little Chute St. John	lose	21-12
1957	Wis. Rapids Assumption	win	34-7
1958	Chippewa Falls McDonell	win	51-7
1959	Stevens Point Pacelli	win	20-7
1960	Wausau Newman	win	13-6
1961	Chippewa Falls McDonell	win	23-0
1962	Wausau Newman	win	25-0
1963	Wis. Rapids Assumption	win	13-6
1964	Prairie du Chien Campion	lose	25-12
1965	Stevens Point Pacelli	win	44-0
1966	La Crosse Aquinas	lose	26-6
1967	Eau Claire Regis	win	16-0
1968	Chippewa Falls McDonell	win	33-0
1969	Wis. Rapids Assumption	win	30-6
1970	Chippewa Falls McDonell	win	24-0
1971	Stevens Point Pacelli	lose	21-6
1972	Wausau Newman	win	6-0
1973	Eau Claire Regis	win	26-6
1974	Chippewa Falls McDonell	win	45-7
1975	Eau Claire Regis	win	13-7
1976	Chippewa Falls McDonell	win	33-7

1977	Wis. Rapids Assumption	lose	14-6
1978	Wausau Newman	win	49-14
1979	Wis. Rapids Assumption	lose	17-10
1980	Wausau Newman	win	35-0
1981	Wis. Rapids Assumption	win	12-7
1982	Chippewa Falls McDonell	win	9-6
1983	Wis. Rapids Assumption	win	13-10
1984	Wausau Newman	win (OT)	17-14
1985	Wis. Rapids Assumption	win	33-0
1986	La Crosse Aquina	win	7-6
1987	Wausau Newman	win	56-22
1988	Wis. Rapids Assumption	win	33-14
1989	La Crosse Aquinas	lose	25-0
1990	Chippewa Falls McDonell	win	43-8
1991	Eau Claire Regis	win	50-16
1992	Wis. Rapids Assumption	win	42-14
1993	Eau Claire Regis	win (OT)	13-10
1994	Wis. Rapids Assumption	win	61-7
1995	Eau Claire Regis	win	14-0
1996	Stevens Point Pacelli	win	38-22
1997	Eau Claire Regis	lose	24-0
1998	Wis. Rapids Assumption	lose	14-6
1999	Eau Claire Regis	lose	21-14
2000	Spencer	win	42-14

Overall Homecoming record: 37-14 (a 72.5% winning percentage)
From 1967-1996, the Dons sported a 26-4 mark in Beell Stadium Homecoming games.

4. Scoring Leaders

Total points

(Extra-point runs and passes counted as one point up until 1969 season)

Points	Name	Years scored	TDs	XP1	XP2	FG
370	Mike Weister	1993-96	60	--	5	--
237	Bob Koch	1963-65	39	3	--	--
206	Mike Scheuer	1991-94	34	--	1	--
196	Jim Moscinski	1950-52	32	4	--	--
191	Russ Truhlar	1956-58	30	11	--	--
189	Dick Stevens	1979-81	11	81	--	14
158	Rob Wagner	1979-81	26	--	1	--
155	David Herkert	1985-87	23	12	1	1
153	Steve Nugent	1988-91	24	1	4	--
148	Jason Linzmeier	1994-96	15	35	1	7
136	Justin Casperson	1990-92	22	--	2	--
128	Chuck Koch	1960-63	14	41	--	1
126	Pat Schueppert	1989-90	21	--	--	--
125	Mike Magistrelli	1989-91	10	61	1	--
120	Joe Henrichs	1974-76	20	--	--	--
120	Jon Radlinger	1979-80	20	--	--	--
118	Eric Heiting	1991-92	19	--	2	--
116	Aaron Rasmussen	1993-95	19	--	1	--
108	Bob Dickman	1972-74	11	28	1	4
108	Ryan Beck	1993-95	18	--	--	--
106	John Rasmussen	1981-83	7	35	2	9
104	Earl Miranda	1985-87	17	--	1	--
104	Joe McCormick	1987-88	17	--	1	--
102	Paul Mancl	1966-68	17	--	--	--
100	Gary Skaya	1978	16	--	2	--

Players scoring in all four years of their high school careers

Years	Name	Career points
1960-63	Chuck Koch	128
1970-73	Steve Seidl	65

1973-76	Tom Stangl	86
1978-81	Dick Stevens	189
1988-91	Steve Nugent	153
1989-92	Jeremy Maurer	56
1991-94	Mike Scheuer	206
1993-96	Mike Weister	370
1994-97	Chris Fredrick	44

Players scoring 100 or more points in a season

Year	Name	Points scored
1965	Bob Koch	132
1978	Gary Skaya	100
1981	Dick Stevens	103
1990	Pat Schueppert	120
1992	Justin Casperson	108
1996	Mike Weister	228
1996	Jason Linzmeier	124

Individual players recording a safety

(CHS also recorded nine team safeties)

Year	Name	Opponent
1953	Gayle Van Ert	Green Bay Catholic Central
1963	Corky Pueschner	Oshkosh Lourdes
1965	Dave Kraus	Eau Claire Regis
1969	Jim Perner	Wausau Newman
1979	Larry Olsen	Eau Claire Regis
1991	Adam Michalek	Stevens Point Pacelli
2000	Justin Poehnelt	Wausau Newman

Fumble recovery touchdowns

Year	Name	Yards & Opponent
1968	Tom Seidl	68 yards vs. Assumption
1970	Greg Higgins	in endzone vs. Assumption
1975	Jim Braem	32 yards vs. Onalaska Luther

1978	Dave Fait	in endzone vs. Aquinas
1980	Larry Olsen	18 yards vs. Auburndale
1982	Steve Jones	2 yards vs. Menominee (MI)
1987	Todd Maurer	in endzone vs. Assumption
1988	Tom Weister	30 yards vs. St. Paul St. Thomas
1991	Steve Nugent	41 yards vs. Regis
1994	Ryan Beck	86 yards vs. Regis
1994	Daryl Konrardy	in endzone vs. McDonell

Scoring leaders (continued)

261 Dons scored for their alma mater

Points	Name	Years scored
98	Brian Fehrenbach	1972-74
94	Steve Scheuer	1988-89
93	Scot Cook	1993-94
87	Jeff Rasmussen	1968-70
86	Don Gust	1958-59
86	Lloyd Hoffman	1963-65
86	Dan Maurer	1965-67
86	Tom Stangl	1973-76
84	Dave Drach	1968-69
84	Jeff Morzinski	1970-71
82	Kevin Ahmann	1991-92
78	Warren Rhyner	1960-61
76	Chris Zygarlicke	1976-78
73	Pat O'Reilly	1957-59
72	John Michalski	1982-84
72	Ben Fredrick	1998-00
69	Tom "Sid" Seidl	1966-67
67	Ted Nikolai	1988-99
66	Steve Jones	1981-82
65	Steve Seidl	1970-73
62	Steve Burr	1972-74
62	Larry Olsen	1979-80
62	Al Talens	1990-92
61	David Scheuer	1985-87

60	Matt Dick	1999-00
57	Terry Mancl	1966-67
56	Jeremy Maurer	1989-92
55	Scott Kundinger	1988-90
54	Jim Weister	1960-62
54	Ed Sheahen	1971
54	Josh Maurer	1998-99
51	Pat Earll	1986-87
50	Jerry Wilkins	1950-51
50	Aaron Dix	1955-57
49	Larry Meress	1960-61
48	Steve McMillan	1969
44	Dave Weber	1964-65
44	Ray Scheuer	1968-69
44	Joel Weigel	1974
44	Ross Gliniecki	1988-89
44	Chris Fredrick	1994-97
42	Mike Dumas	1962-63
42	Al Nikolai	1975-76
42	Dave Fait	1978-79
42	Tom McCormick	1988-89
41	Brian Morgan	1978, 1980-81
40	Andy Pankratz	1987-89
40	Nate Bennington	1992-93
38	Dean Dix	1974-75
38	Kevin Kennedy	1979-80
38	Craig Duellman	1982-83
38	Scott Herkert	1984-85
38	Mike McCormick	1990
38	Adam Michalek	1991
36	Jack O'Reilly	1954-55
36	Bill Bymers	1962
36	Walt "Buster" Sexton	1965-66
36	Jim Hastreiter	1972
36	Ron Swenson	1972
36	Rick Coleman	1974
36	Mark Meyers	1974-75

36	Chuck Hagman	1975-76
36	Steve Meyers	1981, 1983
36	Bill Saviage	1984
36	Todd Maurer	1986-87
36	Craig Lewin	1987-89
36	Joe Seubert	1996
36	Matt Beck	1997-98
32	Chuck Aschenbrenner	1959-60
32	Roger Goldbach	1966
32	Bill "Sudsy" Seidl	1968-69
32	Eric Helms	1985-86
32	Jon Poehnelt	1999-00
31	Bob Schriendl	1951
30	Dave Draxler	1972-73
30	Bruce Norfleet	1974-76
30	John Bersalona	1982
30	Hap Wolfgram	1982-83
30	Mark Mineau	1993
30	Brain McCormick	1994
29	Mark Rae	1981-83
27	Bill Draxler	1967-68
26	Doug Koenig	1957-58
26	Willy Wilcott	1966-67
26	John Adler	1969-70
26	Scott Radlinger	1977
26	Craig Eckes	1993
24	Jim Heinzen	1956-57
24	Pat Johnson	1958, 1960
24	Gary Heiting	1970
24	Wayne Zygarlicke	1975
24	John Olsen	1981
24	Chris Zukowski	1981-82
24	Dan Zygarlicke	1984-85
21	Jim Wein	1958-60
20	Jerry Cherwinka	1950, 1952
20	Ron LaBlanc	1951
20	Vik Vakoc	1955-57

20	Tom Hoff	1956-57
20	Tom Draxler	1972-73
20	Dan Treichel	1999
20	Bo Blenker	2000
19	Bob Mendyke	1950
19	Earl Schlagenhaft	1956-57
19	Jim Morzinski	1967-68
18	Charley Schlagenhaft	1956
18	Ron Maurer	1959
18	Jim Smrecek	1972
18	Frank Baltus	1979
18	Tom Bores	1990
18	Kevin McCormick	1992
18	Daryl Konrardy	1993-94
18	Corey Langreck	1996
18	Pat Michalski	1999-00
17	Ken Kraus	1975
16	Dick Grall	1956
16	John Kleiber	1966
16	Paul Blum	1966, 1968
16	Paul Fehrenbach	1977-78
15	Don Pueschner	1965
14	Pat Esselman	1952
14	Steve Varney	1968-69
14	Tim Dickrell	1975-77
14	Pete Schueppert	1995-96
14	Jacob Hansen	1996-97
14	Eric Kraus	2000
13	Ron Wipfli	1953-54
13	Mike Weber	1960
13	Eddie Fischer	1964
12	Don Flisakowski	1950
12	Jerry Schirpke	1950-51
12	Don Cherf	1950-51
12	Gene Greenwald	1955
12	Bob Keller	1958-59
12	Mert Fischer	1959

Appendices

12	Ralph Jensen	1959
12	Dan Hughes	1959-60
12	Jack Morzinski	1962
12	Bob Vobora	1965-66
12	Kurt Koenig	1968-69
12	Jim Stangl	1970-71
12	Tom Umhoefer	1974-75
12	Tom Huber	1977
12	Chuck Krier	1979
12	Tom Nikolai	1980
12	Lee Pritzl	1984-85
12	Mike Brown	1985
12	Scott Reigel	1986
12	Tom Weister	1987-88
12	Pat Scheuer	1987-88
12	Jason Hertel	1991
12	Andy Dean	1993-94
12	Joe Backaus	1994
12	Mike Wilke	2000
12	Mark Loveland	2000
12	Jason Gorman	2000
11	Jim Bloczynski	1980-81
8	Dave Kraus	1964-65
8	Bill Uthmeier	1971
8	Dave Meyers	1977
8	Tom Kraus	1980-81
8	Ryan Beaver	1989, 1991
7	Bernie Schlagenhaft	1955
7	Bill Heiting	1965-66
7	Mark Smith	1967
6	Elmer Schreiner	1950
6	Paul Umhoefer	1951
6	Don Fischer	1952
6	Jack Kandzela	1952
6	Clarence Blattler	1953
6	Jerry Ledger	1954
6	Bob Baer	1956

6	Mike Wallschlaeger	1960
6	Jim Kundinger	1960
6	Denny Desbrow	1960
6	Tom Heinzen	1960
6	Denny Blum	1962
6	Dan Carsten	1963
6	Denny Goeres	1964
6	Tom Knauf	1965
6	Curt Kaiser	1967
6	Al Hartl	1968
6	Greg Higgins	1970
6	Don Oppman	1972
6	Dave Jaye	1972
6	Clarence Hartl	1973
6	Roger Trudeau	1973
6	Pat Wolf	1974
6	Jim Yaeger	1974
6	Jim Braem	1975
6	Pat Connaughty	1977
6	Brian Rasmussen	1977
6	John Pritzl	1977
6	Tim Connaughty	1979
6	Rick Ploen	1980
6	Joe Baierl	1981
6	Mike Saviage	1982
6	Doug Nikolai	1982
6	John Werner	1984
6	Shawn Carlson	1984
6	Joe Bersalona	1985
6	Mike Earll	1985
6	Jim Pankratz	1986
6	Chris Hendler	1986
6	Sam Zwaschka	1988
6	John Kohlbeck	1988
6	Garret Seebandt	1989
6	Peter Taddy	1989
6	P. J. Wilcott	1991

Appendices

6	Steve Burger	1992
6	Ben Knauf	1995
6	Reed Horswill	1998
6	Joey Altmann	2000
5	Mike Colby	1968
4	Mike Rasmussen	1977-78
3	Nate Albee	1994
2	Gayle Van Ert	1953
2	Corky Pueschner	1963
2	Jim Perner	1969
2	Rich Seubert	1996
2	Luke Knauf	2000
2	Justin Poehnelt	2000
1	Dave Holland	1955
1	Arnold Bevar	1956
1	Tom Pankratz	1958
1	Paul Adler	1959
1	Dave Langreck	1965
1	Jim Haselberger	1967
1	Ed Smrecek	1967
1	Rick Derge	1974
1	Joe Selner	1978
1	Rocky Schueppert	1991

5. Rushing Leaders

Rushing touchdowns

Name	Total	Year(s) TDs scored
Mike Weister	45	1993-96
Bobby Koch	34	1963-65
Mike Scheuer	30	1993-96
Rob Wagner	26	1979-81
Russ Truhlar	22	1956-58
Jon Radlinger	20	1979-81
Justin Casperson	20	1990-92
Pat Schueppert	18	1990
Steve Nugent	17	1989-91
Eric Heiting	17	1991-92
Joe Henrichs	16	1974-76
Aaron Rasmussen	16	1993-94
Gary Skaya	15	1978
Earl Miranda	15	1985-87
Ryan Beck	15	1993-95
Chuck Koch	14	1961-63
Jeff Rasmussen	14	1968-70
Jeff Morzinski	14	1969-70
David Herkert	14	1986-87
Warren Rhyner	13	1960-61
Lloyd Hoffman	13	1963-65
Joe McCormick	13	1987-88
Steve Scheuer	13	1989
Jim Moscinski	12	1950-52
Chris Zygarlicke	11	1976-78
Dick Stevens	11	1981
John Michalski	11	1983-84

*Many with ten and below

Career	45	Mike Weister (1993-96)
Season	26	Mike Weister (1996)
Game	5	Bob Koch (1965) and Mike Weister (1996)

Rushing yards

Career	3362	Mike Weister (1993-96)
Season	2353	Mike Weister (1996)
Game	351	Mike Weister (1996)

Most carries

Career	505	Rob Wagner (1979-81)
Season	283	Mike Weister (1996)
Game	42	Steve McMillan (1969) and Steve Scheuer (1989)

Longest TD run

99 yards	Bob Koch (1965)

200-yard ground games

351 yards	Mike Weister (1996) vs. Burlington Catholic
304 yards	Bob Koch (1965) vs. Pacelli
299 yards	Mike Weister (1996) vs. Aquinas
294 yards	Steve Scheuer (1989) vs. McDonell
292 yards	Bob Koch (1965) vs. St. Paul Cretin
277 yards	Ryan Beck (1995) vs. Assumption
275 yards	John Michalski (1984) vs. McDonell
267 yards	Mike Weister (1996) vs. Manitowoc Lutheran
257 yards	Bob Koch (1965) vs. Madison Edgewood
257 yards	Joe McCormick (1988) vs. Newman
239 yards	Mike Weister (1996) vs. Pacelli
238 yards	Justin Casperson (1992) vs. Onalaska Luther
236 yards	David Herkert (1987) vs. Assumption
218 yards	Mike Weister (1996) vs. Pacelli (Camp Randall)
209 yards	Rob Wagner (1981) vs. Menasha St. Mary's
204 yards	Steve McMillan (1969) vs. Newman
204 yards	Wayne Zygarlicke (1975) vs. Onalaska Luther
200 yards	John Michalski (1984) vs. Madison Edgewood

1,000-yard rushing seasons

Year	Name	Yards	Games	Average per game
1996	Mike Weister	2,353	12	196
1965	Bob Koch	1,648	9	183
1984	John Michalski	1,326	10	133
1981	Rob Wagner	1,247	12	104
1992	Eric Heiting	1,181	12	98
1989	Steve Scheuer	1,061	11	96
1987	David Herkert	1,033	11	94
1990	Pat Schueppert	1,182	13	91
1980	Rob Wagner	1,068	12	89

6. Passing Leaders

Touchdown passes

Name	Total	Year(s) TDs thrown
Mike Magistrelli	30	1989-91
Mike Scheuer	28	1992-94
Bill Draxler	23	1966-68
Dave Draxler	22	1971-73
Pete Schueppert	22	1995-96
Dean Dix	21	1974-75
Brian Morgan	20	1979-81
Eric Helms	20	1985-87
Jon Poehnelt	16	1999-00
Paul Umhoefer	15	1950-52
Mark Rae	13	1982-83
Chuck Koch	12	1961-63
Andy Pankratz	12	1988-89
Bruce Norfleet	10	1975-76
Aaron Dix	9	1955-57
Jim Stangl	8	1970-71
David Scheuer	8	1986-87
Tom Zukowski	7	1978
Doug Koenig	6	1958
Steve Varney	6	1969
Ralph Jensen	5	1959
Dave Weber	5	1964-65
Tim Connaughty	4	1979
Pat Schueppert	4	1988

*Many with three and below

Career	30	Mike Magistrelli (1989-91)
Season	18	Pete Schueppert (1996)
Game	5	Bill Draxler (1967) and Dean Dix (1974)

Passing yards

Career	2605	Mike Magistrelli (1989-91)
Season	1464	Mike Magistrelli (1990)
Game	238	Paul Umhoefer (1950)

Most completions

Career	172	Mike Scheuer (1991-94)
Season	84	Mike Scheuer (1993)
Game	15	Paul Umhoefer (1950)

Most attempts

Career	344	Mike Scheuer (1991-94)
Season	171	Mike Magistrelli (1990)
Game	33	Pete Schueppert (1995)

Longest TD pass

94 yards	Mike Magistrelli (1990)

Most interceptions thrown

Career	24	Andy Pankratz (1987-89)
Season	18	Jacob Hansen (1997)
Game	5	Jim Stangl (1970), Andy Pankratz (1988), Pat Schueppert (1988), Jacob Hansen (1997)

1,000-yard passing seasons

Year	Name	Yards	Games	Average per game
1950	Paul Umhoefer	1,087	8	136
1968	Bill Draxler	1,161	9	129
1990	Mike Magistrelli	1,464	13	113
1993	Mike Scheuer	1,210	11	110
1996	Peter Schueppert	1,209	12	101
1980	Brian Morgan	1,059	12	88

7. Receiving Leaders

Touchdown receptions

Name	Total	Year(s) TDs caught
Jason Linzmeier	15	1994-96
Jim Moscinski	13	1950-52
Bob Dickman	11	1972-74
Brian Fehrenbach	10	1973-74
Steve Jones	10	1981-82
Paul Mancl	9	1967-68
Ed Sheahen	9	1971
Scott Kundinger	9	1989-90
David Herkert	8	1985-87
David Scheuer	8	1985-87
Jerry Wilkins	7	1950-51
Al Nikolai	7	1975-76
John Rasmussen	7	1982-83
Tom McCormick	7	1988-89
Russ Truhlar	6	1956-58
Mike Dumas	6	1962-63
Chuck Hagman	6	1975-76
Dave Fait	6	1978-79
Scott Herkert	6	1984-85
Michael McCormick	6	1990
Adam Michalek	6	1991
Nate Bennington	6	1992-93
Ted Nikolai	6	1998-99
Kevin Kennedy	5	1980
Todd Maurer	5	1986-87
Mark Mineau	5	1993
Brian McCormick	5	1994
Mike Weister	5	1995-96
Dave Drach	4	1968
Ray Scheuer	4	1968-69
Joe McCormick	4	1988
Steve Nugent	4	1990-91

| Joe Seubert | 4 | 1996 |
| Matt Dick | 4 | 1999-00 |

*Many with three and below

Most TD receptions

Career	15	Jason Linzmeier (1994-96)
Season	11	Jason Linzmeier (1996)
Game	3	Paul Mancl (1967, 1968)
		Ed Sheahen (1971)
		Frank Baltus (1979)
		Adam Michalek (1991)
		Jason Linzmeier (1996)

Most receptions

Career	60	David Scheuer (1985-87)
Season	42	Ed Sheahen (1971) and Nate Bennington (1993)
Game	8	Ed Sheahen (1971)
		Ed Sheahen (1971)
		Tom Kraus (1981)
		Scott Kundinger (1990)

Most reception yardage

Career	900	David Scheuer (1985-87)
Season	696	Jason Linzmeier (1996)
Game	167	Paul Mancl (1968)

Longest TD reception

| Game | 94 yards | Steve Nugent (1990) |

8. TD Return Leaders

Kickoff returns

Name	Year	Yards
Russ Truhlar	1957	85
Paul Mancl	1968	85
Bill "Sudsy" Seidl	1969	83
Mike Weister	1996	81, 86
Matt Beck	1997	87

Career	2	Mike Weister
Season	2	Mike Weister (1996)
Game	1	five tied
Longest	87	Matt Beck (1997)

Punt returns

Name	Year	Yards
Jim Moscinski	1951	55, 75, 70, 60, 50
Jack O'Reilly	1958	77
Bob Koch	1964	73
Bob Koch	1965	97
Dave Weber	1965	75
Dan Maurer	1966	60
Walt "Buster" Sexton	1966	55
Paul Mancl	1967	64
Tom "Sid" Seidl	1967	45
Steve McMillan	1969	50
Ron "Sonny" Swenson	1972	82
Brian Fehrenbach	1973	67, 67, 57
Brian Fehrenbach	1974	69, 80
Tom Stangl	1975	55
Tim Connaughty	1979	64
Kevin Kennedy	1979	60
Doug Nikolai	1982	52

Pat Schueppert	1990	60
Steve Nugent	1991	63
Mike Scheuer	1994	72, 53
Mike Weister	1995	83
Mike Weister	1996	64, 75, 62, 47, 39

Career	6	Mike Weister
Season	5	Jim Moscinski (1951) and Mike Weister (1996)
Game	2	Jim Moscinski (1951) and Mike Weister (1996)
Longest	97	Bob Koch (1965)

Free-kick returns

Name	Year	Yards
Jerry Schirpke	1950	40
Jim Bloczynski	1981	67
Ben Fredrick	2000	60

*Note: Schirpke's return was from his own free kick.

Longest	67	Jim Bloczynski (1981)

9. Interception TD Returns

Name	Year	Yards
Jim Moscinski	1950	55
Don Flisakowski	1950	15
Elmer Schreiner	1950	25
Jerry Schirpke	1951	50
Jim Moscinski	1952	30
Jack O'Reilly	1954	45
Russ Truhlar	1956	52
Vik Vakoc	1956	35
Pat O'Reilly	1958	31
Ron Maurer	1959	85*
Jack Morzinski	1962	50
Mike Dumas	1963	50
Bob Vobora	1965	60
Dan Maurer	1967	24
Tom "Sid" Seidl	1967	35
Dave Drach	1968	55
Dave Drach	1968	35
Ray Scheuer	1968	45
Ray Scheuer	1968	55
John Adler	1969	endzone
Tom Draxler	1973	26
Scott Radlinger	1977	85*
Rick Ploen	1980	24
Mike Saviage	1982	60
Shawn Carlson	1984	70
Eric Helms	1985	46
David Herkert	1985	50
David Scheuer	1986	15
David Scheuer	1987	50
Ross Gliniecki	1989	30
Andy Pankratz	1989	35
Steve Nugent	1989	26
Pat Schueppert	1990	28
Al Talens	1992	48

Jeremy Maurer	1992	34
Aaron Rasmussen	1994	50
Ryan Beck	1994	45
Mike Weister	1995	41
Ryan Beck	1995	75
Joe Backaus	1995	42
Mike Weister	1996	35
Joe Seubert	1996	32
Matt Dick	2000	10
Jason Gorman	2000	10

Longest interception TD return

85 yards   Ron Maurer
             Scott Radlinger

Most career int TD returns

2   Jim Moscinski
             Dave Drach
             Ray Scheuer
             David Scheuer
             Ryan Beck
             Mike Weister

Most in a game

2   Dave Drach

10. Place-kickers

Name	Year(s)	XP	FG	Distance(s)
Ron Wipfli	1954	1	--	--
Paul Adler	1959	1	--	--
Chuck Koch	1960-63	40	1	32
Don Pueschner	1965	15	--	--
Ray Scheuer	1968	8	--	--
Mike Colby	1968	5	--	--
Steve Seidl	1970-73	47	4	30, 22, 26, 24
Tom Stangl	1973-76	41	3	28, 27, 26
Bob Dickman	1974	28	4	27, 23, 24, 24
Rick Derge	1974	1	--	--
Ken Kraus	1975	2	5	39, 37, 37, 37, 27
Tim Dickrell	1975-76	2	--	--
Denny Sternweis	1977	2	--	--
Mike Rasmussen	1977-78	4	1	22
Brian Morgan	1978	1	--	--
Joe Selner	1978	1	--	--
Dick Stevens	1978-81	81	14	40, 38, 31, 31, 28, 28, 28, 27, 26, 26, 24, 21, 21, 19
Jim Bloczynski	1980-81	3	1	26
Mark Rae	1981	1	--	--
John Rasmussen	1981-83	35	9	43, 37, 36, 29, 27, 26, 22, 22, 20
Bill Saviage	1984	11	4	36, 27, 22, 20
David Herkert	1985, 1987	12	1	24
David Scheuer	1985	1	--	--
Pat Earll	1986-87	17	4	25, 26, 22, 30
Steve Scheuer	1988	10	--	--
Andy Pankratz	1988	2	--	--
Scott Kundinger	1988	1	--	--
Steve Nugent	1988	1	--	--
Mike Magistrelli	1989-91	61	--	--
Peter Taddy	1989	6	--	--
Kevin Ahmann	1991-92	55	7	40, 28, 18, 32, 25, 30, 35
Rocky Schueppert	1991	1	--	--

Scot Cook	1993-94	57	4	24, 24, 32, 29
Nate Albee	1994	3	--	--
Chris Fredrick	1995-97	26	--	--
Jason Linzmeier	1996	35	7	30, 25, 24, 30, 37, 40, 40
Ted Nikolai	1998-99	22	3	20, 21, 19
Eric Kraus	2000	12	--	--
Luke Knauf	2000	2	--	--

Longest field goal

43 yards   John Rasmussen

All-time leaders

Name	XP kicks	Field goals	Total kick points
Dick Stevens	81	14	123
Kevin Ahmann	55	7	76
Scot Cook	57	4	69
John Rasmussen	35	9	62
Mike Magistrelli	61	--	61
Steve Seidl	47	4	59
Jason Linzmeier	35	7	56
Tom Stangl	41	3	50
Chuck Koch	40	1	43
Bob Dickman	28	4	40
Ted Nikolai	22	3	31
Pat Earll	17	4	29
Chris Fredrick	26	--	26
Bill Saviage	11	4	23
Ken Kraus	2	5	17
Don Pueschner	15	--	15
David Herkert	12	1	15
Eric Kraus	12	--	12
Steve Scheuer	10	--	10

11. All-CWCC Football Selections

Columbus HS All-Conference players

(defensive team selections began in 1968)

Year	Name	Off position	Def position
1956	Vik Vakoc	E	
	Russ Truhlar	RB	
	Bernie Eilers	G	
	Chuck Fellenz	C	
	Charlie Schlagenhaft	RB	
1957	Vik Vakoc	T	
	Russ Truhlar	RB	
	Tom Hoff	E	
	Aaron Dix	QB	
	Larry Dick	G	
1958	Russ Truhlar	RB	
	Pat O'Reilly	RB	
	Mike Biechler	G	
	Leo Fellenz	C	
1959	Pat O'Reilly	RB	
	Leo Fellenz	C	
1960	Russ Adler	T	
1961	Mike Weber	E	
	Larry Meress	RB	
	Warren Rhyner	RB	
1962	Chuck Koch	QB	
	Mike Dumas	E	
	Bill Bymers	RB	
1963	Chuck Koch	QB	
	Mike Dumas	E	
1964	Bob Koch	RB	
	Lloyd Hoffman	RB	
1965	Bob Koch	RB	
	Lloyd Hoffman	RB	
	Tom Knauf	G	
1966	Dave Kraus	C	

Year	Name	Pos	Pos2
1967	Dan Maurer	RB	
	Paul Sinn	T	
1968	Jim Haselberger	G	LB
	Jim Morzinski	E	
	Bill Draxler	QB	
	Paul Mancl	RB	
	Dave Drach		DB
	Ed Smrecek		DL
1969	Bob Rose	T	DL
	Steve McMillan		LB
	Bill Seidl		DB
1970	Bob Rose	T	DL
	John Adler		DE
	Gary Mech		LB
1971	Ed Sheahen	E	
	Jeff Morzinski	RB	
	Bill Uthmeier		LB
1972	No selections		
1973	Dave Draxler	QB	
	Jerry Weinfurtner	G	
	Steve Burr		LB
	Brian Fehrenbach		DB
1974	Steve Burr	RB	
	Bob Dickman	TE	
	Jim Scheuer	T	
	Jerry Weinfurtner	C	
	Brian Fehrenbach		DB
	Greg Herkert		DL
1975	Jeff Jaye	G	
	Steve Huber	C	
	Mark Meyers	RB	
	Ken Kraus	PK	
	Tom Umhoefer		DE
	Greg Herkert		DL
	Bruce Norfleet		LB
1976	Al Nikolai	E	DE
	Mike Kraus	G	

	Bruce Norfleet	QB	
	Tom Stangl	RB, PK	
	Joe Henrichs		LB
	Denny Sternweis		P
1977	Scott Radlinger	RB	DB
1978	Chris Zygarlicke	RB	LB
1979	Paul Hughes		LB
	Larry Olsen		DE
1980	Lyle Lang	G	
	Derrold Martin	T	
	Kelly Kennedy	E	
	Rob Wagner	RB	
	Brian Morgan	QB	
	Larry Olsen		DE
	Kevin Hamann		DT
1981	Lyle Lang	G	
	Greg Sebastian	C	
	Pat Kraus	T	DL
	Rob Wagner	RB	
	Dick Stevens	RB	
	Brian Morgan	QB	
	Rich Nikolai		DE
1982	Steve Jones	E	
	Randy Spencer	T	
	Paul Rasmussen	G	
	John Rasmussen	PK	
	Rich Nikolai		DE
	Pat Mancl		LB
	Mark Rae		P
1983	Al Gripentrog	G	
	Mark Rae	QB	P
	John Rasmussen	E, PK	
1984	John Michalski	RB	
	Bill Saviage	PK	
1985	Dan Zygarlicke		LB
1986	Brian Louis	C	
	Rob Cooper	T	

	Mike Nikolai		DE
	David Herkert		DB
1987	Chris Hendler	G	
	David Scheuer	E	LB
	Eric Helms	QB	DB
	David Herkert	E	
	Todd Maurer		DE
1988	Eric Gordee	G	
	Joe McCormick	RB	
1989	Jeff Burrill	G	LB
	Steve Scheuer	RB	NG
	Tom McCormick		DB
1990	Pat Schueppert	RB	DB
	Adam Michalek	T	DT
	Keith Nikolay	C	
	Steve Nugent	RB	
	Mike Magistrelli	QB	
	Michael McCormick		DE
1991	Mike Magistrelli	QB, PK	P
	Adam Michalek	T	DL
	Jeremy Maurer		DE
	Steve Nugent	RB	DB
	Tom Backaus	T	
	Jeremy Sternweis	G	
	Eric Heiting		LB
1992	Eric Heiting	RB	LB
	Tom Backaus	T	DL
	Jeremy Sternweis	G	
	Kevin Ahmann	PK	
	Justin Casperson		DB
	Jeremy Maurer		DE
1993	Ryan Kolbeck	T	DL
	Rocky Schueppert	G	
	Nate Bennington	E	
	Scot Cook	PK	
	Craig Eckes		DB
	Brian McCormick		DE

	Andy Dean		P
1994	Mike Scheuer	QB	DB
	Ryan Beck	RB	
	Mike Weister	RB	
	Peter Spencer	C	
	Steve Burger	G	
	Brian McCormick		DE
	Daryl Konrardy		DL
1995	Ryan Beck	RB	
	Jerry Bennington	T	
	Aaron Rasmussen		LB
1996	Pete Schueppert	QB	
	Mike Weister	RB	LB
	Jason Linzmeier	E, PK	DB
	Richie Seubert	G	DL
	Mike Seelen	T	
1997	Josh Klumb		DE
1998	Matt Beck		LB
	Matt Schmitt	G	
1999	Josh Maurer	RB	
	Matt Knauf	C	
	John Geldernick	G	
	Matt Lang		DL
2000	No Marawood selections		

Multiple-year Columbus High School CWCC picks

Times selected	Name	Years selected
3	Russ Truhlar	1956, 1957, 1958
2	Vic Vakoc	1956, 1957
2	Pat O'Reilly	1958, 1959
2	Leo Fellenz	1958, 1959
2	Chuck Koch	1962, 1963
2	Mike Dumas	1962, 1963
2	Bob Koch	1964, 1965
2	Lloyd Hoffman	1964, 1965
2	Bob Rose	1969, 1970

2	Steve Burr	1973, 1974
2	Brian Fehrenbach	1973, 1974
2	Jerry Weinfurtner	1973, 1974
2	Greg Herkert	1974, 1975
2	Bruce Norfleet	1975, 1976
2	Larry Olsen	1979, 1980
2	Lyle Lang	1980, 1981
2	Dick Stevens	1980, 1981
2	Rich Nikolai	1981, 1982
2	John Rasmussen	1982, 1983
2	Mark Rae	1982, 1983
2	David Herkert	1986, 1987
2	Mike Magistrelli	1990, 1991
2	Steve Nugent	1990, 1991
2	Eric Heiting	1991, 1992
2	Jeremy Sternweis	1991, 1992
2	Tom Backaus	1991, 1992
2	Jeremy Maurer	1991, 1992
2	Adam Michalek	1990, 1991
2	Brian McCormick	1993, 1994
2	Mike Weister	1994, 1996

Acknowledgments

All things are created twice. First, the idea. Later, if lucky, the culmination. John Adler, Ed Sheahen, and I spent hours talking about the Dons on many levels after we graduated from Columbus. It was always a theme I would come back to when I returned home to Marshfield and Johnny would routinely state, "Not that again!" Sadly Eddie Bear passed in 2008. To these two, alone, I owe a real debt for keeping me abreast of the Dons after I left Marshfield for good in 1977.

The local central Wisconsin newspaper reporting scene from the 1950-2000 era will probably never be matched. I used 17 newspapers for my research. The main one, *The Marshfield News-Herald*, had a newly arrived sports editor in 1949 by the name of Bob Stevenson. He remained there till 1985. The breadth-and-depth of his *News-Herald* sports pages remain unmatched. Watching him in action and then reading his game summaries afterwards influenced my start in life as a journalist. To me, he was the paramount small city sports editor. Others thought so too; he was inducted into the Wisconsin Football Coaches Hall of Fame in 2010. Stevenson mentored or cast a long shadow over others who covered the Dons over the years. The list starts with Doug Zaleski and ends with Tim Johnson. In between, game reports from Kirk Holmes, Alan Lemke, Keith Wandrei, Dan Kohn, Alan Kay, Larry White, Denny Tauscher, Jim Pryse, Jennifer Eisenbart, and Paul Lecker helped add rich detail to this book.

Besides the *News-Herald*, the *Wisconsin Rapids Daily Tribune, Stevens Point Journal, Wausau Daily Herald, La Crosse Tribune, Eau Claire Leader-Telegram, Chippewa Falls Herald-Telegram, Green*

Bay Press-Gazette, Oshkosh Northwestern, Appleton Post-Cresent, Manitowoc Herald-Times-Reporter, Fond du Lac Reporter, Madison Wisconsin State Journal, Madison Capital Times, Austin (Minn.) *Daily Herald, Sioux Falls Argus-Leader,* and *Kansas City Star* served as cross references. Again, the detail of local sports reporting during the last half of the 20th century is enviable. Thank you to the sports staffs of these papers. May we one day see robust reporting of this nature again.

Every city should be blessed to have a radio sportscaster the likes of Gene Delisio. He's a renaissance man and has been covering the entire sports scene in Marshfield and central Wisconsin since 1985. We all build on the backs of others and I hope this book will encourage others to add to Columbus football lore. For really all I'm doing here is adding to the statistics that Gene painstakingly accumulated over the years and was so gracious in sharing.

Valuable contributions were also made by Adrian R. Martin and his book on Marty Crowe, and Mark Felker and the select research he provided.

Kim Krueger, Don Schnitzler, and Kibby Arkulary from the North Wood County Historical Society aided me in getting photos from the *News-Herald* archives and of Fred Beell. They do valuable, tireless work for the Marshfield community. Also a shout out to Marshfield Senior High's Jackson Hein and Nathan DeLany, principal and athletic director respectively, for their help with a *Tiger* yearbook photo we ended up not using. Thanks also to Joe Benash at Mapping Specialists, in Fitchburg, for creating the customized four-state map of places football took the Dons.

The folks at Columbus Catholic High School were very accommodating with access to the school's *Columbian* yearbooks. Thank you to David Eaton (president) and Michael Lambrecht (principal) for ensuring all the yearbooks were available for research. Joe Konieczny shares many qualities with Walt Kroll: both successful coaches, both athletic directors, both loyal beyond logic. The Columbus Catholic family is fortunate to have a man of his character aboard.

What do I know about publishing a book? Absolutely nothing. I leaned on my undergraduate alma mater, UW-Stevens Point, to point me in the right direction. After all they had one of the nation's few student-staffed university presses. Ross Tangedal, the head of Cornerstone Press, took off his professor's hat and tossed his freelance designer expertise my way. I am the better for it. Thank you, Ross.

I know a bit more about media strategy, but not much more. To keep matters simple, I insisted on a website-alone strategy (columbusdonsfootball.com). The folks at Walzak Marketing Communications in Milwaukee seemed to understand this odd request and launched a website well beyond my vanilla tastes. Kevin and Toni, your creativity and friendship is valued more than you know.

I met Tom Stanton over forty years ago when he was starting a string of weekly newspapers in suburban Detroit. He allowed me to fulfill my doctoral internship writing sports for his *Bay Voice* newspapers. We remain best friends to this day. His editing of the original manuscript made this book a better product. Writing about 489 games over a five-decade span is no walk in the park. Thanks, buddy.

My last thank you is reserved for my wife Georgia and our two adult children—Kirk and Thea. No one knows me better than them. Georgia saw that bringing this "Kroll thing" to some finality brought me great joy. How great was my fortune the night I met her in Oxford those many decades ago.

Any mistakes contained within these pages, and there no doubt will be many with all the moving parts associated with a 51-year span, are mine and mine alone. I apologize for them in advance. I tried my best.

MIKE VARNEY is a retired Air Force lieutenant colonel. Before embarking on a 24-year military career, Varney earned accolades as a student journalist in Wisconsin. A former William P. Pors Award winner at UW-Marshfield, he also wrote for *The Colfax Messenger* and the suburban Detroit *Bay Voice* newspapers after graduating in Communication from the University of Wisconsin-Stevens Point. He currently lives on Milwaukee's east side with his wife.

www.ingramcontent.com/pod-product-compliance
Lightning Source LLC
Chambersburg PA
CBHW030919140626
46545CB00016B/1545